Essays in Ancient Greek Philosophy VI
Before Plato

Edited by

Anthony Preus

STATE UNIVERSITY OF NEW YORK PRESS

Published by
State University of New York Press, Albany

© 2001 State University of New York

For information, address State University of New York Press,
90 State Street, Suite 700, Albany, NY 12207

Production by Judith Block
Marketing by Dana Yanulavich

Library of Congress Cataloging-in-Publication Data

(Revised for vol. 5)
Essays in ancient Greek Philosophy.
    Papers originally presented at the annual meetings
of the Society for Ancient Greek Philosophy, 1953–
    Vol. 2–5 edited by John P. Anton and Anthony Preus.
    Includes bibliographical references and indexes.
    Contents: v. 1–2. [without special title]—
v. 3. Plato—v. 4. Aristotle's ethics. 5. Aristotle's Ontology.
    1. Philosophy, Ancient—Congresses. I. Anton, John
Peter, 1920–   . II.Kustas, George L. III. Preus,
Anthony. IV. Society for Ancient Greek Philosophy (U.S.)
.B171.A56   180   69-14648
ISBN 0-8739-5050-X (v.1)

ISBN 0-7914-4955-6 (alk. paper)—ISBN 0-7914-4956-4 (pbk. : alk. paper)

10 9 8 7 6 5 4 3 2 1

Essays in Ancient Greek Philosophy VI
Before Plato

Contents

Introduction

Anthony Preus

This volume is dedicated to the study of ancient Greek philosophy before Plato—not including Socrates, since it is next to impossible to disentangle the study of Socrates from the study of Plato. The essays included here have been selected from the best of those that have not been previously published, and a very few previously published, mostly in relatively inaccessible places, presented at the meetings of the Society for Ancient Greek Philosophy since 1980. The Society sponsors panels at the meetings of each of the divisions of the American Philosophical Association, and at the annual meeting of the American Philological Association. It also sponsors a large joint meeting with the Society for the Study of Islamic Philosophy and Science (SSIPS) each year.

The essays selected as chapters in this volume explore many of the liveliest topics in the study of early Greek philosophy today; they deal with a significant range of the most important figures in the period, and represent several varying methodological approaches.

At least since the publication of Martin Bernal's *Black Athena* historians of ancient Greek philosophy have had to be prepared with some sort of answer to the question of the origins of Hellenic speculation—did philosophy pop into being out of the genius of the Ionians like Athena out of the head of Zeus? or were some sixth-century BCE Greeks, conversant with the wisdom of civilizations far older than their own (for example the Egyptian or the Mesopotamian), importers of leading philosophical ideas from the south and east? One approach to answering questions of this kind must certainly be the careful reexamination of the thought of the earliest Hellenic thinkers who have traditionally been counted among the "philosophers"— Thales, Anaximander, Xenophanes, Pythagoras, for example. In this volume, the chapters by McKirahan, Couprie, Naddaf, and Huffman (at least), address issues that would potentially connect Hellenic and pre-Hellenic thought.

Although speculative thought in Hellas may be said to be at least as old as the texts of Homer and Hesiod, Sappho and Solon, the Milesians— Thales, Anaximander, and Anaximenes—as well as Pythagoras and Xenophanes, appear to us to be qualitatively different from the earlier poetic tradition. We may imagine them motivated by a desire for something that we

1

would recognize as a "scientific" or "naturalistic" explanation of terrestrial phenomena—their subject matter is "Nature."[1] And we recognize in the contributions of these people the beginnings of methodologies that would later pay large dividends in natural science. We have three chapters on the "scientific" findings of Anaximander—McKirahan, Couprie, and Naddaf; several chapters that look at early Greek views of natural process (Matson, Wilcox, Bodnár), and several that examine early Greek skepticism (Curd, Gagarin, Robinson).

Another way that the earliest "canonical" philosophers differ from their predecessors in the poetic tradition is that in classical antiquity Thales, Pythagoras, Xenophanes, Parmenides, Empedocles, Democritus, Protagoras, and even Heraclitus, were thought to be founders of "schools" of philosophy, to have had disciples or admirers who followed their lead, working out the implications of the primary intuitions and arguments of the "founders" of each tradition. While recent scholars have been critical of the schematism upon which Diogenes Laertius structures his *Lives*, there is also something right about the traditional format: philosophy both in antiquity and today operates most often and best as a dialogue carried on from one generation to the next about what most truly exists, how we can know it, how we can communicate what we think we know to others—and why the answers provided to those questions by our predecessors are clearly insufficient. Huffman's chapter explores the ways that Pythagoreanism leads to Plato; Matson reformulates the significance and potential influence of Zeno of Elea; Bodnár relates the thought of Democritus to the history of atomism, and Curd to ethical and epistemological theory.

Aristotle saw the philosophy of his predecessors as dominated by the question of *ousia*—what is the primary being? But he also realized that those same philosophers were concerned with the question of how we can know or understand primary being, that they had epistemological concerns as well as ontological. In the twentieth century the question of the identity of primary being has often been left to physics or some other mode of investigation, while philosophy has claimed for itself issues of how we know—then turned around and called into question the possibility of knowledge. Recent skeptics and postmodern philosophers have often found anticipations of their positions among the Sophists and others in the immediately pre-Platonic era; several of the chapters in this volume explore the degree and kind of skepticism that may be discerned in philosophers of that period. The chapters by Curd, Gagarin, Robinson, and Gould can be read in this light.

---

1. Aristotle calls them *physiologoi*, people who give an account of nature.

Aristotle also thought that "in the time of Socrates the investigation of nature went out of fashion and philosophers turned toward the useful virtues and politics."[2] It may be some exaggeration to say that the study of nature was neglected—certainly Democritus and the Pythagoreans were among those who continued to interest themselves in natural philosophy—but pressing problems in the nature of human life in its social context did indeed take precedence. Thus the chapters by Curd, Gagarin, Robinson, and Gould can be seen as focusing on "the useful virtues and politics" as those issues were understood in the days of Socrates.

We have called this volume *Before Plato*. Normally the group of texts examined in this volume are called "Presocratic"; that denomination suggests either that those texts lead up to the work of Socrates—and that might well be said about Antiphon's *Truth*, the *Dissoi Logoi*, or the plays of Sophocles, for example—or that Socrates marks a more or less clean break away from what had gone before, as we mentioned earlier—and that could be said about very nearly everything else in this volume. But in looking at the chapters in this volume, we are struck by the degree to which they demonstrate *Plato's* reliance on the thought of his predecessors. This is of course quite explicit in the chapters by Gould on Sophocles's *Philoctetes* and Huffman on the Pythagorean background of Plato's *Philebus*, but connections to Plato are pervasive throughout the volume. The "cosmological" chapters that begin the volume provide a context for the science, especially the astronomy, of the *Timaeus*; Wilcox's chapter also has several points of contact with the *Timaeus*. Matson's chapter on Zeno is constantly in dialogue with Plato's account of Eleatic philosophy in the *Parmenides* and elsewhere; Gagarin and Robinson point out ways in which Plato may have relied on Sophistic texts rather more than his heated attacks on Sophism might lead us to believe. Only one chapter in the volume concerns a text not generally included in the "canon" of "Presocratics," Gould's on the *Philoctetes*. But this chapter should be seen from the perspective of the development of Plato's synthesis of the moral, political and aesthetic with the epistemological, ontological, and natural thought of his predecessors. The dramatists preceded Socrates and Plato in taking very seriously the problem of understanding, and judging, human values and motivations. Plato has been called "dramatist of the life of reason"[3]; using the art of Aeschylus, Sophocles, Euripedes (and yes, Aristophanes too), Plato brings to the stage of the mind the life of the intellect in Hellas in the two hundred years that precede his day. This volume is dedicated to studies from a variety of viewpoints of the materials that went into the construction of Plato's dramatic representations.

---

2. *Parts of Animals* I. 1, 642a28.
3. That is of course the title of J. H. Randall Jr.'s introductory book (1970) about Plato.

PERMISSIONS

Chapter 1, Gerald Naddaf's "On the Origin of Anaximander's Cosmological Model" was originally published in the *Journal of the History of Ideas*, volume 59. Copyright 1998. Reprinted with permission of Johns Hopkins University Press.

Figure 2.7 in Chapter 2, reproduced with permission of the Trustees of the British Museum. See also W. Treue (ed.), Achse, Rad und Wagen. Fuenftausend Jahre Kultur—und Technikgeschichte., Goettingen, 1986, pp. 68 and 78.

Chapter 5, Wallace Matson's "Zeno Moves!", is a revised version of "The Zeno of Plato and Tannery Vindicated" published in *La Parola del Passato*, volume 43. Copyright 1988. Reprinted here in revised form with permission of *La Parola del Passato*.

Chapter 7, István M. Bodnár's "Atomic Independence and Indivisibility" was originally published in *Oxford Studies in Ancient Philosophy*, volume XVI. Copyright 1998. Reprinted with permission of Oxford University Press.

Chapter 10, Thomas M. Robinson's "The *Dissoi Logoi* and Early Greek Skepticism" was originally published in Richard H. Popkin, ed., *Scepticism in the History of Philosophy*. Copyright 1996. Reprinted here in revised form with permission of Kluwer.

Chapter 1

Anaximander's Measurements Revisited

Gerard Naddaf

The capacity for critical thought that appeared within generations after the advent of writing in the Hellenic world did not manifest itself as critical historiography. Rather, the skepticism generated by the inherent inconsistencies between the past and the present first resulted in what we would call science and philosophy. The first Hellenic thinker traditionally counted as a philosopher to write a prose book was Anaximander of Miletus (c. 575 BCE). The Milesian's *historia* (or investigation) is both rational and argumentative; it meets the two prerequisites of distinctively Hellenic philosophy. Anaximander's *historia* is distinctively important in that it helps us understand just what is involved in the movement from a mythopoeic to a speculative account. Although we have just one extant fragment from Anaximander, the doxographies reveal a surprising consistency in his application of rational or natural causes to explain not only the origin and evolution of the present order of things, but also how this order is maintained. Certainly one of the most interesting facets of Anaximander's *historia* is his cosmological model. While the *origin* of the cosmological model has been the subject of a great deal of controversy, the interpretations relative to the numbers and/or measurements associated with this model are no less controversial.

According to the doxographical tradition, Anaximander of Miletus held that the earth remains at rest (*menein*) at the center (*epi tou mesou*) of the universe[1] and that its form is cylindrical (*kulindroeidē*) and that its *depth* is a third of its *width*, that is, its *diameter* is three times its *height* (*echein de [sc. tēn gēn] tosouton bathos hoson an eiē triton pros to platos*).[2] He imagined the heavenly bodies

---

1. Aristotle, *On the Heaven* 295b10 (=DK 12A26); Hippolytus (*Refutation* I.6.3 = DK 12A11). For a similar description and perhaps a reference to Anaximander himself by Plato, see *Phaedo* 108e-109a and *Timaeus* 62c-63a. For a discussion of the common interpretations of these passages, see *Appendix* at the end of this chapter.

2. Pseudo-Plutarch, *Miscellanies* 2 (=DK 12A10, 32–33). Further, it is confirmed, in a certain sense, by both Hippolytus (*Refutation* 1.6.3 = DK 12A11) and Aetius (3.10.2 = DK 12A25) who inform us that the earth for Anaximander is shaped like a column drum (*kioni lithōi paraplēsion*). Although this interpretation has not gone uncontested (for example, O'Brien [1967], 424–425, would prefer to translate it as the *height* is 3✕ the *width*), it is held by the vast majority of commentators. The fact

(*continued on page 6*)

as rings (*kukloi*) of fire somewhat like chariot wheels (*harmateiōi trochōi paraplēsion*), encased in *aēr* or mist except for an aperture (*stomion, ekpnoē*) through which the fire emerges.[3] He postulated three of these rings: one for the sun, one for the moon, and one for the fixed stars.[4] As for their position relative to the earth, Anaximander placed the sun the furthest of all, then the moon and, finally, the fixed stars.[5] The texts are clear on this point and are not contested by anyone. However, as soon as one turns to the actual sizes and distances of the three rings, one enters into the realm of conjecture, because of the *lacunae* in our testimonia.

According to Hippolytus, the sun ring (*ton kuklon tou hēliou*) is 27 times (*heptakaieikosaplasiona*) the size (diameter) of the earth. Although the moon is mentioned in the text, the number corresponding to its size is missing because of a mutilated text.[6] The number 27 for the size of the sun ring is confirmed by

---

2. (*continued from page 5*)
   that both Hippolytus and Aetius (see below) state that Anaximander's earth is shaped like a *kioni lithōi* which translates as "stone column," appears to be behind O'Brien's reasoning. This may explain why a number of commentators prefer "column drum" e.g., KRS (1983), 133–134, Guthrie, vol. I (1962), 98, and West (1971), 87. According to Hahn (1995), 99–100, the form of a column drum was an Ionian technical innovation of the first half of the sixth century and its proportions were roughly compatible with Pseudo-Plutarch's ratio of three to one. The fact that a *kulindros* ("rolling stone") is wider than it is thick would seem to confirm this.
3. There are a number of doxographies in which these descriptions appear: Pseudo-Plutarch, *Miscellanies* 2 (=DK 12A10, 37); Hippolytus *Refutation* 1.6.4–5 (=DK 12A11, 9–16); Aetius 2.13.7 (=DK 12A18, 28–29); Aetius 2.20.1 (=DK 12A21, 11–13); Aetius 2.21.1 (=DK 12A21, 14–15); Aetius 2.24.2 (=DK 12A21, 16–17); Aetius 2.25.1 (=DK 12A22, 19–21); Aetius 2.29.1 (=DK 12A22, 23).
4. Anaximander speaks of rings (*kukloi*) in the case of the fixed stars. There are a number of problems associated with these, mostly in conjunction with their position relative to the earth.
5. It is not clear why Anaximander would have placed the fixed stars closest to the earth. Scholars are very much divided on the issue. However, if Burch (1949–1950), 156 is correct that distance is not discernible with the naked eye, then the order proposed by Anaximander (and this would also hold for the numbers corresponding to the sizes and distances of the heavenly bodies) cannot be based on observation. Ironically, if it is true, as astronomers assure me, that it is not that difficult to discern the occultations of the stars by the moon, then this also leads to the conclusion that the order proposed by Anaximander cannot be based on observation.
6. Hippolytus *Refutation* 1.6.5 (=DK 12A11). Some scholars like Neuhäuser (1883), 399 and Dreyer (1906), 15 n.1, hold that the text is not mutilated and Anaximander is stating that the circle of the sun is 27 times *that of the moon*. However, this would entail that Anaximander was using a unit of measure other than the earth (it would also make the earth appear many times smaller than it actually appears) and this is highly unlikely (see below p. 12ff). For this reason, I do not discuss the options associated with it below.

one of Aetius's doxographies.[7] However, in another doxography, he informs us that the circle of the sun is 28 times (*oktōkaieikosaplasiona*) the size of the earth (*ison einai tēi gēi*).[8]

Although the number 28 has been ignored by some[9] and considered as corrupt by others,[10] it is the source of a great deal of speculation on the part of the majority. However, before examining this more closely, it is important to turn to the size of the moon and star rings. Indeed, prior to Paul Tannery,[11] the speculation was limited to the sun ring, whereas since Tannery the speculation has spilled over to the moon and star rings.[12]

The reason for this is, I believe, because the only ratio to have come down to us for the size of the moon ring is 19 times (*enneakaidekaplasiona*) that of the earth,[13] and since the moon ring should, like the sun ring, be a multiple of 3, this has led a powerful group of scholars, since Tannery, to conclude that the number missing in the text of Hippolytus for the size of the moon ring must be 18. Although there are no recorded figures for the size of the fixed star ring (or rings), since it forms the innermost ring, in conformity with the examples of the sun and the moon, the same chorus, again since Tannery, recommends 9 and 10 as the corresponding ratios. In sum, what we have here are two series of numbers: 9,18,27 and 10,19,28. But why two series of numbers?

According to Tannery and a host of others[14] the smaller series of numbers (9,18,27) represent the inner diameters of the rings and the larger series of numbers (10,19,28), the outer diameters of the rings. However, according to Geoffrey Kirk and his group of followers,[15] this involves an error in computation for if diameters are meant[16] and if we assume that the rings themselves are one earth diameter thick (and the fact that the sun is said to be the same size as the earth seems to substantiate this),[17] then 2 and not 1 should be

---

7. Aetius 2.2.1 (=DK 12A21).
8. Aetius 2.20.1 (=DK 12A21).
9. Sambursky (1956/1987), 15–16; Hahn (1995).
10. Kahn (1960), 62; West (1971), 86.
11. Tannery (1887/1930²).
12. For an interesting analysis of speculation prior to Tannery (1930), cf. O'Brien (1967), 423–424.
13. Aetius 2.25.1 (=DK 12A22).
14. Tannery (1930), 94ff, followed by Burnet (1930⁴), 68; Diels (1897), 231; and Heath (1913), 37.
15. KRS (1983), 136 n.1 followed by Guthrie (1962), 96; Burkert (1962; 1972), 309 n.59; Conche (1991), 209–210.
16. According to Kirk (1955), there seems little doubt that what are being compared are the *diameters* (my italics) of the rings of the heavenly bodies with the diameter or width of the circular surface earth.
17. Aetius 2.21.1 (=DK 12A21).

added to the multiple to give 29,20,11, respectively.[18] Consequently, Kirk holds that the larger series "might represent the diameter of the ring from outer edge to outer edge" and the smaller series "from points halfway between the inner and outer edges of the actual felloe of air."[19] In sum, according to Kirk's calculations, the distance from the inner edge to inner edge of the rings would be 26,17,8.

O'Brien,[20] in one of the more detailed and coherent accounts of the problem, holds that there is no reason (contra Kirk) that we should not think of the thickness of the rings as equal to one half of the earth's diameter, that is, the same thickness as the radius of the earth.[21] Consequently, if we compare the radius of the earth with the radius of the rings, that is "like with like," then the numbers will hold.[22]

However, while it is true that O'Brien's construction shows that the celestial rings are equidistant, and therefore Anaximander's propensity for *equality* (something everyone appears to agree with),[23] Anaximander appears obsessed with units of 3 and not with units of 4 which follow from O'Brien's analysis.[24] But what is more important, the language (a *kuklos* 27× the size of the earth) implies that the earth's *radius* is not the unit of measure.

There has been a great deal of controversy (and confusion) surrounding these numbers and much of this is due to the fact that commentators do not seem to agree on just what is being compared and measured: is it the *size* of the rings? or the *distance* of the rings? or *both*? and what is the unit of measure: the *radius* of the earth? the *diameter* of the earth? the *circumference* of the earth?

---

18. Although the accent in KRS is put on the sun ring, this is of course valid for all three rings.
19. KRS (1983), 136 n.1.
20. O'Brien (1967), 423–432.
21. O'Brien (1967), 424.
22. In fact, according to O'Brien, as long as we "retain the comparison of the radius of the earth with the thickness or width of the rim of the sun wheel then the figures 'will hold' whether we think of the *distance* (my italics) of the sun wheel from the earth in terms of radius, diameter, or circumference" (425). Due to the fact that O'Brien holds that the rings are one half the earth's diameter, his calculations are in halves with the number 4 being dominant (425).
23. One of the few exceptions to this is Joyce Engmann (1991), 22. She is clearly wrong.
24. O'Brien arrives at units of 4 by halving the diameters of the three rings (which he assumes, like the majority, to be 9,18,27, respectively) and postulating the thickness of the rings themselves as 1/2 the earth's diameter. Consequently, the distance between each ring is 4 earth diameters and if we add 1/2 for the thickness of the star ring and 1/2 for the thickness of the moon ring, then the distance from the *center* of the earth to the inner circumference of the sun ring is 13 1/2 earth diameters (1/2+4+1/2+4+1/2+4).

the *thickness* of the earth? or a combination of two or more?[25] There also seems to be a great deal of controversy (and confusion) with respect to the thickness of the ring itself and its role in coming to terms with the numbers.

In this chapter, I will argue that the dimensions of the earth and, therefore, the number 3 is the key to the whole problem and when put into perspective most, if not all, of the problems and confusion are abated.

I concur with those who hold that the series 9,18,27 is due to Anaximander himself.[26] Indeed, since it would be rather odd that Anaximander would use more than one unit to account for the size of the rings, since the earth is said to be the unit which served for the size of the rings (and the fact that the sun is said to be the same size as the earth appears to confirm this), and since the diameter of the earth is said to be three times its height, that is, a multiple of 3, then the smaller rather than the larger series would appear to be correct. Although I believe that the larger series 10,19,28 (or perhaps only the numbers 28 and 19) is due to a "commentator's refinements"[27] or is quite simply corrupt,[28] my solution will also make sense of them.

For what follows, it is important to note that I will be taking the *diameter* of the earth as the unit of measure for each possibility. Further, I will be assuming that Anaximander would have postulated a value of 3 for π—something I believe to be historically appropriate.

Let us begin with the example of the sun ring—what follows will also hold for the moon ring and the star ring. When Anaximander says that the sun ring (*kuklos tou hēliou*) is 27 times the size of (*-plasios*) the earth, does he mean that the sun ring's circumference (as opposed to the circumference of the sun disk) is $27\times$ the earth's circumference (A.1)? diameter (A.2)? or radius (A.3)? that the sun ring's diameter is $27\times$ the earth's circumference (B.1)? diameter (B.2)? or radius (B.3)? or then again, that the sun ring's radius is $27\times$ the earth's circumference (C.1)? diameter (C.2)? or radius (C.3)? And, is the accent put on the size of the sun ring, its distance from the earth, or both?

A.1 (the sun ring's circumference is $27\times$ the earth's circumference), B.1 (the sun ring's diameter is $27\times$ the earth's circumference), and C.1 (the sun ring's radius is $27\times$ the earth's circumference) entail that the *diameter* of the

---

25. See O'Brien (1967), 425.
26. The number of scholars who consider that the series 9,18,27 is due to Anaximander himself is indeed impressive. In reality, virtually everyone who has written on the subject of the three rings (I list twenty-five or so in [1998], n.64). Even Charles Kahn who believes that there is "little documentary evidence" for the numbers (1960, 62) vigorously challenges those who argue that the numbers have a sacred or mythical significance rather than a rational one (94–97).
27. Guthrie (1962), 93.
28. Kahn (1960), 62; West (1971), 86–87.

sun ring would be 27, 81, and 162 earth diameters, respectively. However, A.1 and B.1 put the accent on the *diameter* and, therefore, on the *size* of the sun ring, whereas C.1 puts the accent on the *radius* and, therefore, on the *distance* of the sun ring or *circumference* from the earth or *center*. In sum, in the case of A.1 and B.1, *distance* is implied, but is secondary, whereas in C.1, *size* is implied, but is secondary. Most commentators, O'Brien is the exception, fail to distinguish between *distance* and *size*.

A.2 (the sun ring's circumference is 27× the earth's diameter), B.2 (the sun ring's diameter is 27× the earth's diameter), and C.2 (the sun ring's radius is 27× the earth's diameter) entail that the *diameter* of the sun ring would be 9, 27, and 54 earth diameters, respectively. However, A.2 and B.2 put the accent on the *diameter* and, therefore, on the *size* of the sun ring, whereas C.2 puts the accent on the *radius* and, therefore, on the *distance* of the sun ring from the earth.

A.3 (the sun ring's circumference is 27× the earth's radius), B.3 (the sun ring's diameter is 27× the earth's radius), and C.3 (the sun ring's radius is 27× the earth's radius) entail that the *diameter* of the sun ring would be 4 1/2, 13 1/2, and 27 earth diameters, respectively. However, A.3 and B.3 put the accent on the *diameter* and, therefore, on the *size* of the sun ring, whereas C.3 puts the accent on the *radius* and, therefore, on the *distance* of the sun ring from the earth.

According to O'Brien, as long as we compare "like with like" the *proportions* of the universe will remain the same. In reality, the *proportions* of the universe will remain the same whether or not we compare "like with like." This is clear from the possibilities just listed. It still remains that some possibilities are more defensible than others.

This may explain why some of these possibilities have not been held, at least to my knowledge, by anyone: A.3, B.3, C.1. Indeed, A.3 (the circumference of the sun ring is 27× the earth's radius), B.3 (the diameter of the sun ring is 27× the earth's radius), and C.1 (the radius of the sun ring is 27× the earth's circumference) are all nonsensical.

Of the remaining six, A.1, B.2, and C.3 all compare like with like: A1, circumference with circumference; B.2, diameter with diameter; and C.3, radius with radius. According to O'Brien, these three are the only real possibilities since they alone entail that "the *proportions* of the universe will remain the same."[29] As we already saw, this is not the case. Nonetheless, the vast majority of commentators fall into this category. Of these three possibilities, the comparison of the sun's radius with that of the earth[30] appears the least probable for the

---

29. O'Brien (1967), 425.
30. This is O'Brien's thesis, but also that of A.E. Taylor (1928), 163.

reasons already mentioned. The two other possibilities (A.1 and B.2) both make perfectly good sense, especially since the expressions "the sun is the same size as the earth" and "the sun ring is 27× the size of the earth" can both be taken in the sense of *circumference* or *diameter*. Although in both cases the proportions remain exactly the same, if we consider that Hippolytus stresses that the *diameter* of the earth is 3× its *height*, then *diameter* (or B.2)[31] rather than the circumference (or A.1)[32] appears to be the most likely. I concur with this, but before examining it in more detail, I would like to look at the other possibilities.

The three last possibilities—A.2 (the circumference of the sun ring is 27× the earth's diameter), B.1 (the diameter of the sun ring is 27× the earth's circumference), and C.2 (the radius of the sun ring is 27× the earth's diameter)—make sense from different points of view, but are difficult to sustain.

A.2 meanwhile was held by at least two commentators, Forbiger and Röper,[33] in the pre-Tannery period, that is, before the accent was put on all three rings. They hold that if such is the case then the figure 27 could represent the circumference minus the size of the hole for the sun and 28, of course, the circumference with the sun.[34] Albeit, in my view, an obvious *petitio principii* argument (anyone looking to the sky would see that it would take more than 27 sun disks to form a circle or ring), a closer examination of A.2 in light of this position leads to some interesting results, especially if we consider that the accent is not on the diameter, but on the word *kuklos*.[35]

If it is assumed that Anaximander took the circumference to be 27× the diameter, then he may have reasoned that if 27 earth columns or diameters (remember the sun's disk is said to be the same size as the earth—*ison einai tēi gēi*) were placed together in the form of a circle or ring, the result would be a circle 9 times the size of the earth's circumference. Meanwhile, if such is the case, it is possible that the number 28× would indeed be a "refinement": someone looking for the approximate ratio of the circumference of the sun ring to its diameter or π (3.14 × 9 = 28.26). Of course, the same would hold for the moon

---

31. For a partial list, see note 38.
32. Burnet (1930), 68; Zeller (1892⁶), 300 n.2; Rescher (1969), 22; West (1971), 86.
33. Forbiger (1842), 523 n.57 and Röper (1852), 608.
34. O'Brien (1967) 424 n.4 criticizes the thesis of Forbiger and Röper for whom the figures 27× and 28× represent the circumference minus the size of the hole for the sun. According to O'Brien this "confuses circumference and diameter, for it makes the *circumference* (his italics) of the sun's orbit 27 or 28 times the *diameter* (his italics) of the earth." This is because O'Brien is of the opinion that we can only compare "like with like" (425), that is diameters with diameters or radii with radii etc.
35. This may explain why Burkert (1972), 307, puts the key word circle in quotation marks: "the sun is as large as the earth; its 'circle' is 27 or 28 times as large as the earth."

ring and the star ring. If 18 earth columns were placed together in the form of a circle or ring, the result would be a circle 6 times the size of the earth's circumference (19× being a "refinement" once again of 3.14 × 6 = 18.84). Finally, if 9 earth columns were placed together in the form of a circle or ring, the result would be a circle 3 times the size of the earth's circumference (10× being a "refinement" again of 3.14 × 3 = 9.42—or perhaps a lack of one). Of course, I am only trying to be exhaustive here. As I noted above, this is quite obviously a *petitio principii* argument.

The second possibility, B.1 (the diameter of the sun ring is 27× the earth's circumference) is plausible,[36] if one considers that it makes the sun appear only about 3× closer (at π =3) than it actually does.[37] However, in the final analysis, even this would appear indefensibly large. Indeed, since the sun's angular diameter is about 30′ or 21 (which means that its distance is approximately 100 times its linear diameter), it would take 720 sun disks (or earth columns) placed in a circle to conform to the reality (whereas B.2 entails 243 sun disks placed in a circle).

The last possibility, C.2 (the sun ring's radius is 27× the earth's diameter)[38] seems to be based on the assumption that Anaximander's primary preoccupation was with the *distance* of the heavenly bodies rather than their sizes. Consequently, Marcel Conche[39] insists that this is the case because what Anaximander understands here by diameter is in fact the *démi-diamètre*, that is the *radius* of the *kuklos*.[40]

This (C.2) also appears to be, at least in part, Couprie's solution to the problem.[41] In fact, Couprie gives us the most detailed (and intricate) account of any commentator on the problem in question. It is, therefore, important to examine his solution in more detail.[42]

One of the major problems I have with Couprie's solution is that on the one hand, he explicitly states that the numbers 9, 18, and 27 have nothing to

---

36. Teichmüller (1874/1966), 16–17.

37. On this, see Burch (1949–1950), 154–155.

38. Cornford (1934), 12 and 15; Conche (1991), 209–210; Hahn (1995), 17 (at least Hahn's diagram seems to imply this). C.2 would work out to the sun appearing approximately 4× larger than it actually does.

39. Conche (1991), 209–210.

40. Ironically, Conche is directing his fire at O'Brien who insists that we must compare "like with like." According to Conche, if this were not the case then the diameter of the *kuklos* as measured from outer edges of the rings (agreeing in this with Kirk) would be 11, 20, and 29. But this is *not* what Kirk means, as we have seen.

41. This is explicitly mentioned with reference to Kirk on pp. 34f of Couprie, Chapter 2, this volume.

42. Couprie's general thesis (Chapter 2, this volume) is that Anaximander discovered "space", that is, depth in space. I largely concur with this thesis.

do with observation[43] "for depth in the universe cannot be *observed*,"[44] but on the other hand, he does his best to make the numbers conform to observation.[45] According to Couprie, the solution to the series 9,18,27 is found in Hesiod's *Theogony*. Hesiod employs the number 9 in the *Theogony* to indicate that the distance from sky to earth (or then again from earth to Tartarus) is very great indeed.[46] Thus, what Anaximander means by the numbers 9, 18, and 27 is simply far (the star ring), farther (the moon ring), and farthest (the sun ring).[47] He also wants to account for the numbers 10, 19, and 28. However, Couprie feels compelled to make the numbers conform to observation because he feels that Anaximander's numbers could not be in "disagreement with the most obvious observational data."[48] In sum, he argues that Anaximander must have been aware that the angular diameter of the sun was close to 30' or 1/2° and, therefore, the number 27 must somehow conform to this. This is the impetus behind Couprie's solution. But just what is his solution? He begins by arguing (following O'Brien) that the numbers refer to *radii*, but *radii* multiplied by *diameters*, that is, the *distance* from the earth to the sun ring is 27 earth *diameters* or 54 earth *radii* (thus 27 *radii* equal 54 *radii*).[49] However, this still entails that it would only take 162 sun disks to make the circle (instead of 720), and an angular diameter of 2°15', which means that the sun would appear 4.5 times larger than it actually appears. To resolve this "flagrant discrepancy," Couprie conjectures, rather ingeniously, that we must imagine Anaximander's cosmological model from an elevated (or three-dimensional) view rather than a plan (or two-dimensional) view. From this perspective, according to him, it is the *height* rather than the *width* which we see in the sky; and since the *height* is one third the *width* (like that of the earth),[50] this entails that it would take 486 sun disks (that is, 162 × 3) to make

---

43. Couprie (Chapter 2, this volume), 33.

44. Couprie (Chapter 2, this volume), 38.

45. See in particular the remark on Thales, Couprie (Chapter 2, this volume), 41.

46. The text in question is found in *Theogony* 722–725. Hesiod states that it would take a brazen anvil 9 days falling from heaven to reach the earth (which it would do on the tenth day). Couprie, therefore, sees Hesiod as the forerunner of Anaximander in that he was already trying to imagine distances (p. 40).

47. Couprie (Chapter 2, this volume), 40.

48. Couprie (Chapter 2, this volume), 41.

49. Since the rings are, according to Couprie (again following O'Brien), one earth *radius* thick, this accounts for the numbers 28, 19, and 10 earth *diameters* as the distance between the *outer* rims of the 3 rings.

50. Couprie's corresponding figure 2.8 would then be somewhat like my own figures 1.1 and 1.2—albeit inverted. My figures or diagrams were developed prior to (and thus independently of) his.

the circle, and an angular diameter of 45′, which means that the sun would only appear 50% larger than it actually appears.

The major problem I have with this solution is that it attempts to make Anaximander's figures correspond at any cost (and thus, in my view, another *petitio principii* argument). Indeed, Couprie begins by stating that the numbers draw their inspiration from Hesiod and yet he still insists that they correspond to observation. In fact, if, as he suggests, "Thales had already discovered that the sun's apparent diameter is 1/720 times its orbit,"[51] then why would Anaximander be off by as much as 50% (45′ as opposed to 30′). Assuredly 486 sun disks instead of 720 sun disks to form a circle is still a gaffe if Anaximander is as keen an observer as Couprie suggests.[52] Further, the fact that Anaximander places the star ring closest to the earth suggests that observation did not play a prominent role in his cosmological model. The occultations of the stars by the moon are not as difficult to discern as Couprie suggests. Finally, the expression that the sun ring is 27× the size of the earth (as noted above) seems to exclude this interpretation.

I, therefore, concur with those who argue that Anaximander is comparing the diameter of the ring or rings with the diameter of the earth (B.2).[53] I also concur with those who argue that only the series 9,18,27 is Anaximander's and that these numbers represent the *sizes* and *distances* of the three rings, that is, the heavenly bodies, although the accent is initially on the *diameter* and thus on the *size*.[54] However, my analysis, as we will now see, differs in a number of ways from those of my predecessors.

It is worth beginning with the *thickness* of the rings itself. It should be assumed that the rings are one earth diameter *thick*, but again, for reasons not hitherto recognized. Many commentators assume that since Anaximander's sun

---

51. Couprie (Chapter 2, this volume), 41.
52. See my note 5. And again, if Anaximander were as keen an observer as Couprie suggests, assuredly he would have observed the occultations.
53. Diels (1897), 231; Dreyer (1906), 14–15; Heath (1913), 32; Tannery (1930²), 94; Baccou (1951), 76; KRS (1983), 136; Kahn (1960), 62; Guthrie (1962), 95; Couprie (1995), 160. Of course, B.2 would make the sun appear 9× larger (4°30′) than it actually does appear. If this conclusion is correct, it is a clear indication that observational astronomy, strictly speaking, could not have played a role in the series in question. In fact, only C.1 is a close acceptable approximation (45′) and it was not held by anyone for obvious reasons. This also concurs with what was stated above with respect to the position of the star rings.
54. This is in opposition to others (in particular Kirk, 134) who insist on putting the accent on the *distance* rather than the *size* of the rings which, in my view, only adds to the confusion.

is said to be the same size (*ison*) as the earth then the thickness of the rings also must be one earth diameter thick.[55] However, a distinction must be made between the *width* and the *height* of the rings and this necessitates a return to the image of the earth. The earth, as noted, is described as a column drum 3× as wide as it is high. Now, when the sun disk is said to be the same size as the earth, this must be understood to mean the *width* of the sun disk (as opposed to the *width* of the sun ring) is the same size as the earth (figure1.1).[56]

It must also be understood that the sun disk is on the *inner* face of the sun ring. The *inner* face, lying aslant,[57] looks down on the earth from above; the *inner* face has the aperture through which the visible sun or sun disk appears (figures 1.1 and 1.2).[58] We therefore have in figure 1.2 an elevated view reflecting the obliquity of the heavenly axis.

---

55. See for example, Burch (1949–1950), 155 n.41; KRS (1983), 136; Guthrie (1962), 95; Burkert (1972), 309 n.59; Conche (1991), 209; McKirahan (1993), 39 n.16. It is this contention that O'Brien tries to refute (1967, 424–425) but not for the same reasons as my own. O'Brien, to defend his position, argues that the ring is one half of the earth's diameter. This was also Tannery's position (1930²), 94 and, I believe, Rescher (1969), 23. On page 24 of his article, Rescher states that "the wheels of the celestial bodies also had a height that is one-third their breadth, just like the earth . . ." The difference between the former and the latter in the case of Rescher is one of perspective (plane view versus elevated view).

56. See figures on pp. 16 and 18. It is important to note for the case at hand that I am making a distinction between the *ring of fire* and the *sun ring*. The *sun ring*, as we shall see, also includes the ring of dark mist that encases the *ring of fire*.

57. *keimenon loxon* DK A22. The tilting of the ring of the sun has nothing to do with the obliquity of the ecliptic but with the obliquity of the heavenly axis with respect to the earth around which the heavenly bodies turn. This entails, as I noted above, that the celestial rings stand for the daily paths of the sun, moon, and stars. Since Anaximander thought the earth to be flat, the obliquity of the axis (some 38.51 at Delphi, the earth's navel) would be the same all over the earth. For a rendition of the astronomical model which would follow from this, see Couprie (1995), 159–181. Couprie's thesis only reinforces my own thesis that Anaximander's numbers are not based on astronomical data of any sort. In fact, as Couprie himself notes, the discovery of the ecliptic (the yearly path of the sun along the stars) was only ascribed to Oinopides several generations later (DK 41A7) and appears "to be a too sophisticated conception for Anaximander's more primitive astronomical ideas in general" (1995), 161–162.

58. It is worth noting, using my figures as references, that whereas I see the ring of fire (or sun disk) from the perspective of the width as shining down on us, Couprie sees the ring of fire (or sun disk) from the perspective of the height (which is one third the width) as shining down on us.

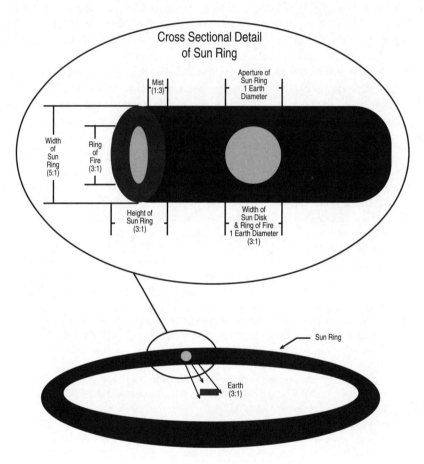

Figure 1.1
Cross sectional detail of sun ring

Figure 1.2
Sun disk in perspective

If such is the case then the *height* or *thickness* will be the *distance* from the *inner* to the *outer* face (figure 1.1). But what is the *height*? Again, this necessitates a return to the dimensions of the earth. If the *width* or diameter of the earth is 3× its *height*, then the *height* is 1/3 the *width*. What must be envisioned, in my view, to be consistent, is a ring (or rings) of fire 3× as *wide* as it is (or as they are) *thick* (figure 1.1). But the rings of air (*aēr*) or dark mist which encases the rings of fire must also be factored in (this is consistent with the expression "like bark around a tree").[59] If it is assumed that each side of the encasement is of the same *thickness* as the fire ring, this will give a *height* of one earth diameter: 1/3 (air) + 1/3 (fire) + 1/3 (air) (figure 1.1). These figures would hold for the plane view (figure 1.3). However, the *height* in the elevated view (figure 1.1), would become the *width* in the plane view.

There are several advantages to this. First, the *distances* (in *radii*) from center to center can still be understood in multiples of 3 and if one were to add one earth *radius* as the distance from the *center* of the sun ring to the outer face of the sun ring, this would give 28 *radii* from the *center* of the earth to the outer face of the sun ring.[60] Second, it accounts for the *thickness* of the ring itself being one earth diameter which in turn explains why the distance from outer face to outer face of the sun ring amounts to 28 earth diameters. Third, it means that although the visible heavenly bodies are obviously of different sizes, their rings have the same *height* or thickness. Last, the ring can thus be understood as oval or flat rather than round (figure 1.2) which is

---

59. *hōs tōi dendrōi phloion* in Pseudo-Plutarch's *Miscellanies* 2 = DK 12A10, 36. Rescher (1969) also sees the thickness of the ring of fire as 1/3 the diameter of the earth, but he sees the dark mist as comprising the entire space between the rings of fire. In fact, he seems to understand the rings of dark mist/air as the wheels them-selves (see, in particular, the diagrams on page 24). This is the case because he sees the rings as "like a broad wheel without spokes" (20). He therefore translates the phrase *harmateiōi trochōi paraplēsion, tēn hapsida echonta koilēn, plērē puros* (Aetius 2. 20.1 = DK 12A21) as "like a chariot wheel, having a hollow center, and this is full of fire" (20). I understand it as: "like chariot wheels, with its rim hollow, and full of fire." In sum, I do not understand a solid wheel "without" spokes, but a wheel that would entail spokes (albeit, not strictly speaking, with spokes). Aetius describes the moon ring with almost identical language: *homoion gar einai harmateiōi trochōi koilēn echonti tēn hapsida kai puros plērē* . . . (Aetius 2.25.1 = DK 12A22) and the stars are *pilēmata aeros trochoeidē, puros emplea*, that is, "wheel shaped compressions of air filled with fire" (Aetius 2.13.7 = DK 12A18). Moreover, all three descriptions are consistent with the expression: *hōs tōi dendrōi phloion* ("like bark around a tree") which could be understood in a similar sense.

60. O'Brien's analysis gives multiples of 4.

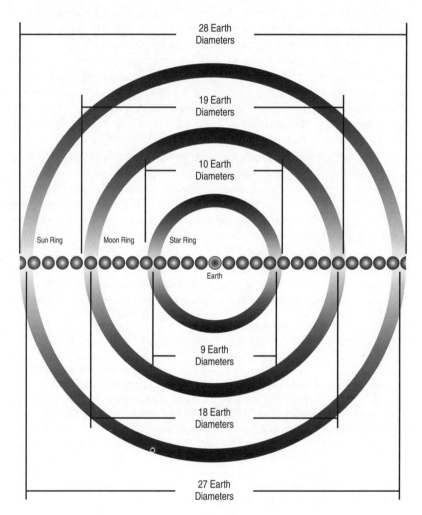

Figure 1.3
Plan view of cosmological model

consistent with the description of the celestial rings as "like chariot wheels."[61] Let us now put this into context.

In Anaximander's model, the *diameter* of the earth is 3× its *height* and the *circumference* of the earth is 3× its *diameter*. According to the hypothesis that the series 9,18,27 refers to the *sizes* and *distances* of the three rings with respect to the dimensions and position of the earth, this is what follows.

The *circumference* of the star ring is 9× the *circumference* of the earth (or 1 × 3 × 3); the *diameter* (or *size*) of the star ring from *center* to *center* is 9× the *diameter* of the earth (or 1 × 3 × 3); the *distance* from the *center* of the earth to the *center* of the star ring is 9× the *radius* of the earth (or 1 × 3 × 3).[62]

The *circumference* of the moon ring is 18× the *circumference* of the earth (or 2 × 3 × 3); the *diameter* of the moon ring is 18× the *diameter* of the earth (or 2 × 3 × 3); the *distance* from the *center* of the star ring to the *center* of the moon ring is again 9× the *radius* of the earth (or 1 × 3 × 3) and from the *center* of the earth to the *center* of the moon ring 18× the *radius* of the earth (or 2 × 3 × 3).

The *circumference* of the sun ring is 27× the *circumference* of the earth (or 3 × 3 × 3); the *diameter* of the sun ring is 27× the *diameter* of the earth (or 3 × 3 × 3); the *distance* from the *center* of the moon ring to the *center* of the sun ring is again 9× the *radius* of the earth (or 1 × 3 × 3) and from the *center* of the earth to the *center* of the sun ring 27× the *radius* of the earth (or 3 × 3 × 3).

In sum, just as the measurements of the earth stand in a relation of 1:3:9 to each other (height:width:circumference) so do the sizes and distances of the 3 rings stand in a relation of 1:2:3 both to each other and to the dimensions of the earth.

What can one deduce from all this? Simply that Anaximander conceived his universe or cosmological model according to a mathematical or geometrical

---

61. On the importance of flatness, see Burch (1949–50), 155 n.41. Further to this, it should be clear that if mist is the same thickness throughout, then the shape of the ring would be oval or flat rather than round (figure 1.3). What I understand by "round" is if a straight round column were to take on the form of a circle. I don't mean to imply here that "chariot wheels" at that time had an oval shape, but that "rings" or wheels in the sky would not, in my view, have been perceived as being perfectly tube shaped or having square shaped edges. My figure follows from taking the column drum earth with its ratio of 3 to 1 (and encased in dark mist) as a model. For some interesting figures of chariot wheels in perspective, see Greenhalgh (1973).

62. Although it is generally agreed that the star ring or rings become smaller as the stars are nearer to the poles, this, in fact, would only be the case for the star ring or rings at the celestial equator. But it seems obvious that Anaximander did not give this any thought. This again seems to entail that observational astronomy, strictly speaking, was not the inspiration behind his cosmological model.

plan that reflects a propensity for both *geometrical* equality and symmetry following the series 3. In fact, the vast majority of commentators has adopted this hypothesis.[63] My aim here was to try to resolve the controversy and confusion surrounding the measurements associated with Anaximander's cosmological model (thereby reinforcing the validity of this hypothesis) and to offer some visual representations of the results.

Appendix

Aristotle, *On the Heaven* 295b10 (=DK 12A26), says that according to Anaximander the earth is held at rest at the center of the celestial sphere because of its equilibrium (*dia tēn homoiotēta*), meaning that it is equidistant from all the points on the circumference (*homoiōs pros ta eschata*). Hippolytus (*Refutation* 1.6.3 = DK 12A11), for his part, states that the earth is at rest because it is not dominated by anything (*hupo mēdenos kratoumenēn*), in that it is equidistant from everything (*dia tēn homoian pantōn apostasin*).

The most common interpretation of these passages is that Anaximander's reasoning behind the earth's immobility and position is mathematical and *a priori*. See, for example, Francis M. Cornford (1952), 165; Kirk, Raven, and Schofield (1983²), 134; Charles Kahn (1960), 77; W.K.C. Guthrie vol. I (1962), 99; Richard D. McKirahan (1993), 40; Rosemary Wright (1995b), 39. In sum, the principle of "sufficient reason" is: if there is no reason for an object to move in one direction rather than another, it stays where it is. This has been vigorously contested by some scholars, notably John Robinson (1971), 111–118, and David Furley (1987), vol. 1, 23–30. Robinson argues, with what he sees from

---

63. The commentators are, however, far from agreeing about the origin of the numbers and consequently about the origin of the cosmological model. There are, in the main, four hypotheses: 1) they are the result of a sacred or mythical inspiration; 2) they are the result of an astronomical inspiration; 3) they are the result of an architectural or technical inspiration; 4) they are a result of a political inspiration. In my *JHI* paper, I attempt to show that the only valid hypothesis is the political one, but not for reasons hitherto evoked. I argue that the numbers which translate the *sizes* and *distances* of the heavenly bodies in relation to the earth correspond in some way or other to the three social groups of which the *polis* of Anaximander's time was composed: the aristocracy, the (new) middle class, and the peasantry (or poor). Anaximander's cosmological model reflects what he saw as the only possible way of ridding the *polis* of the political dissension of his time: *isonomia*. Thus, each of the three social groups would correspond to one of the three celestial rings whose numbers translate the same relation of equality, symmetry, and reciprocity (1:2:3) in relation to the center of the universe, the earth, as the three social groups in relation to the *agora*. Consequently, since Anaximander, like Plato, is advocating a sociopolitical model that has yet to be realized, he may be considered as the first known utopian.

Aristotle (*On the Heavens* 2.13, 295a8-15 where Aristotle states that all those who hold that the earth came together at the center, attribute it to a vortex [*dinē*] and its flatness) and Simplicius (*Commentary on Aristotle's On the Heavens* 532.13) as textual support, that it is the vortex and air which are behind the earth's immobility. Furley, for his part, argues that certain images (like the tree trunk in Pseudo-Plutarch's *Miscellanies* 2 = DK 12A10, 36) imply that the overall shape of the cosmos was not important for Anaximander. He argues further that only a spherical earth could be equidistant from all extremes. Consequently, if the earth is at rest, it is because it is flat, evenly balanced, and floating on air, in sum, for purely physical reasons. While there is little doxographical evidence in support of a vortex (there is no doxographical evidence of a vortex before Empedocles) or the earth resting on air in Anaximander, the cosmogonical development leaves clearly understood that the explanation for the earth's stability is *physical*. The earth remains at rest at the center of the sphere because of its *inertia* occasioned by the cosmogonical development (see, in particular Pseudo-Plutarch's *Miscellanies* 2 = DK 12A10, 33–36). Indeed, the two primary opposites behind this cosmogonical development—hot (and dry), and cold (and wet)—are characterized by mobility and immobility, respectively and this, in turn, explains the earth's inertia. Further, at the end of the cosmogonical development the earth finds itself at the center of a *plenum* for it is surrounded, as we will see, by a sphere composed of three concentric rings (which contain the heavenly bodies) of fire and mist, with air between them. However, if we consider (A) that the earth is at the *center* of the sphere surrounded by three concentric rings, (B) that the ratio (as we will see) of the dimensions of the earth is analogous to the sizes and distances of the three rings, (C) that the earth is, therefore, equidistant from all the points on the celestial circumference as well as the three rings, then we may conclude (D) that the reasoning behind the physical structure of Anaximander's world is mathematical or geometrical. In sum, Anaximander's reasoning may have been something like the following: How can I make the physical structure of the universe, which definitely exhibits order, conform to the most perfect geometrical form, the circle.

Chapter 2

Anaximander's Discovery Of Space

Dirk L. Couprie

One of the ideas that is most characteristic of Western thought, and distinctive for Western civilization, is the idea of space—the space of the universe. Western man is the conqueror of space. Western civilization has sent people to the moon, has sent unmanned spacecrafts beyond the farthest planet of our solar system, has searched for signs of extraterrestrial civilizations in our galaxy, and has looked through telescopes billions of light-years into the universe. Whether you call it a blessing or not, no other civilization has ever accomplished these things. These were successes of Western technology, but they were not only technological achievements. In order to send machines to other planets, you must be convinced of the possibility, the conceptual possibility, of doing such a thing. All of these achievements presuppose a concept of the universe in which they might be done. If you conceive of the universe as a firmament, a big dome or ceiling, onto which the celestial bodies are glued in some way or another, you will never even consider the possibility of sending people to walk on the moon or to other planets. The Western concept of the heavens is of a three-dimensional universe, a universe with depth, in which the celestial bodies lie behind one another. We are so used to this concept that it is difficult to recognize how unusual it is. If you have been in a planetarium, where the stars, the planets, the sun, and the moon are represented by lights, spotted on a curved ceiling, perhaps you may realize that this is the way we *see* the universe. The depth of the heavens is not something we *see*, but something we *know*. We do not *see* that the celestial bodies are behind one another, but we *know* that this is the case. The universe, conceived as three-dimensional, with depth, is a highly artificial one, and it is completely different from the more natural way of looking at it as a firmament, onto which the celestial bodies are glued, all at the same distance.

How did this conception of the stratified universe, this idea of space, originate? I claim that it was the discovery of the Greek Anaximander, who lived in Miletus, in the Asian part of Greece, from about 610 to 547 BCE. He taught three epoch-making theories: (1) that the celestial bodies make full circles, and thus go underneath the earth, (2) that the earth hangs free and unsupported in the center of the universe, and (3) that the celestial bodies lie behind one another: first the stars, then the moon, and farthest away the sun, at nine, eighteen and twenty-seven earth diameters distance from us. The important thing in this last theory is not that he was wrong about the order of the celestial bodies, or that his estimates of their distances were far from correct, but that he said that they were *behind* one another. I argue that these three ideas together, and the third one in particular, mark the origin of Western astronomy; Anaximander is the discoverer of space. My aim is to show that Anaximander's astronomy, strange as it may seem, makes perfect sense, and it led eventually to our picture of the universe. In understanding Anaximander's view of the universe, we may gain a better understanding of our own.[1]

In interpreting Anaximander's thoughts, we have the difficulty of placing ourselves in the mind of someone who thinks that the earth is flat and situated in the center of the universe, someone who has no other astronomical instruments at his disposal than the naked eye and a gnomon. In order to achieve this, we have to do a kind of mental gymnastics. If we fail to do that, we may be misled by what I call "the anachronistic fallacy"; as we shall see, scholars from the earliest doxographers until the present have been so misled.

The doxography has two conflicting stories about Anaximander's description of the earth. Diogenes Laertius tells us that Anaximander taught the sphericity of the earth.[2] However, Pseudo-Plutarch, Hippolytus, and Aetius tell us that Anaximander said that the earth was cylindrical, like a column of stone.[3] Generally, modern scholars agree that Diogenes Laertius was mistaken, and that "column of stone" must mean "column-drum," as is suggested by the ratio 3:1 for the diameter and the height given by Hippolytus (figure 2.1).[4] These scholars argue that on the whole Diogenes Laertius's reports are not always very reliable, that the image and the words in which it is put in the other reports are so curious and yet precise that they must be authentic, and that the cylindrical form is a kind of missing link between the flat earth of the primitive world-picture and the spherical earth of the more sophisticated conception from

---

1. Critical remarks, made by István Bodnár, Robert Hahn, and Gerard Naddaf, made it possible to clarify my thoughts on Anaximander, especially where they disagree with me.

2. DK 12A1(1).

3. DK 12A10 and 12A11(3).

4. Some take the ratio the other way around. So, e.g., Dumont: "un cylindre dont la profondeur est trois fois plus grande que la largeur," which certainly is a wrong translation. See Dumont (1988) 28. See also O'Brien (1967), 424–425, and Wright (1995b), 39. The figure is from Hahn, *Anaximander and the Architects. The Contribution of Egyptian and Greek Architectural Technologies on the Origins of Greek Philosophy* (State University of New York Press, 2001); we gratefully acknowledge Hahn's cooperation in printing this figure.

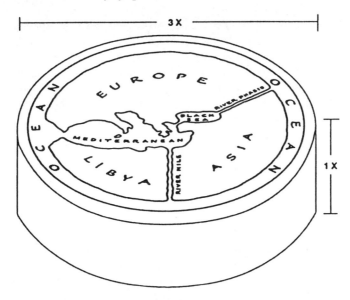

Figure 2.1
The drum-shaped earth (after Hahn)

Plato and Aristotle onward. So we may say with certainty that Anaximander did *not* teach the sphericity of the earth.

Why is it so important to stress this point, although it is not much discussed by scholars? The cylindrical earth is a kind of permanent reminder of what I call the danger of the anachronistic fallacy. This is the fallacy that results from our inability to give up our familiar interpretation of the universe and look at Anaximander's astronomical teachings with an unbiased eye. We shall meet this fallacy over and over again, and in various disguises. As a matter of fact, Diogenes Laertius is a good example of an early victim of the fallacy: he could not imagine that anyone would believe the earth to be other than a sphere.

But the dangers of an anachronistic interpretation of Anaximander's astronomical teachings go much further. Since Aristotle the universe as a whole, like the earth, has been conceived as a sphere, or better, as a number of concentric sphere-shells. This image of a spherical universe has been strengthened by the concept of the sphere as the most perfect body. The image is so strong that it is hard to imagine that people before Aristotle might have had another idea about the universe. So almost all commentators take it for granted that Anaximander too taught a spherical universe. But did he? We read that the earth is cylindrical, that the celestial bodies are wheels, like those of a chariot,[5] and that during the genesis of the universe a sphere of fire grew around the air encircling the earth "like the bark around a tree."[6] The common view is that this image of the bark around a tree must go back to Anaximander himself.[7] If we try to look at the doxography with an unbiased eye, not so much the image of spheres pops up, as those of cylinders and wheels. The very word "sphere," used here by Theophrastus in Diels and Kranz (hereafter: DK) 12A10, has to be viewed as an anachronism as well: even when describing the Anaximandrian image of telescoping cylinders (the bark around a tree), Theophrastus is not able to abandon the spherical universe of his teacher, Aristotle. I agree with Furley that "it should be noticed that the idea of circular orbits for all the heavenly bodies does not itself entail that the whole cosmos is spherical."[8] If we want to understand Anaximander's astronomical thought, we must begin from the idea that he did *not* teach the sphericity of the universe either.

The difficulty of imagining Anaximander's cylindrical earth entails another anachronism. Pliny tells us that Anaximander should have understood the obliquity of the zodiac or ecliptic.[9] It is a matter of dispute between scholars whether this tradition is correct or not. The main arguments for doubt are: 1) that even in Babylonian astronomy the first time the zodiac is mentioned is in a cuneiform tablet dated about 410 BCE,[10] a considerable time after Anaximander, 2) that the same discovery is also ascribed to Oinopides,[11] who lived a century or so later, and 3) that it is not in accordance with Anaximander's rather primitive astronomy. This latter point can be made stronger. First, it has to be stressed that the zodiac (i.e., the broad band of constellations through which the planets, the sun, and the moon wander), is not exactly the same thing as the ecliptic, which is the sun's path through those constellations. The zodiac is presumably a much older concept, and we may presume that the Babylonians, who paid much attention to the rather complex movements of the planets, were acquainted with it, even though there seems to be no written evidence of this. But it is more difficult to observe that the sun describes a circular annual path along those stars, if only because the brightness of the sun itself is a serious hindrance to an exact determination of its place among the stars. But most of all, the *obliquity* of the ecliptic is a concept which belongs to the conception of a spherical earth within a spherical universe. For the plane, with respect to which the ecliptic is inclined, is that of the equator

---

5. DK 12A18, 21, and 22.
6. DK 12A10.
7. Cf. DK 12B5.
8. Furley (1987), 27.
9. DK 12A5.
10. Cf. Thurston (1994), 66.
11. DK 41A7.

of both the earth and the spherical universe. Anaximander's earth was cylindrical, and, consequently, the concept of the equator doesn't make sense in this context. So we may conclude that Anaximander did *not* teach the obliquity of the ecliptic.

Now that we have looked at the heavens with Anaximander's eyes, we are prepared to appreciate his major astronomical discoveries. Anaximander is famous for his teaching that the earth hangs free in space. Most commentators focus on the way he argues why the earth does not fall, as it is not supported by anything. Or even more sophisticated, why it does not fall down or move up, or float away laterally. We will come back to this famous argument later on, but let us stay for a while with the conception of a free-floating earth. This idea meant a complete revolution in people's conception of the universe. Here is put forward, for the first time in history, the image of an unsupported earth. How revolutionary this conception was is illustrated by Anaximenes, Anaximander's successor, who apparently found the idea too daring and let the earth float like a lid on the air. Obviously, the earth hanging free in space is not something Anaximander could have *observed*. It was more than 2500 years later when astronauts *saw* the unsupported earth floating in space and thus made the ultimate confirmation of Anaximander's conception. Without the benefit of space travel, how did Anaximander *conclude* that the earth hangs unsupported in space?

This question leads us to Anaximander's second epoch-making discovery. And again, it is so self-evident to us that it is hard to understand how daring an idea this was. It is the idea that the celestial bodies in their daily course make full circles and thus go also underneath the earth—from Anaximander's standpoint. Again, this is not something he could have *observed*, but a *conclusion* he must have drawn. We would say that this is a conclusion that lies at hand. We can see—from the northern hemisphere, like Anaximander—the stars around the Polar star making full circles, and we can also observe that the more southerly stars sometimes disappear behind the horizon, and that the arcs they describe are smaller, the more to the south they are. So we may argue that the stars, of which we see only arcs, in reality also describe full circles, just like those near the Polar star. With regard to the sun and the moon, we can observe that the arcs they describe are sometimes bigger and sometimes smaller, and we are able to predict exactly where they will rise the next day. So it seems not a bold guess to say that these celestial bodies also make full circles. Nevertheless, it was a daring conclusion, just because it necessarily entails the conception of the free hanging earth. In other cultures, we now and then meet a representation of, for example, the sun being transported by a boat through the waters underneath the earth. Those ideas are, as far as I can see, quite different from the idea of hoops at a distance from the earth, leaving the earth unsupported, as Anaximander imagined. How daring his conception was is shown by the fact that his follower, Anaximenes, taught that the celestial bodies do not go underneath the earth, but around it "like a felt hat turns about our head."[12] It is important, however, to recognize that the conception of the celestial bodies as hoops and that of the unsupportedness of the earth are not independent of one another. When Anaximander concluded from the daily appearance and disappearance of the celestial bodies that they make full circles and go underneath the earth, he must have concluded as well that the earth must be unsupported in the center of those circles. As far as I know this connection has been made nowhere in the literature.

For Anaximander, as he realized that the celestial bodies make full circles and that as a corollary of this the earth must be unsupported, the urgent question that had to be answered was, why the earth, being unsupported, does not fall. The argument is that the earth, being in equilibrium with equal distances to "everything," has no reason whatsoever to go in either direction and so necessarily remains in the center of the universe.[13] This argument is glorified as the first instance of the so-called "Principle of Sufficient Reason," according to which everything which is true or real implies a reason why it is so and not otherwise."[14] It is the same argument, and in the same connection, that is ascribed to Parmenides,[15] and that is used by Socrates in Plato's *Phaedo*.[16] As a general principle, it is formulated by Leucippus.[17] The argument definitely deserves better than the way Aristotle ridicules it by reducing it into a kind of Buridan's ass: on the basis of the same principle, a hair which is pulled from both sides with equal strength would not snap in two, and a man who is as hungry as thirsty and is placed on equal distances of drink and food, would not be able to move to either side.[18]

Moreover, there is a link here with another one of Anaximander's astronomical ideas, the conception of the celestial bodies as rings or wheels. One of the reasons for this strange (to our modern minds) idea, is that these rings incorporate the argument why the earth doesn't fall: each point on a ring has the same distance to (the center of) the earth as any other. If the celestial bodies had been free-floating bodies themselves—as we now know they are—Anaximander's argument on the basis of the Principle of Sufficient Reason would not have made sense. Let us look at the same problem from the other side. There is no doxographical evidence of it, but it is quite certain that the question, why the celestial bodies do not fall upon the earth must have been as serious a problem to Anaximander as the opposite question, why the earth

---

12. See DK 13A7(6).
13. Cf. DK 12A11 and 12A26.
14. Kahn (1960), 77.
15. DK 28A44.
16. Plato, *Phaedo* 108E4-109H8.
17. DK 67B2.
18. Aristotle, *De Caelo* 295b31-34.

does not fall. The conception of the celestial bodies as rings, then, provides an answer to both questions: just like the earth, the celestial bodies have no reason whatsoever to move otherwise than in circles around the earth, as each point on them is always as far from the earth as any other. It is because of reasons like this that for a long time thereafter the celestial bodies were thought of as somehow attached to sphere-shells, and not as free-floating bodies. In fact, astronomy had to wait until Newton for a more convincing answer to the question, why the celestial bodies don't fall. These considerations give the tradition about Anaximander's hoops more trustworthiness than Dicks believes.[19]

The ideas of a free-floating earth and the celestial bodies as rings, making full circles around the earth, are the first and second marks of the new Anaximandrian conception of the universe. And they are completed by a third, namely, the conception of the different distances of the celestial bodies to the earth. Together, these three insights (the free-floating earth, the celestial bodies as rings, and the different distances of these rings) result in a three-dimensional world-picture. When Anaximander looked at the heavens he imagined, for the first time in history, *space*, in our sense of the word. In order to understand better Anaximander's achievement, let us dig deeper into his conception of *depth* in the universe, the idea that the celestial bodies lie *behind* one another. One gets an impression of the enormous difference between Anaximander's idea of the universe and older mythological ones, when comparing it with the picture of the covering of the holy tree with the mantle of the heavens on an Assyrian seal cylinder, as shown in figure 2.2.[20] The conception of the celestial vault, rejected by Anaximander, can also be found in the Egyptian representation of the heaven goddess Nut, held up by the sky god Shu, standing on the earth god Keb, as shown in figure 2.3.[21] The Egyptian and Mesopotamian cultures apparently did not imagine a depth dimension in the universe, or perhaps they were not interested in it. This knowledge does not serve direct practical

---

19. See Dicks (1970), 45–46.
20. From Eisler (1910), 592, fig. 70 (ca. 800 BCE). There exists, however, some doubt whether this is the right interpretation of this picture: ". . . apodictic statements about the meaning of the Tree are carefully avoided in recent studies" (Parpola [1993], 165n.). Elsewhere (1993, 183), a similar picture is interpreted by Parpola as 'the distributing of the Divine Stream.'
21. From Lerner (1991), 59, fig. 2.1 (ca.1000 BCE). This picture, many specimina of which exist, hardly changes through the ages. Sometimes, Nut is pictured as the Celestial Cow, on whose underbelly stars appear, and whose legs are obviously considered as the support of the vault of the heavens. See Clagett (1989) *Tome Two*, 817 (and 531–546 in the 'Book of the Divine Cow'). Other Egyptian symbols of the sky were such different images as the wings of a vulture and an ocean. (Cf. Clagett [1989] *Tome One*, 270–271).

Figure 2.2
The covering of the holy tree with the mantle of the heavens
on an Assyrian seal cylinder

purposes, for the data it delivers are neither religiously or astrologically interesting, nor are they of help in making calendars. The image of the celestial
vault is still present with Anaximander's contemporary Anaximenes, who
thinks that the stars are like nails hit into, or like fiery leafs painted on, the crys-
talline celestial vault.[22]

However, there seem to be some Iranian parallels to the conception of celestial bodies behind one another. Eisler was one of the first to hint at some
texts in the Avesta in which the stars, the sun, and the moon (in that order) are
mentioned as stations in the journey of the soul to heaven to the throne of
Ahura Mazda.[23] He and other authors have claimed that Anaximander was

22. DK 13A14.
23. Eisler (1910), 90–91 n.3. See also: Bousset (1901) esp. 24ff. Later scholars like
    Burkert and West point out similar parallels. See Burkert (1963), 106 and 110–112,
    and West (1971), 89–90.

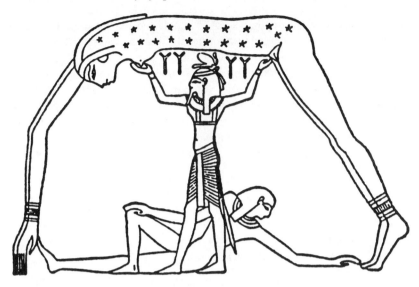

Figure 2.3
Egyptian painting of the heaven goddess Nut,
held up by the sky god Shu,
standing on the earth god Keb

dependent on Iranian cosmogony. Some others, however, point out that the Iranian texts are rather late and wonder whether the influence wasn't the other way around.[24] Be this as it may, there is a real and significant difference between these texts and Anaximander's universe. The Iranian texts are embedded in mythological and religious contexts, whereas Anaximander designs a completely rational and, as we would call it, scientific cosmology. Of all the numerous Mesopotamian astronomical clay tablets there is only one that possibly has to do with depth in the universe. It is a tablet, dating from ± 1150 BCE, and which may be read as follows: "19 from the Moon to the Pleiades; 17 from the Pleiades to Orion; 14 from Orion to Sirius, 11 from Sirius to δ canis majoris, 9 from δ canis majoris to Arcturus, 7 from Arcturus to Scorpius, and 4 from Scorpius to AN.TA.GUB," and ending with the question "how much is one god

---

24. Most recently by Schmitz (1988), 77–78. See also Kahn (1960), 90 n.1; and Duchesne-Guillemin (1966), 425. The counterargument of Burkert and West, that Anaximander was almost the only Greek who arranged the heavenly bodies in that order, is not very convincing. See Burkert (1963), 103, and West (1971), 96. See also Classen (1986), 86 n.111. According to Aetius, Metrodorus of Chios and Crates of Mallos were the only others who held Anaximander's order (see DK 12A18).

(i.e., star) distant from another god?"[25] Scholars differ on the question of whether this text is about radial or transversal distances. I suspect that the last, the angular distance between the constellations, is meant, and not distances from the earth. However, in both cases the figures are clearly wrong. Scholars tend to think that the numbers "are not astronomically significant but purely the outcome of a mathematical problem as it is set up in the text."[26] But even if not, this is a stray note, whereas Anaximander's distances play their part in the context of his doctrines of the free-floating earth and the full circles of the heavenly bodies. There exists one other cuneiform tablet on which there is talk of a stratified heaven; it can be translated as follows:

> The upper heavens, of *luludanitu*-stone, are the property of *Anu*.
> The middle heavens, of *saggilmut*-stone, are the property of the *Igigi*.
> The lower heavens, of jaspis, are the property of the *lumasi*-stars of
> the gods;
> He (i.e., Marduk) drew them thereon.[27]

As far as I can see, it is only the lowermost heaven in this text associated with heavenly bodies painted on them, not unlike Anaximenes' conception. The other two layers apparently have a more religious meaning. This becomes clearer when we see that in the next lines of the text the three layers of the heavens are mirrored by three layers of the earth: the upper earth, where human beings, frail like a gust of wind, live; the middle earth, where he settled his father *Ea*; and the lower earth, where the 600 *Anunnaki* dwell. We may conclude that in the neighboring civilizations there exists hardly any evidence before and during Anaximander's time of a conception of the heavens that can be compared with his.

Perhaps it is not too daring to read in his cosmogony a recognition that Anaximander was fully aware that he was exploding the old conception of the universe. It is reported that originally a sphere of fire, originating from the γόνιμον, grew around the earth like the bark of a tree, before falling apart in the separate rings of the sun, the moon, and the stars.[28] When we take the tree as a usual metaphor of the heavenly tree, the axis of the heaven, the bark of that tree can be regarded as an image of the celestial vault that explodes in a kind of heavenly firework.

---

25. This concerns the so-called Hilprecht text HS 229. See Neugebauer (1952), 94 (part of the quoted text), and Rochberg-Halton (1983), 212. AN.TA.GUB is an as yet unidentified star. I thank Dr. W. H. van Soldt from the University of Leiden for his kind information on this issue.
26. Rochberg-Halton (1983), 216. See also van der Waerden (1974), 62–63.
27. From the tablet KAR 307, lines 30–38. See Ebeling (1931), 30 and 33. Cf. Lambert (1975), 58.
28. See DK 12A10.

In order to understand better Anaximander's conception of *depth* in the universe, let us look at his strange order of the celestial bodies. Some scholars wonder why Anaximander made the stars the nearest celestial bodies, for he should have noticed the occurrence of star-occultations by the moon. On the contrary, however, he placed them nearest to the earth. I think that Anaximander is not too much to blame for the wrong position of the stars. In contradistinction to Dicks,[29] I think that occultations of stars by the moon are not so easy to observe (how many of us have ever consciously witnessed the occultation of a star?) or, rather, that they could be easily interpreted otherwise. Let us try again to put ourselves into the position of someone (Anaximander) who thinks—for whatever reason— that the brightest celestial bodies are farthest away. Nowadays, we *know* that the stars are behind the moon, and thus we speak of star occultations when we see a star disappear behind the moon. But Anaximander had no reason at all, from his point of view, to speak of a star occultation when he saw a star disappear when the moon was at the same place. So it is a *petitio principii* to say that for him occultations of stars were easy to observe. He perhaps observed stars disappearing and appearing again, but he did not observe—could not see it as—the occultation of that star, for that interpretation did not fit his paradigm. The easiest way to understand his way of looking at it—if he observed the phenomenon at all—is that he must have thought that the brighter light of the moon outshines for a while the much smaller light of the star. And when the moon is waxing or declining it is even the sun whose light outshines that of the star, for at those occasions the moon is near the sun in the sky. Also the fact that the stars look much smaller than the sun and moon does not automatically lead to the conclusion that they are farther away. In other words, those who, like Dicks, think that Anaximander is to blame for not having understood the true meaning of star occultations, are again victim of an anachronistic fallacy. Our conclusion must be that Anaximander neither could have *observed* the spatial relations of the celestial bodies, nor that he could have *inferred* those relations in the way we are used to. So there must be another reason why he put the celestial bodies in that strange order.

Krafft points to the curious fact that in German it is idiomatic to say "Sonne, Mond und Sterne" when enumerating the celestial bodies.[30] The same idiomatic expression also occurs in English: "sun, moon, and stars," in that order, which is Anaximander's order and not the real one. So in daily language we still use the order of decreasing brightness. It is like an Anaximandrian fossil in our language. A plausible suggestion is that the original sphere of fire, which originated from the γόνιμον and grew around the earth like the bark

---

29. Dicks (1970), 226 n.51. Here Dicks himself is victim to what he calls "the 'tacit assumptions' so often made . . . by modern commentators on ancient science" (175).
30. Krafft (1971), 106.

around a tree, and which fell apart in the separate rings of the sun, the moon, and the stars, still resides at the periphery of Anaximander's universe.[31] This fire, however, remains invisible, hidden by the air, which hides also the fire within the celestial wheels, except where the openings are that we see as sun, moon, or star. The farther away from the surrounding fire, the less bright the celestial bodies are, and this should explain the order of the celestial bodies. So it must have been the difference in brightness between the celestial bodies that made Anaximander think that they must lie behind one another.[32]

Let us now turn to Anaximander's numbers, the expression of his conception of depth in the heavens. The doxography gives the following numbers: 27 for the sun hoop;[33] 28 for the sun hoop;[34] 19 for the moon hoop.[35] If Anaximander did distinguish the planets at all, he certainly placed them at the same distance from the earth as the stars,[36] but our sources give us no numbers for either the stars or the plants. Building on the work of earlier scholars like Tannery and Diels,[37] O'Brien, in the first two parts of his article "Anaximander's Measurements,"[38] describes the distances of the celestial bodies in Anaximander's universe as based on calculations which were simple numerical proportions. According to this reconstruction, the diameters of the inner and outer rim of the sunwheel measure 27 and 28, the inner and outer diameters of the moonwheel 18 and 19, and those of the stars, which are nearest to the earth, 9 and 10 earth-diameters. Figure 2.4 shows this conception in Diels's rendition. Others have argued that the numbers must not refer to the diameters but to the radii of the rings, that is to say, to their distances to the earth.[39] I think they are right, for three reasons. The first reason has to do with a problem that has been delineated by Kirk.[40] It is recorded that according to Anaximander the sun has the same size as the earth.[41] This means, Kirk

---

31. Kahn (1960), 91; Robinson (1968), 29; Rescher (1958/1969), 724, fig. 5. West (1971, 92) suggests the number 36 as the diameter of this "outer οὐρανός."
32. So already Diels (1897), 229. Reprinted in Diels (1969), 14. See also Bodnár (1988), 50.
33. DK 12A11, a mutilated text, corrected by Diels; idem DK 12A21.
34. DK 12A21.
35. DK 12A22.
36. Cf. DK 12A2: ὑπὸ δὲ αὐτοὺς (sc. sun and moon) τὰ ἀπλανῆ τῶν ἄστρων καὶ τοὺς πλάνητας.
37. Tannery (1887), 94–95. Diels (1897), 236.
38. O'Brien (1967), 423–427.
39. In an original way, Naddaf thinks that it is possible to have his cake and eat it: "the numbers represent the sizes and distances of the three rings" (Naddaf [1998], 14). According to him, taken as multiples of the earth diameter, the numbers represent diameters; taken as multiples of the earth radius, they represent distances (15).
40. Kirk and Raven (1957), 136 n.1.
41. DK 12A21: Ἀναξίμανδρος τὸν μὲν ἥλιον ἴσον εἶναι γῇ.

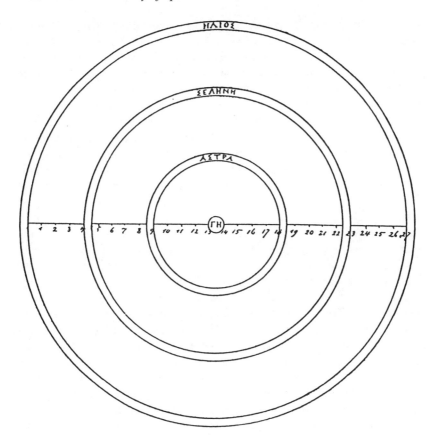

Figure 2.4
Diels's map

assumes, that the width of the sun ring must be the same as the diameter of the earth. But this would result in a difference of 2 earth diameters between the inner and outer rim instead of 1. A quick look at Diels's figure shows that Kirk is right. O'Brien tries to solve this problem by maintaining that "there is no reason why we should not think of the thickness or width of the rim of the sun wheel as equal to one half of the earth's diameter."[42] As O'Brien

---

42. As O'Brien himself remarks (1967, 424n.), this was in fact the intention of Tannery and Diels. Tannery says explicitly: "la double épaisseur du cerceau est ainsi égale au diamètre de la Terre" (1887, 94). And Diels says: "so ist die Breite dieser Ringe auf einen Erdradius zu veranschlagen" (1897, 232).

expresses it, we must "compare the thickness or width of *each side* of the rim of the sun wheel with the *radius* of the earth."[43] Although he is right, that "this will give a difference of one between the inner and the outer diameter of the sun wheel,"[44] I don't agree with him on this point, because he never explained how to press a whole sun into a ring that measures half its width. And thus he leaves Kirk's problem unanswered. The second reason why I think the numbers must indicate radii has to do with what I call Anaximander's main discovery, that the celestial bodies are at different distances from the earth. In contradistinction with diameters, radii indicate distances, and those were exactly what Anaximander was interested in. The third reason is that I tend to read the numbers as a kind of instruction for drawing a map of the universe. Anaximander's conception of the universe presupposes the possibility of elevating oneself in thought from the earth to a virtual point of view from which one has a survey of the universe as a whole. This is the point of view of a mapmaker. We know from the sources that Anaximander was the first to make a *mappa mundi*, a map of the world.[45] If we suppose that Anaximander also made a map of his universe,[46] not unlike that produced by Diels, then he must have used certain measurements for his drawing. In other words, Anaximander's numbers also must have played a role in his attempt to visualize his universe. The instruction, then, reads somewhat like this: "take a pair of compasses and draw a little circle; this is the earth. Call its diameter 1 unit. Now leave one of the legs of the compasses in the center, put the other leg at a distance of 9 units and draw a circle; this is the inner rim of the star ring. Now put the same leg of the compasses at 10 units; this is the outer rim of the star circle, etc." Moreover, I do not only agree with Kirk, that the clause Ἀναξίμανδρος τὸν μὲν ἥλιον ἴσον εἶναι τῇ γῇ

---

43. O'Brien (1967), 424.
44. O'Brien (1967), 423–424.
45. See DK 12A6.
46. I take it that where the doxography anachronistically speaks of a sphere (DK 12A1 and 12A2), these reports in reality go back to a *map* (a two-dimensional model) of the universe, drawn by Anaximander. Perhaps even the words ὅλως γεωμετρίας ὑποτύπωσιν ἔδειξεν (DK 12A2) must be understood as a reminiscence of such a map. Drawing or constructing a three-dimensional model with wheels and cylinders like the one I published earlier (Couprie [1995], figs. XIII–X) was, I think, beyond Anaximander's possibilities, although *we* can draw such a model that fits his conception of the universe. On the other hand, it is quite easy to explain the movements of the celestial bodies with the help of a plan view, by making broad gestures, describing circles in the air with your hands and indicating their inclination, the speed with which and the direction in which they move; something like that is told of a quarrel between Anaxagoras and Oinopides (See DK 41A2).

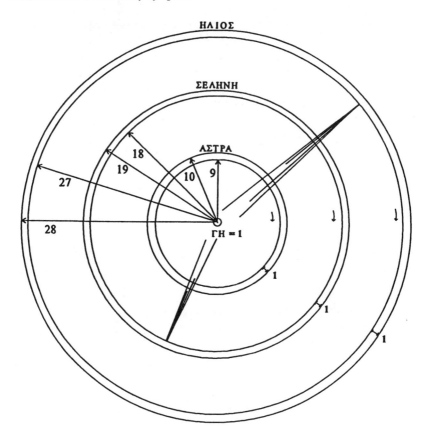

Figure 2.5
Map of Anaximander's universe

("Anaximander [says that] the sun is equal to the earth") means that the width of the sun ring must be the same as the diameter of the earth, but I tend to see it also as a kind of drawing-instruction: "make sure that the width of the ring(s) is one earth-diameter." My rendering of a map of Anaximander's universe is shown in figure 2.5.

The question, however, why Anaximander chose exactly these numbers (9 and 10 for the stars, 18 and 19 for the moon, 27 and 28 for the sun) to indicate the distances of the celestial bodies has remained just as mysterious. O'Brien offers one answer: "In Anaximander's system, as we have reconstructed it, the earth and the celestial wheels are *equidistant*. This was probably one of the primary factors influencing Anaximander's choice of measurements."[47] Making the distances between the rings equal lies at hand, be it only for aesthetic reasons, when we imagine Anaximander for the first time drawing his map. Still in pictures of the Ptolemaic or Copernican systems the rings usually are rendered as equidistant. Perhaps there is a reminiscence of the equidistance of Anaximander's rings in what has become a report on innumerable worlds being at equal distances: τῶν ἀπείρους ἀποφηναμένων τοὺς κόσμους Ἀναξίμανδρος τὸ ἴσον αὐτοὺς ἀπέχειν ἀλλήλων.[48] Both Cornford and Kahn come to the conclusion that the doctrine of innumerable worlds is not Anaximandrian, but must be a later, anachronistic, misinterpretation. And Cornford remarks: "Being familiar with the Atomist doctrine of innumerable coexistent worlds, they (sc. the doxographers, DC) would readily interpret what they found in that sense."[49] I tend to read this text as another (distorted) instruction for drawing a map of the universe: "make sure that the distances between the rings are equal." Obviously, however, O'Brien offers only part of an answer, for equidistance can be obtained with other numbers as well. It is important to realize that Anaximander's numbers cannot be based on observation, not only because they are apparently wrong, but particularly for the same simple reason that with the naked eye one does not *see* distances (depth) in the heavens.[50] What is more, he couldn't have *measured* those distances.[51] In order to know *how much* farther the sun is than the moon, and how far they are from the stars,

---

47. O'Brien (1967), 427. Engmann's opinion, that "the figures do not yield equal distances" is clearly wrong (Engmann [1991], 22). Whether we take radii or diameters, the result will always yield equal distances between the rings.

48. DK 12A17. Cornford (1934), esp. 12. Cf. also Kahn (1960), 46–53, esp. 50.

49. Cornford (1934), 2. Cf. also Kahn (1960), 46–53, esp. 50.

50. Dicks is right in saying that "there is not the remotest possibility that the numbers are based on observational data" (Dicks [1966], 36). Conche's conjecture, that Anaximander put the sun at such a distance that it appeared as a disc and not as a point, doesn't lead to any numbers at all, notwithstanding what he seems to imply. (See Conche [1991], 218–219).

51. The only exception, perhaps, is the sun. In ± 120 BCE, Chinese astronomers, thinking, like Anaximander, that the earth was flat, measured the distance to the sun with the help of two gnomons. Of course, their result was wrong, due to their false assumption of a flat earth. But, as the method these Chinese astronomers used was in principle the same as that by which Thales is said to have measured the distance of a ship at sea, Anaximander could have used the same method. See Thurston (1994), 91. See also: Needham (1959), 225; Cullen (1996), 77–80. However, if Anaximander had really *measured* the distance to the sun, the doxographers certainly would have reported it.

we need rather sophisticated instruments and geometry.[52] For me, this is the main reason to think that O'Brien's terminology is somewhat misleading, when he speaks of "Anaximander's Measurements," and why I prefer the word "numbers."

For similar reasons, Anaximander's numbers cannot be traced back to Babylonian astronomical observations. The kind of data he could have obtained from the Babylonians have to do with the movements of the celestial bodies, and with the periods in which they return to the same relative positions. But these data do not concern the distances to the celestial bodies. The interest of the Babylonians in astronomy was, so to speak, two-dimensional. They described the movements and relative positions of the celestial bodies as if they were on the screen of the heavens. This was what they needed, because for them astronomy was subordinate to the requirements of religion, astrology, and the making of calendars. So they studied thoroughly the movements and the times of appearance and disappearance of the celestial bodies at the horizon, and the constellations of stars. Anaximander's numbers, on the contrary, are of no help whatsoever for astrological goals or for making calendars. It is characteristic that the doxography gives us hardly any information on Anaximander's opinion of the planets, whereas the movements of these wandering stars are of the utmost importance for religious and astrological questions. It is also characteristic that there is only one concrete example of an observation made by Anaximander of a stellar constellation,[53] whereas there is an abundance of this kind of observation from the Babylonians, dating roughly from 700 BCE onward. Anaximander's interest was, so to speak, purely scientific: He was concerned with a three-dimensional astronomy that breaks through the two-dimensional ceiling of the heavens.

The usual explanation of Anaximander's numbers is that they are somehow based on mathematics. The doxography tells us that the earth, according to Anaximander, resembles a column drum.[54] The ratio 1:3 between the height of the earth and its diameter he could have derived from that kind of

---

52. Aristarchus of Samos (310–230 BCE) was the first to seriously try to measure the (relative) distances of the sun and the moon. Astronomers did not have the instruments necessary to calculate the sun's distance, and thereby its size, until the telescope was invented. Even with the use of a telescope, measuring distances in the universe is still a big problem for astronomers.

53. DK12A20. It can be shown that Anaximander's observation is the most accurate of the three mentioned there.

54. κίονι λίθῳ παραπλήσιον, DK 12A11; cf. 12A25.

building-stone, some of which show roughly those dimensions.[55] I think it must be considered as typically Anaximandrian to rephrase into mathematical ratios the tradition of the holy number 3. We may understand a little bit more of Anaximander's universe when we follow a suggestion made by West and Krafft.[56] They both point to Hesiod's *Theogony* 722–725, where it is said that a brazen anvil (according to Krafft: a meteorite) would take nine days to fall from heaven to earth, and again nine days to fall from earth to Tartarus. Or more precisely, it takes nine days to fall, while arriving on the tenth day.[57] It is not a bold guess to say that Anaximander must have known this text. The agreement with his numbers is too close to neglect, for the numbers 9 and 10 are exactly those extrapolated by Tannery for Anaximander's star ring. Moreover, according to Krafft, in the Greek counting system Hesiod's numbers mean "a very long time." Thus Troy was conquered in the tenth year after having stood the siege for nine years; and Odysseus scoured the seas for nine years before reaching his homeland in the tenth year.[58] Hesiod can be seen as a forerunner to Anaximander, for he tried to imagine the distance to the heavens, and even to the depths underneath the earth, although apparently he did not connect these distances with the celestial bodies, let alone with celestial bodies at different distances. We may infer that Anaximander, with his numbers 9 and 10 for the star ring, simply was trying to say that the stars are very far away. Then the other numbers can easily be interpreted as "farther" (for the moon ring) and "farthest" (for the sun ring). And this is exactly what we should expect from someone who has discovered that the image of the celestial vault is wrong, that the celestial bodies are behind one another, and who wishes to share this new knowledge with his fellow citizens. This solution explains why Anaximander used the measures which have been handed down to us: he wished to express, by using numbers that

---

55. See Hahn (1995), 118. Hahn's daring thesis is "that the cosmos is measured in column-drum proportions" (p. 96). Nevertheless, he does not account for Anaximander's numbers (9, 18, 27), and only suggests "that the horizontal face of the column drum . . . bears a striking resemblance to a *plan* model rendition of Anaximander's cosmos" (118). In his 2001 book (see n.4), Hahn defends his position more extensively. In order to see the intended resemblance we have to look at Rescher's version of that map (Rescher [1958], figs. 2–5 and 7).

56. West (1971), 94; Krafft (1971), 107. See also Burkert (1962), 288 n.63.

57. Hesiod measures distances in terms of time. This is an old method. So, for example, a παρασάγγης is the distance of one hour's marching. In modern astronomy a similar method is used when we speak of a "light-year" (the distance light travels in one year) as a measure for distances in the universe. Hesiod's unit of measure was, so to speak, the "anvil-day." Anaximander, on the contrary, used spatial measures to express distances.

58. Krafft (1971), 107–108. See also: Germain (1954), 13.

his readers could understand, that the stars, the moon and the sun are far, farther and farthest away.[59]

On a map as shown in figure 2.5, the radius of the inner rim of the sun hoop equals 28, and that of the outer rim of the sun hoop 29 earth diameters.[60] However, in this conception we seem to get a sun ring of 162 (2π (= 3) $\times$ 27) suns, put one after another,[61] and, accordingly, an angular diameter of some $2°15'$ for the sun, which is about 4.5 times too big (see figure 2.6).[62] In reality, some 720 suns one after another make up a full circle. The outcome of this option is so much in disagreement with the most obvious observational data that Anaximander must have noticed it.[63] Even Anaximander would have been able to see that his sun ring (the daily path of the sun) was much bigger than 162 suns, put one after another. This would be all the more the case if we can trust the report that Thales had already discovered that the sun's apparent diameter is 1/720 times its orbit.[64]

---

59. Burkert (1962), 449 n.72, mentions 9 and 27 as "Steigerung" of 3, which played a part in the death-cult. Quite another solution has been proposed by Eggermont. He maintains that Anaximander selected the number 27 "because it occurred in the formula 27 $\times$ 13 1/3 = 360, which on the one hand represented the actual observation of the sidereal lunar year and on the other hand embodied a mystic truth, viz. the equivalence of the sun to gold and of the moon to silver," the contemporary gold/silver ratio being 13 1/3. Eggermont (1973), 128. This theory is as strange as it is unverifiable. Baccou suggests that Anaximander derived the numbers of the sun ring somehow from a comparison of the angular diameter of the sun and the supposed measurement of the earth (Baccou [1951], 77). Baccou does not, however, show how Anaximander managed this. Recently, Naddaf has tried to connect Anaximander's numbers with the equality of parties in a (utopian) political situation. This, however, does not lead to specific numbers, as equality of distances can be expressed by any number (1998, 16–28).

60. In Couprie (1995), 162, I still followed the usual view, which makes the numbers refer to the *diameters* of the rings of the celestial bodies. This does not invalidate the conclusions of that article.

61. I owe the idea of putting suns after one another on the circumference of the circle of the sun ring, in order to visualize the angular diameter of the sun, to Stritzinger (1952), 63. The number 3 is a rough approximation of π (the ratio of the circumference of a circle to its diameter), which Anaximander could have found by unrolling a wheel and comparing the distance thus found with the diameter of the wheel.

62. Rescher notes the discrepancy between the resulting and the real angular diameter of the sun, without offering a solution (1958, 727 n.21a and fig. 8).

63. On this point I strongly disagree with Dreyer, who says that "no doubt this might have escaped his attention" (Dreyer, 1906/1953, 15 [see note]).

64. Not 1/27, as Hölscher maintains. See Hölscher (1970), 318n. See DK 11A1(24) and 11A19. Diogenes Laertius's report, however, seems inconsistent with what we know about Thales's cosmology.

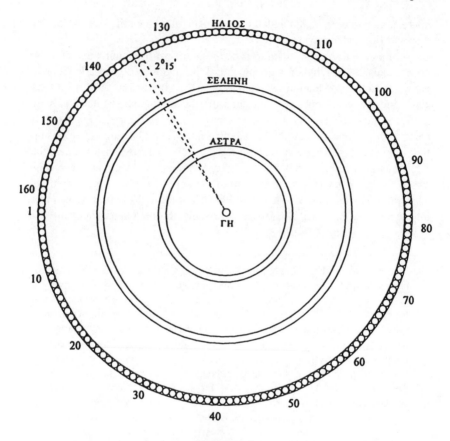

Figure 2.6
The problem of the sun's angular diameter

In order to find a solution to this problem, we have to remember that the doxography tells us that Anaximander conceived of the heavenly bodies as rings or wheels.[65] That they must be thought of as three-dimensional is clear from the doxography; we are told that they are "wheel-like, compressed masses of air filled with fire."[66] "Wheel-like" seems, according to Diels/

---

65. See DK 12A11, 18, 21, and 22.
66. DK 12A18: πιλήματα ἀέρος τροχοειδῆε πυρὸς ἔμπλεα. Kahn's translation (1960), 86.

Kranz,[67] to be the most authentic, and, I might add, thus also the additions: "wheel of a chariot" and "rim of the wheel."[68] "Rings" is, I think, an anachronistic expression which belongs to later models of the universe called "armillary spheres." In the doxography we still can see how later authors wrestled with Anaximander's concept of wheels, which was strange to them. Achilles Tatius definitely no longer understood it, for he took it to mean that the sun is the hub of a wheel, which sends its beams out like spokes to the rim. Modern authors tend to think that the wheels are like bicycle tubes. I think that this is another anachronism playing games with these authors.[69] Let us take Anaximander's image seriously: Contemporary pictures of (chariot-)wheels look much like coach-wheels such as are still used today; see figure 2.7.[70] The cross section of those wheels (i.e., of their rims) is a rectangle not a circle, as in the tube-like figures. Perhaps the form of the earth also has to do with the image of the wheels, for it might be seen as the hub of the concentric celestial wheels, especially when drawn on a map.[71] In order to understand what I propose as the right solution, we ought to realize that on a map the *width* of the celestial wheels is important, but their *height* is not depicted, as such a map is necessarily two-dimensional. We have to remember too that, due to the inclination of the axis of the heaven, the celestial bodies do not circle around the earth in the same plane as the earth's—flat—surface. The wheels "lie aslant" with respect to the surface of the flat earth. If it is agreed that Anaximander was not acquainted with the obliquity of the ecliptic, this is the natural interpretation of the words κείμενον λοξόν.[72] This entails, moreover, that the wheels of the sun and the moon simply

---

67. See DK 12B5: "auch τροχός A 21, 22 wohl echt."
68. DK 12A21 and 22.
69. See DK 12A21. Achilles seems also to be misled by the image of the "nozzle of a bellows" or "flute." One modern example is Krafft's romantic drawing in his article, "Anaximandros" (297). In both other versions of his article (see n.30), this picture is missing. Unfortunately, Krafft's erroneous picture has been reproduced recently by Saltzer (1990), 67. That Krafft's picture is altogether misleading, I have argued earlier. See Couprie (1995), 173–174. Brumbaugh (1981, 21) describes the wheels as follows: "rings of hollow pipe (a modern stove-pipe gives the right idea)." And also Naddaf draws such pipelike rings (1998), 10. However, he seems to feel a little uneasy at this point, for he writes: "I don't mean to imply by this that 'chariot wheels' at the time were oval shaped" (15n). In an earlier article, I too was guilty of drawing tube-like rings (Couprie [1995], 177 and 178).
70. Reproduced with permission of the Trustees of the British Museum. See also: Treue (ed.) (1986), 68 and 78.
71. This seems to me a more natural interpretation than O'Brien's (1967, 424), who considers Anaximander's earth as "as it were, an 'unexploded' wheel."
72. DK 12A22.

(a)

(b)

Figure 2.7
Contemporary (chariot) wheels:
(a) A clay model of a four wheeled vehicle, Athens 720 BCE; and
(b) a wheel on an Attic vase, ± 530/520 BCE

coincide with their daily motion, and not with their annual or monthly path.[73] The tilting of the heaven's axis makes it possible that "the inner face of the wheel, with the opening for the sun in it, could look down on the earth from above," as O'Brien[74] puts it. Now the supposition lies at hand, that "the wheels of the celestial bodies also had a height which is one-third their breadth, just like the earth," to use Rescher's words.[75] So it is the sun wheel's *height*, being one third of its width, which we see from the earth, whereas it is the wheel's *width*, and not its height, which appears on the map of the universe. The sun as we see it is a hole in the sun-hoop, according to Anaximander. This hole is in that part of the sun-hoop that is turned towards the earth, and thus in what I called its *height*, which is not visible on a map of the universe.[76] So, if I am right that the doxographical report that the sun is as big as the earth originally was an instruction for drawing a map of the universe, it says everything of the width of the sun-ring, but nothing of the size of the sun. In that case, the sun— that is, the hole in the sun's wheel—can be any size, and especially that which

73. On this point I fully agree with Kahn's answer to Dicks, in which he reconsiders his earlier view Kahn (1970), 102. The tilting of the heaven's axis must have been one of the biggest riddles of the universe to Anaximander's mind. Why is it tilted at all? Who or what is responsible for this phenomenon? Why is it tilted just the way it is? Unfortunately, the doxography has nothing to tell us about this problem. Later on, other presocratics like Empedocles and Anaxagoras mention the tilting (ἔγκλισις) of the heavens. This inclination amounts to about 38.50 at Delphi, the world's navel, and must have the effect, in Anaximander's opinion, that the celestial bodies are, at a given time, almost at the same height above the horizon everywhere on the surface of the flat earth. See, for example, DK 31A59 and 59A1(9). The atomists Leucippus and Democritus describe the same phenomenon as the tilting of the earth. (See DK 67A27 and 68A96). This seems to presuppose knowledge of the global form of the earth, for otherwise it must be explained why we do not slide off the earth. Strangely enough, however, the atomists thought that the earth was flat. (See DK 67A26 and 68A94).

74. O'Brien (1967), 424.

75. Rescher (1958), 727. In his figures, however, Rescher doesn't stick to his own prescription (see his figures 9 and 10). Naddaf, in a rather speculative way, even tries to reconstruct the inner measurements of the sun ring (1998, 10 [fig. 1] and 15). Some notations in his picture that seem to refer to ratios are not understandable, as they lack a fourth term; for example, "Width of Sun Ring (5:1)," or "Mist (1:3)."

76. For Naddaf, the words width and height change meaning, depending on the kind of representation of Anaximander's universe: "the *height* in the elevated view . . . would become the *width* in the plane view" (1998, 15). He needs this strange consequence as he takes the report that the sun is as big as the earth to refer to the sun disk. In any case, his conception makes the rings even more unlike chariot wheels. Moreover, it leads to an unacceptable angular diameter of the sun of about 4030', which is 9 times too big.

fits with the angular diameter of the sun as we see it. *Mutatis mutandis*, the same holds true for the moon. If we imagine such an Anaximandrian celestial wheel, it will look like figure 2.8, which shows the sun wheel on a summer day.[77]

A last difficulty concerns the stars. On a map like that presented above, they also appear as a ring, which is nearest to the earth, at a distance of 9 to 10 earth-diameters. Many authors have wondered how the stars can be rendered by a ring. Tannery apparently thought that Anaximander meant the Milky Way with his ring of the stars.[78] This suggestion has the obvious disadvantage that it does not explain stars outside the Milky Way. I think the simple solution is that on a map, where the main concern is to indicate the different distances of the celestial bodies from the earth, the stars appear naturally as a ring, just like the sun and the moon. The same holds for many maps of the universe in later ages, on which celestial bodies are thought to be attached to spheres, rendered as circles.[79]

Finally, we will consider a much-discussed question: How can the hoops of the moon and the stars be transparent to the sunlight without letting their own fire appear except through the apertures? Some have sought the solution in the order of the celestial bodies: the farther, the brighter, so that the light of the bodies in the outer rings can penetrate the inner rings.[80] This solution is unsatisfactory, for it would mean that the light of the sun is sometimes brighter and sometimes less bright (when it passes a ring, e.g., that of the moon). It is evident that such phenomena do not occur. I think we lack sufficient information from the doxography to understand fully how this problem could be solved. On the other hand, Dreyer is wrong to say that "these matters of detail had probably not been considered by Anaximander,"[81] for his answer to the question of the visibility of the sun and the moon is, as far as I can see, somehow hidden in the words πρηστῆρος αὐλός.[82] This "nozzle of a bellows" or, perhaps better, "funnel of a tornado"[83] apparently accounts for the visibility of the outer celestial bodies

---

77. In Naddaf's drawing "Sun Disk in Perspective" (1998, 10, fig. 2), although he says that it is "an elevated view which reflects the obliquity of the heavenly axis" (15), the sun ring does not lie aslant, but lies in the plane of the earth disk. This would be an astronomical impossibility.
78. Tannery (1887), 97.
79. So still in the fifteenth century on a celestial map by Johan Tolhopf. See Snyder (1984), 47.
80. So Bodnár (1988), 50.
81. Dreyer (1953), 15.
82. DK 12B4 and 12A21.
83. See Hall (1969), 57–59. This translation was suggested earlier by Teichmüller (1874), 13n.

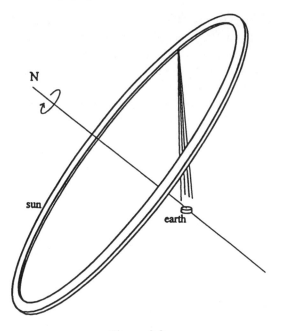

Figure 2.8
The tilted sun wheel on a summer day

through the rings of the inner ones. The image of a pipe stuck through the inner rings is rather striking when we try to show, on the map that we suppose to be much like Anaximander's, how the beams of the sun and the moon reach the earth, as can be seen in figure 2.5.

In this chapter, I hope that I was successful in showing that, staying as close as possible with the texts and trying to look with Anaximander's eyes, we are able to tell a consistent story about and make a consistent picture of his conception of the universe. Even if some parts of this reconstruction might be wrong, the conclusion still stands that Anaximander is the originator of the Western world picture or, in other words, the discoverer of space. It is the combination of his three teachings of the full circles of the celestial bodies, the free-floating earth, and the distances of the celestial bodies, which makes him deserve that honor. Together, they constitute Anaximander's most important achievement in astronomy, involving a completely new way of looking at the skies. He no longer considered the firmament as a huge screen, the ceiling of a tent or dome, on which we observe the constellations of the celestial bodies, but he imagined a universe in which the celestial bodies circle at different distances from the earth. Primitive though Anaximander's astronomy may be, these insights meant a step forward, the importance of which can hardly be overestimated. They mark, in fact, the origin of the Western three-dimensional world-picture of a universe that has depth, in contradistinction with the primitive two-dimensional world-picture of the celestial vault. In my opinion Anaximander not only was a great philosopher but a great astronomer as well. In this he reminds me of that other great philosopher, Immanuel Kant, who, more than two millennia later, and also on the basis of scant observational data,[84] brought about the modern view of the universe, as he discovered the real nature of the Milky Way and the star nebulae, and offered a famous theory of the origin of the solar system and of the universe as a whole.[85]

---

84. See Jones (1971), 29–34.
85. Kant (1755/1981). See also: Couprie (1996).

Chapter 3

Anaximander's Infinite Worlds

Richard McKirahan

INTRODUCTION

The old question whether and in what sense Anaximander believed in an infinite number of worlds has taken on new importance in the light of Furley's recent discussion of ancient cosmologies in terms of the distinction between the Closed World and the Infinite Universe.[1] At stake is no longer just an isolated point within a cosmology but a key element in an entire world view.[2] Much depends on whether Anaximander thought the earth is at the center of a single finite-sized world-system or a part (and not necessarily the central part) of but one of an unlimited number of world-systems scattered throughout an infinite universe, each coming to be and in turn being destroyed. Of these two worldviews, the Closed World was championed in antiquity mainly by Aristotle, and the Infinite Universe by the fifth-century atomists and Epicurus. Furley sees Anaximander as a predecessor of Aristotle, even though his theory does not contain all the features of Aristotle's Closed World.[3]

An embarrassment for this interpretation is the fact that many of the testimonia on Anaximander speak of *apeiroi kosmoi*, apparently in the sense of "infinite worlds." In Furley's opinion, "If this theory is to be ascribed to Anaximander, then we shall have to accept him as the founder of the Infinite Universe theory."[4] However, there is a widely accepted interpretation, which Furley adopts, that Anaximander's "infinite worlds" are not coexistent but successive: "our world, although unique in its time, is born, dies, and is reborn in an infinite succession."[5] This is not how Aristotle viewed the history of the cosmos, but at least it provides a way to avoid regarding Anaximander as the founding member of the Infinite Universe club. I shall return to Furley at the end of this chapter; my purpose so far has been to show that deciding on the nature of Anaximander's *apeiroi kosmoi* is important for understanding not only

---

1. Furley (1987) and (1989)
2. Furley (1987, 1–8) lays out the elements of the two worldviews.
3. Furley (1987), 27–28.
4. Furley (1987), 29.
5. Ibid. It is odd that Furley adopts Cornford's interpretation, but refers to Kirk's discussion, which rejects that interpretation. We return to this issue later in the chapter.

Anaximander's theory but also the history of the concepts of the Closed World and the Infinite Universe, and the universality of the contrast between those two world views.

This century has seen three principal interpretations of Anaximander's views on this topic. According to one, there are at any time an infinite number of worlds in existence, all of them generated and subject to destruction. On the second, there is only one world in existence at any time; it has a beginning and an end, and when it passes away it will be followed by another world and then another in endless succession. On the third, there is only one world—our world—which had a beginning but will have no end. I shall call these interpretations, respectively, the coexistent worlds theory, the successive worlds theory, and the one world theory. Note that the coexistent worlds theory involves temporal succession in that at any moment some worlds are being destroyed and others are coming to be.

Burnet argued for the coexistent worlds theory,[6] but his arguments were bad ones and were vigorously attacked in 1934 by Cornford,[7] who reinstated the successive worlds interpretation earlier proposed by Zeller.[8] The Zeller-Cornford interpretation has, I think, been the dominant one ever since. However, in 1955 Kirk proposed the one world theory,[9] seconded five years later by Kahn.[10]

I think it is fair to say that the successive worlds and the one world theories are the ones most widely held today,[11] and also that most scholars have been reluctant to go back to the evidence for a fresh look; the testimonia are so numerous and so many arguments and counterarguments have been put up concerning their meaning and their value as sources. However, I think the evidence deserves another look and as I have said, there is a good deal at stake in this matter, which might otherwise seem to have only antiquarian interest. In the rest of this chapter I will reexamine the most important ancient evidence that bears on this question (part I). In part II, I will examine the assumptions governing the current interpretations. To tip my hand, I think that the most

---

6. Burnet (1930), 58–61.
7. Cornford (1934).
8. Zeller (1919), 306ff.
9. Kirk (1955), reiterated with further arguments in Kirk, Raven, and Schofield (1983), 122–126.
10. Kahn (1960), 47–53.
11. Recent champions of coexistent worlds are West (1971), 80–81, and Conche (1991), 100–126. Conche (1991, 125) provides a valuable critique of Zeller and Cornford, although his readiness to accept the testimonia at face value means that he is unlikely to persuade partisans of the successive worlds theory or the one world theory to change their minds.

straightforward reading of the evidence favors a version of the discredited coexistent worlds theory, and I am not convinced by the reasons that have been given for rejecting that reading. I shall conclude in part III by returning to Furley's interpretation and challenging his account of Anaximander as a Closed World theorist.

I. TESTIMONIA ABOUT ANAXIMANDER'S INFINITE WORLDS

The relevant testimonia are given below. In general I have nothing new to say about their relative value. It does appear, though, that those who want to deny infinite worlds to Anaximander have a great deal of evidence to impugn.

T1. Simplicius, *in Physica* 24.16 (DK 12A9)

λέγει δ' αὐτὴν μήτε ὕδωρ μήτε ἄλλο τι τῶν καλουμένω εἶναι στοιχείων, ἀλλ' ἑτέραν τινά, φύσιν ἄπειρον, ἐξ ἧς ἅπαντας γίνεσθαι τοὺς οὐρανοὺς καὶ τοὺς ἐν αὐτοῖς κόσμους.

> He says that it is neither water nor any of the other things said to be elements, but some other nature which is infinite (*apeiron*), out of which come to be <u>all the heavens and the worlds in them</u>.

T2. Hippolytus, *Refutatio* 1.6.1 (DK 12A11)

οὗτος ἀρχὴν ἔφην τῷ ὄντων φύσιν τινὰ τοῦ ἀπείρου, ἐξ ἧς γίνεσθαι <u>τοὺς οὐρανοὺς καὶ τὸν ἐν αὐτοῖς κόσμον.</u>[12]

> He declared the principle of existing things to be some nature coming under the heading of the infinite (*apeiron*), from which come to be <u>the heavens and the world in them</u>.

T3. [Plutarch], *Stromateis* 2 (DK 12A10)

τὸ ἄπειρον . . . ἐξ οὗ δή φησι <u>τούς τε οὐρανοὺς</u> ἀποκεκρίσθαι <u>καὶ καθόλου τοὺς ἅπαντας ἀπείρους ὄντας κόσμους.</u>

> The infinite (*apeiron*) . . . from which he declares have been separated off <u>both the heavens and generally all the worlds, which are infinite</u>.

---

12. I give the manuscript reading, accepted by DK. Ritter, followed by Diels and now by Conche (1991, 101), emends to τοὺς ἐν αὐτοῖς κόσμους, to agree with Simplicius in T1. It makes no difference to the present argument which reading is adopted, since on the evidence of T1 and T3 we must conclude that the plural (τοὺς . . . κόσμους) is what Theophrastus wrote.

T4. Simplicius, *in De Caelo* 615.15 (DK 12A17)

ἄπειρον δὲ πρῶτος ὑπέθετο, ἵνα ἔχη χρῆσθαι πρὸς τὰς γενέσεις ἀφθόνως· καὶ <u>κόσμους δὲ ἀπείρους</u> οὗτος καὶ ἕκαστον τῶν κόσμων ἐξ ἀπείρου τοῦ τοιούτου στοιχείου ὑπέθετο <u>ὡς δοκεῖ</u>.

He was first to posit an infinite (*apeiron*), in order to be able to put it to use in generation without fear of its being used up. And, <u>as it seems</u>, he posited <u>infinite worlds</u> and that each of the worlds is generated from such an element, which is infinite.

T5. Simplicius, *in De Caelo* 202.14 (not in DK)

Ἀ. μὲν ἄπειρον τῷ μεγέθει τὴν ἀρχὴν θέμενος <u>ἀπείρους ἐξ αὐτοῦ τῷ πλήθει κόσμους</u> ποιεῖν <u>δοκεῖ</u>.

Having posited a principle that is infinite in size, A. <u>seems</u> to produce <u>from it worlds that are infinite in number</u>.

T6. Simplicius, *in Physica* 1121.5 (DK 12A17)

οἱ μὲν γὰρ <u>ἀπείρους τῷ πλήθει τοὺς κόσμους</u> ὑποθέμενοι, ὡς οἱ περὶ Ἀ. καὶ Λεύκιππον καὶ Δημόκριτον καὶ ὕστερον οἱ περὶ Ἐπίκουρον, γινομένους αὐτοὺς καὶ φθειρομένους ὑπέθεντο ἐπ' ἄπειρον, ἄλλων μεν ἀεὶ γινομένων ἄλλων δὲ φθειρομένων, καὶ τὴν κίνησιν ἀΐδιον ἔλεγον.

Those who posited <u>worlds infinite in number</u>, like A., Leucippus, Democritus and later Epicurus, posited them coming to be and being destroyed ad infinitum, with some coming to be and others being destroyed at any moment, and they said that motion is eternal.

T7. Aetius 1.3.3 (= [Plutarch] 1.3, Stobaeus, *Ecl.* 1.10.12) (DK 12A14)

Ἀ. . . . φησι τῶν ὄντων ἀρχὴν εἶναι τὸ ἄπειπον· ἐκ γὰρ τούτου πάντα γίγνεσθαι καὶ εἰς τοῦτο πάντα φθείρεσθαι. διὸ καὶ γεννᾶσθαι <u>ἀπείρους κόσμους</u> καὶ πάλιν φθείρεσθαι εἰς τὸ ἐξ οὗ γίγνεσθαι. λέγει γοῦν διότι ἀπέραντόν ἐστιν, ἵνα μηδὲν ἐλλείπη ἡ γένεσις ἡ ὑφισταμένη.

A. . . . declares that the infinite (*apeiron*) is the principle of existing things. For from this all things come to be and into this all are destroyed. This is in fact why <u>infinite worlds</u> come to be and are in turn destroyed into that from which they arise. Anyway he says why it is unlimited—to prevent the existing process of generation from ceasing.

T8. Aetius 1.7.12 (Stobaeus, *Ecl.* 1.1) (DK 12A17)

Ἀ. ἀπεφήνατο τοὺς <u>ἀπείρους οὐρανοὺς</u> θεούς. (The version in [Plutarch] 1.7 has A. τοὺς ἀστέρας οὐρανίους θεούς.)

A. maintained that <u>the infinite heavens</u> are gods. ([Plutarch] has: A. held that <u>the stars are heavenly gods</u>.)

T9. Aetius 2.1.3 (= Stobaeus, *Ecl.* 1.21.6) (DK 12A17)
Ἀ., Ἀναξιμένης, Ἀρχέλαος, Ξενοφάνης, Διογένης, Λεύκιππος, Δημόκριτος, Ἐπίκουρος <u>ἀπείρους κόσμους</u> ἐν τῷ ἀπείρῳ κατὰ πᾶσαν περιαγωγήν. (The version in [Plutarch] 2.1 mentions only Democritus and Epicurus and has περίστασιν for περιαγωγήν.)

> A., Anaximenes, Archelaos, Diogenes, Leucippus, Democritus, and Epicurus held that there are <u>infinite worlds</u> in the infinite (*apeiron*), in every direction.

T10. Aetius 2.1.8 (= Stobaeus, *Ecl.* 1.22.3) (DK 12A17)
τῶν <u>ἀπείρους</u> ἀποφηναμέων <u>τοὺς κόσμους</u> Ἀ. τὸ ἴσον αὐτοὺς ἀπέχειν ἀλλήων.

> Of those who claimed <u>the worlds</u> to be <u>infinite</u>, A. held that they are equidistant from one another.

T11. Cicero, *N.D.* 1.10.25 (DK 12A17) Anaximandri autem opinio est nativos esse deos longis intervallis orientes occidentesque, eosque <u>innumerabilis</u> esse <u>mundos</u>.

> Anaximander's opinion is that gods are born, that they come to be and pass away at long intervals, and that they are <u>innumerable worlds</u>.

T12. Augustine, *Civ. Dei* 8.2 (DK 12A17) Non enim ex una re sicut Thales ex umore, sed ex suis propriis principiis quasque res nasci putavit. Quae rerum principia singularum esse credidit infinita, et <u>innumerabiles mundos</u> gignere et quaecumque in eis oriuntur; eosque mundos modo dissolvi modo iterum gigni existimavit, quanta quisque aetate sua manere potuerit, nec ipse aliquid divinae menti in his rerum operibus tribuens.

> He did not think that all things are born from a single thing (as Thales thought that all things are born from water), but that each is born from its own proper principles. He believed that these principles of individual things are infinite and that they generate <u>innumerable worlds</u> and all that arises in them; and he thought that those worlds perish at some time and at another time are generated again, depending on how long each can survive, and he attributed nothing in these processes to divine intelligence.

T1, T2, and T3 are different versions of Theophrastus's account, and I concur with those who have treated the doxography in detail[13] that T1 sticks closest to the source. In fact, in what follows, T1, which comes from Simplicius, will be the star exhibit. It mentions multiple worlds, not infinite ones, and says nothing about whether they are coexistent or successive.

---

13. Especially Kahn (1960), 29–35.

T4, T5, and T6 are other statements from Simplicius that bear on the matter. The confident statement in T6 that Anaximander posited infinite worlds is tempered in T4 and T5 by the words "as it seems" (T4) and "seems" (T5). T4 and T5 are best taken as speaking of coexistent worlds; T6 stresses their succession, but also implies their coexistence. (This is the best way to account for the plurals "some . . . others.")

Of Aetius's several references to Anaximander's infinite worlds (T7–T10), T7 emphasizes that the worlds are successive, while the argument in its final sentence points towards their being coexistent.[14] T9 says that they are either coexistent or successive, depending on what *kata* and *periagōgē* (or *peristasis*) mean, and T8 and T10 are unhelpful on the matter. In any case Aetius is a witness of limited trustworthiness and I do not rest my case on his testimony.

The Ciceronian passage, T11, has been taken by some to mention coexistent worlds and by others to mention successive ones; it depends on how we interpret *intervallis*. Since the entire context in Cicero is severely flawed as a doxographic source,[15] I do not base my argument on it.

Finally, in T12 Augustine stresses the succession of worlds, though what he says is compatible with there being infinite coexistent worlds.

The discussion that follows is based entirely on passages T1, T4, T5, and T6—all of which come from Simplicius, who is agreed to be our best authority.

T1 asserts that Anaximander believed in a plurality of worlds and heavens, and although it does not say whether this plurality is infinite, it is perfectly compatible with passages that do.[16] T6 implies that he believed in infinite worlds that are coexistent as well as successive. T4 is best taken as claiming that he believed in infinite coexistent worlds, since the existence of infinite worlds is given as a reason for positing an infinite principle. If the worlds were successive there would be no need to posit an infinite principle.[17] T5 is best taken as concurring with T4.

The most favorable way for a supporter of infinite coexistent and successive worlds to line up this evidence would be to hold that T6 represents

---

14. We return to a discussion of this issue later in the chapter.
15. McKirahan (1996).
16. Pace Cornford (1934), 11.
17. This argument is also implicit in the last sentence of T7. Aristotle gives a related argument as a reason for believing in the infinite: "this is the only way coming to be and destruction will not fail, if that from which what comes to be is taken, were to be infinite" (*Phys.* 3.4 203b18)—a fallacious argument, as Aristotle later points out (*Phys.* 3.8 208a8): "since the destruction of one thing can be the origin of another, the totality being finite." But given a belief in an infinite number of coexistent worlds, this argument gives a good reason to believe in an infinite source of generation.

the considered view of Simplicius or his source, that T4 and T5 agree with T6, their qualifications "as it seems" and "seems" being merely urbane *façons de parler*, and that in T1 Simplicius simply chooses not to mention the fact that the plurality of worlds is an infinite plurality. On this assessment, Simplicius maintains consistently that Anaximander believed in infinite coexistent worlds, and since Simplicius is our best source, there is no need to search further. In that Aetius and other testimonia agree, they support the view that the infinite coexistent worlds reading goes back at least to Theophrastus. In fact, there is no need to see a substantial amount of disagreement, with Aetius in T7 favoring coexistent and successive worlds, Cicero in T11 saying something that could quite well be taken in the same way, and Augustine in T12 stressing succession but by no means excluding coexistence. I shall call this the best-case picture, and I think that it must remain a live possibility.

However, this is not the only way to assess the passages from Simplicius. T4 and T5 could equally well be Simplicius's (or his source's) considered view,[18] T6 being a less careful statement of the same point. On this reading, Simplicius (or his source) believed Anaximander to be committed to infinite coexistent and successive worlds, but found no clear proof that he actually stated that view.[19] As long as we take Simplicius's evidence at face value, this is a worse-case picture, for as far as we can tell from Simplicius, either Anaximander claimed that there are infinite worlds or someone (Simplicius or his source) thought he was committed to infinite worlds.

T1 is the best of all four testimonia. It is found in Simplicius's version of Theophrastus, which is agreed[20] to follow Theophrastus closely. It is found in Simplicius's summary of Theophrastus,[21] and it occurs shortly before Anaximander's fragment for which Simplicius is our only source. Kahn[22] goes further, arguing that Theophrastus took the expression "all the heavens and the worlds in them" directly from Anaximander, because it is not what Theophrastus, a peripatetic, would say. If he is correct, we definitely have a plurality of worlds in Anaximander. However, Kahn's view has been rejected for being inconsistent with claims in the testimonia that Pythagoras was the first to use the word *kosmos* in this sense.[23]

---

18. This is the view of Kahn (1960), 49.
19. I disagree with Conche's interpretation of ὡς δοκεῖ (Conche [1991], 111–113).
20. Kahn (1960), 33, quoted with approval by Kirk in KRS (1983), 105–106.
21. σύντομος περίληψις τῶν ἱστορημένων περὶ ἀρχῶν (Simplicius, *in Phys.* 28.30).
22. Kahn (1960), 49, following Reinhardt (1959), 175.
23. See West (1971), 81 and especially n.4. The primary testimonia are Aetius 2.1.1 (DK 14A21) and Diogenes Laertius 8.48 (DK 28A44), which credit Pythagoras with being the first to call the *ouranos* (or the *periochē tōn holōn*) by the name *kosmos*.

In any case, as I shall maintain later in this chapter, Theophrastus might well have used this expression.

So far it seems that Simplicius had solid evidence going back at least to Theophrastus, if not to Anaximander himself, that Anaximander believed in plural worlds. On the worst-case interpretation of T4, T5, and T6, Simplicius or his source thought that the evidence implied that Anaximander was committed to infinite coexistent worlds.

Cornford, following Zeller, challenged this straightforward interpretation of the texts in his influential 1934 article, maintaining that at any given time there is only one *kosmos* in the sense of "world-system," and claiming that in T1, *ouranoi* means not "heavens," but "the rings of the heavenly bodies" and *kosmoi* means not "worlds" or "world-systems" but "the regions of the [single] world-order framed by [the rings]."[24]

First, on *kosmoi*. Kahn surveys the early history of the philosophical use of the word *kosmos*, which he contrasts with the ordinary meanings of the word,[25] and concludes that "all extant examples of *kosmos* and *diakosmos* in the early philosophical fragments illustrate the idea of an all-embracing 'arrangement' or ordering of parts: the natural world is conceived of as a structured whole in which every component has its place."[26] Nevertheless, Kahn favors the Zeller-Cornford interpretation of *kosmos*, for which the only parallels he cites[27] are found in the Hippocratic work *On Seven* (chaps. 1 and 2)—parallels which I confess I find unconvincing.[28] So, if the phrase "all the *ouranoi* and the *kosmoi* in them" goes back to Anaximander as Kahn thinks it does, *kosmoi* is more likely to mean "worlds" than "regions within the world," and if it goes back to Theophrastus, it is also more likely to bear this meaning, which is the usual meaning of the term for the Peripatetics.

Second, *ouranoi*. Here the Zeller-Cornford line is that the *ouranoi* are the rings of the heavenly bodies—one for each body—so that "all the *ouranoi*" refers not to a plurality of *sets* of stars, suns, and moons, but only to *our* stars, sun, and moon. If we accept this interpretation, we pretty much have to accept

---

24. Cornford (1934), 11.
25. Kahn (1960), 219–230.
26. Kahn (1960), 229.
27. Kahn (1960), 224.
28. In none of the five occurrences that Kahn cites is the word *kosmos* found by itself. In all five we have phrases like "the *kosmoi* beneath the earth," in which the context signals the restricted sense of *kosmos*. What Kahn needs to make the point are cases where *kosmos* bears the restricted sense all by itself, since that is how the word occurs in T7.

the Zeller-Cornford reading of *kosmoi* as well. But this meaning of *ouranos* is even harder to defend. Some[29] say that this sense of *ouranos* corresponds to one of the senses of the word given by Aristotle: "the body continuous with the farthest periphery of the universe, in which are the moon, the sun, and some of the stars, for we say that these too are in the heaven" (*De Caelo* 1.9 278b16-18). But Aristotle speaks of a single *ouranos in which* the celestial bodies are located, not of a separate *ouranos* for each celestial body.[30]

All this effort to reinterpret the meanings of *kosmos* and *ouranos* stems from the alleged difficulty of the expression in T1, "out of which come to be all the *ouranoi* and the *kosmoi* in them," which has been thought to require there to be plural *kosmoi* within a single *ouranos*. However, if we can make reasonable sense of it without recourse to odd meanings of the two key words *kosmos* and *ouranos*, there is no reason whatsoever not to take them in their most natural senses of "world" or "world-system," and "heaven" in the sense of a system of celestial bodies.

In fact, there is no difficulty in the expression, which I think Theophrastus could have written himself. Taken at face value, the phrase refers to a plurality of worlds, each with its associated heaven. *Ouranos* indeed means "heaven"— that is, system of celestial bodies; *kosmos* means "world" or "world-system"; and *en* means not "within" or "inside" but "at"—that is, "located there."[31] Therefore, the entire phrase means "out of which comes to be every one of the world-systems and the system of celestial bodies that defines its location and that partly constitutes it." There is no need to understand the phrase as suggesting that one heaven can contain many world-systems. This is the most natural way to read T1; it also makes perfect sense.

Summary of Part I. A great deal of evidence supports the interpretation that Anaximander believed in infinite coexistent and successive worlds. Even though some of that evidence is questionable, the message of the most reliable testimonia is that this was Anaximander's belief, or at least that his known beliefs commit him to this view. It takes a great deal of argument to impugn all this evidence, and much of the argument that has been made, such as that which relies on an unknown meaning of *ouranos*, sounds very much like special pleading.

---

29. For example, Guthrie (1962), 111–112.
30. This sense would help Kirk's interpretation, but even he confesses that he does not think "that Cornford adequately demonstrated that *ouranos* might be used in precisely such a sense" (Kirk in KRS 1983, 31).
31. Cf. LSJ s.v. A.I.4. Alternatively, it could have the same meaning as in the πήρασε ἐν τόξοις, which LSJ translates as "equipped with" (s.v. A.I.3). Each *kosmos* is equipped with—partially constituted out of—its own *ouranos*.

II. CONCEPTUAL ANALYSIS OF ANAXIMANDER'S INFINITE WORLDS

Where there is special pleading about evidence further considerations are likely to be in play. In this case they are not hard to find. The scholarly literature on Anaximander frequently employs the expression "atomist worlds." The fifth-century atomists believed in infinite coexistent worlds. In fact, the principles of their system entail the existence of such worlds, which is to say the atomists had theoretical grounds for believing in them. These theoretical grounds include the atomists' distinction between what is and what is not, which they forged in response to Parmenides—"what is" being the atoms and "what is not" being the infinite void. But, the critics say, Anaximander did not believe in what is not, or in the existence of void, and he did not have the conception of the infinite needed to suppose that there are infinite worlds. Hence, Anaximander had neither theoretical grounds nor the conceptual apparatus to believe in infinite worlds, and, therefore, he could not have believed in atomist worlds. Any statements that he did must result from confusing him with the atomists.[32]

So far I have shown that there is good evidence that Anaximander held or was committed to a belief in *apeiroi* coexistent worlds, and up to now I have translated this word as "infinite." It remains to be seen whether he could have conceived of such worlds, and if so, whether he had theoretical reasons for positing them.

"There is nothing in nature to suggest innumerable worlds," wrote Cornford.[33] "No intelligible reason why the theory of innumerable worlds should have been formulated within the context of Milesian thought," wrote Kahn.[34] "Nothing whatever in 'the appearance of nature' to suggest *successive* worlds," wrote Kirk, taking Cornford's argument a step further, "no reason to assume that the whole world was going to be destroyed, or that if destroyed it would be succeeded by another."[35] And, to quote Kirk one more time, "the idea of different worlds in time would be, surely, an absolutely extraordinary one for an early Ionian thinker, whose object, judging from the other evidence, was to explain *our* world and account for its coherence. This necessitated, as it seemed to the Milesians, the description of a cosmic evolution from a single kind of matter. It did *not* necessitate the irrelevant and bizarre hypothesis of the world disappearing again into that same kind of matter."[36] I concede that Anaximander had

---

32. This position is held by supporters of both the successive worldviews and the one worldview, and is well put by Guthrie (1962), vol. 1, 113–114.
33. Cornford (1934), 15.
34. Kahn (1960), 50–51.
35. Kirk, Raven, and Schofield (1983), 122.
36. Kirk (1955), 29.

no empirical grounds for positing *apeiroi* worlds, but I dispute the claims that he could not have conceived of them and that he had no theoretical grounds for positing them.

First, Anaximander is standardly praised for the boldness and originality of his thinking. I need only mention his revolutionary ideas about cosmogony, cosmology, meteorology, and the origin of life. It is a mistake to reject out of hand the idea that such a thinker might have conceived the equally bold and original idea of a plurality, perhaps an *apeiros* plurality, of worlds.

Second, several prominent features of Anaximander's system could not be based on empirical evidence. There is, in Kirk's phrase, "nothing whatever in the appearance of nature to suggest" that the evident stability of the earth is due not to its being supported by something beneath it, but to its "similar relation to the extremes."[37] There is "nothing whatever in the appearance of nature to suggest" that humans originated from fish-like creatures,[38] or that our world had a beginning, or that it originated out of a substance that is *apeiron* in Anaximander's sense of the word, or that there is such an *apeiron* substance at all. In view of the fact that there is no doubt that Anaximander believed in these entities, events, and processes without having empirical evidence for their existence, the absence of empirical evidence that there is more than one world simply falls flat as an objection.

Third, even if Anaximander did not have the conception of the infinite needed to hold that there are infinite worlds, he did (clearly) have what he considered a workable conception of the *apeiron*. Even if it is right that his *apeiron* originative substance ("the *apeiron*") is not *infinitely* large or long-lasting, it is widely agreed that it is "indefinitely huge in [its] extent"[39] and also in its temporal duration.[40] And there seems no reason why he could not have supposed that the *apeiron* gives rise to a plurality, even an *apeiros* plurality, of worlds just as it gave rise to ours. Further, as his account of the origin of our world does not make use of the notions of void or of what is not, there is no need for him to utilize those notions to account for other worlds either. So, even if the number of worlds is not *infinite*, Anaximander's system still leaves room for *apeiroi* worlds in the sense of indefinitely, boundlessly, or unlimitedly many, scattered through the vast bulk of the living, divine *apeiron*, coming to be and being destroyed throughout its unlimited duration. We can tailor the claims in the testimonia that Anaximander believed in *apeiroi kosmoi* to fit the conception of *apeiron* that he used. In order to avoid the

---

37. Aristotle, *Cael.* 2.13 295b14 (DK 12A26).
38. Censorinus 4.7, Plutarch, *Symp.* 730E (both DK 12A30).
39. Kirk, Raven and Schofield (1983), 110.
40. Kahn (1960), 237–238.

potential anachronism inherent in the word "infinite," from now on I shall speak of these *apeiroi kosmoi* as "limitless worlds."

There seems, then, no reason why Anaximander *could* not have conceived of worlds limitless in number, both coexistent and successive. I now want to show that he *ought to have* conceived of them and to have posited them. Three features of his system point in this direction.

First, his system has strong tendencies towards symmetry, as we find in the highly symmetric structure of our world: a cylindrical earth, round rings for the celestial bodies, the axis of the rings coinciding with the axis of the earth, and the distances between successive rings being apparently equal and equal to the distance of the nearest ring to the earth. More to the point, the surviving fragment asserts that events in our world take place according to principles of symmetry. Kirk and Kahn (who hold the one world interpretation) maintain that the fragment does not refer to the generation and destruction of the world, even though Simplicius thought it did.[41] Instead, it refers to the alternate predominance of such "opposites" as hot and cold in summer and winter, of light and dark in day and night, and so forth—each one encroaching a limited amount upon its opposite for a fixed period of time, after which its opposite in turn encroaches a like amount upon it, also for a fixed, presumably equal, period. But if the major events around us go on in this pattern of alternate waxing and waning, of generation and destruction, and if Anaximander held that the world was generated, then it would in a literal sense be "absolutely extraordinary" for him not to have held that the world will be destroyed in turn, and another world generated afterwards "according to the judgment of time."[42]

Second, Anaximander's system is remarkably efficient: A small number of principles and mechanisms accounts for a large number of phenomena. Again, the fragment is a prime example, making use of a single regulative pattern to account for day and night, the seasons, floods and droughts, and perhaps other events as well. Also worth recalling is Anaximander's deployment of a single process, "separation off" (*apokrisis*), to explain events in the realms of cosmogony, meteorology, and biology. Now anyone who thinks like this, who explains phenomena by fitting them under a general principle that covers other phenomena as well, is unlikely to make so noticeable an entity as the entire world an exception to his general approach. Specifically, Anaximander's tendency to see events as instances of general patterns that occur in other places and at other times and in different contexts might well have led him to hold that the process that generated our world is not unique and in consequence unintelligible. To be understood it must be seen as an instance of a general pattern

---

41. Kirk in KRS 1983, 119; Kahn (1960), 34–35.
42. Anaximander, fr.1 (DK 12B1).

which at the very least will cover the generation of other worlds as well. So, even if he is, in Kirk's words, "an early Ionian thinker, whose object, judging from the other evidence, was to explain *our* world and account for its coherence," Anaximander's conception of explanation, as far as it can be reconstructed, should require him to account for our world in a way that can be generalized to cover other worlds as well.

The third feature of Anaximander's system that points toward a belief in limitless worlds is his use of an argument that relies on something like the Principle of Sufficient Reason. Aristotle tells us that Anaximander declared "that the earth is at rest on account of its similarity. For it is no more fitting for what is established at the center and equally related to the extremes to move up rather than down or sideways. And it is impossible for it to make a move simultaneously in opposite directions. Therefore, it is at rest of necessity."[43] Anaximander began by taking a supposed case and generalizing it: if it were fitting for the earth to move in one direction it would be equally fitting for it to move in all directions. He then pointed out that the generalized situation is impossible and by *modus tollens* infers that the supposed case is false.

A related sort of reasoning yields the conclusion that there are multiple worlds. If the *apeiron* originative substance generated a world in one place, it would generate worlds elsewhere too—without limit. But it *did* generate *our* world *here*, so it *did* generate others elsewhere. Likewise, if the *apeiron* generated a world at one time, it would generate other worlds at other times. But it did generate our world at a particular time, so it has generated, is generating, and will generate others at other times too—again without limit. In these two arguments as in the previous one, we begin with a supposed case and generalize from it. But this time the antecedent is taken to be true, and so the conclusion follows by *modus ponens*: the *apeiron* generates limitless worlds. That is not to say that it follows that the *apeiron* generates worlds at *all* times and places; Anaximander need not have held that there are worlds so close together that they occupy the same space at the same time. Nor is it to say that he worked out the details of this wrinkle in his system, or even that he actually drew these inferences. My only claim is that he could have drawn them and that it would be in keeping with what we know of his thinking if he did so.[44]

What, then, of Kirk's claim that Anaximander's "object . . . was to explain *our* world and account for its coherence" and that "this necessitated . . . the description of a cosmic evolution from a single kind of matter" but "did *not* necessitate the irrelevant and bizarre hypothesis of the world disappearing again

---

43. Aristotle, *Cael.* 2.13 295b11-16 (DK 12A26).
44. Conche employs the Principle of Sufficient Reason to similar effect, though somewhat less cautiously (1991, 107, 126).

into that same kind of matter"?[45] I am inclined to accept Kirk's account of Anaximander's objective, but as I have indicated, I think that Anaximander's conception of explanation required him to give an account that would apply not only to our world, but to any other worlds there might be, and that would leave open the possibility that our world is not unique.

Of course this does not mean that he *did* talk about limitless worlds, only that the account he gave of our world should have been generalizable. So when Simplicius or his source considered Anaximander's cosmogony along with other features of his system, he reasonably inferred that Anaximander *seemed* to believe in limitless coexistent and successive worlds. Still, our best evidence, which is also Simplicius's most reliable testimonium—T1—speaks definitely of a plurality of worlds, and once we accept that there are more worlds than this one of ours, it is difficult to see how to put a limit on how many there might be at any given time.

I conclude that, according to our best evidence, Anaximander mentioned more than one *kosmos*, in the sense of "world" or "world-system," and that he envisaged all worlds to be structured at least broadly like ours, with a heaven (*ouranos*), consisting of light celestial bodies, surrounding a dense mass located at the center. It is reasonable to think that they are all generated out of the *apeiron* by means of the same sort of cosmogonic process as the one that generated our own world.[46] Further, although the claim that Anaximander actually asserted the existence of a limitless plurality of worlds (what I called the best-case picture) is not proved, it is certainly not disproved either and is by far the simplest way to account for the many testimonia in addition to Simplicius that report that he held this view. The only reasonable alternative is the interpretation I have been presenting (my worst-case picture), that to the knowledge of our sources, Anaximander did not pronounce on the subject, but that what he did say committed him to limitless worlds.

III. FURLEY ON ARISTOTLE'S TESTIMONY: CONCLUSION

My case depends to some extent on the claim that Anaximander employed in a cosmogonic context reasoning like what he is reported by Aristotle to have used in explaining why the earth stays still. However, Furley has denied that this is how he argued for the earth's stability,[47] and if Furley is right the plausibility of my case is severely weakened. I do not have the space to go into depth on this issue, but I do think that Furley's reasons for rejecting Aristotle's

---

45. Kirk (1955), 29.
46. The evidence for this process is found in [Plut.] *Strom.* 2 (DK 12A10).
47. Furley (1989), 16–22.

testimony can be questioned and that his alternative, that Anaximander believed like Anaximenes that the earth stays put because it rides on a cushion of
air, is not well supported by the evidence. Roughly speaking, I think that each
world is generated in a given region of the *apeiron*, that as it develops it is differentiated by means of "separation off," with the lighter materials collecting
at the spherical periphery and the denser materials collecting at the center of
that world (not, of course, at the center of the *apeiron* itself).[48] In our own case,
the dense materials formed a cylinder rather than a sphere. (Anaximander will
have had empirical rather than theoretical reasons for thinking the earth's surface flat.)

Anaximander's world is quite small, so that a relatively small motion of
the earth in relation to the celestial bodies would be easily noticeable. Since we
apparently do not get progressively closer to some stars and more remote from
others, but each of the celestial bodies revolves around the earth at an unchanging distance, it is apparent that the earth's position within our world does
not change, and also that the earth occupies the center of the world.

Because the earth is so much denser than the air and fire surrounding it, I
do not think that Anaximander supposed that these flimsy materials could keep
the earth from falling. Anaximenes did believe that air could hold up the earth,
but he believed that the air is *apeiron*[49] and so his cushion was vastly deep,
whereas with Anaximander the cushion could be only as deep as the radius of
the *kosmos*, or perhaps only as deep as the distance from the earth to the nearest celestial ring (presumably four times the earth's diameter[50]). Rather, the reason why the earth does not fall is that it occupies the center of our world, for
that is where it wound up after it was condensed out of the mass of material that
turned into the world we know, and there is no sufficient reason for it to move
away from that place.[51]

In *Cosmic Problems* Furley insists that if Anaximander argued for the
earth's motionlessness as Aristotle says he did, he must have had a dynamical

---

48. This answers Furley's question, "What exactly could the earth be at the center of?"
    (Furley 1987, 25).
49. Simplicius, *in Phys.* 24.26-27 (DK 13A5).
50. This is not the place to argue this matter. I shall simply say that I accept the widely
    held view that the circles of the sun, the moon, and the stars, are, for Anaximander,
    27, 18, and 9 times the earth, respectively. I take it that this means that the circum-
    ferences of the celestial rings are 27, 18, and 9 times the circumference of the earth,
    so that the diameters of the rings will be the same multiples of the diameter of the
    earth. When the earth is located in the middle, the distance from the surface of the
    earth to the nearest ring turns out to be four earth-diameters.
51. This is my answer to Furley's second question, "Why should being at the center en-
    tail being in a state of equilibrium?" (1987, 25).

theory to account for motion towards the center. Furley's treatment of the issue in *Cosmic Problems* dovetails with his overall project in *The Greek Cosmologists*, which is to contrast the two models of the universe I mentioned earlier, the Closed World and the Infinite Universe. These two models contain many antitheses of which the question of size (finite vs. infinite) is only one. Another important antithesis is found in the respective positions on natural, unimpeded motion: either "centrifocal" (towards the center of the closed, finite world) or moving in parallel straight lines as Epicurus declares. Thus (and I am severely abbreviating Furley's argument)[52] if Aristotle is trustworthy and Anaximander believed that "the earth needs no underpropping," we must attribute to him some kind of centrifocal dynamics too. That is to say, we have no minor difference between him and his two Milesian colleagues, Thales and Anaximenes, but a difference of enormous significance: nothing less than the abandonment of the archaic worldview, and the substitution of something that Plato presents as a surprising novelty nearly 200 years later."[53] In short, Furley finds this too much to take and opts for the alternative mentioned above.

    In reply, all I can say is that Furley may be demanding too much of Anaximander in insisting that he have a dynamical theory. There is little evidence that he was interested in problems of forces and motion, much less that he worked out a consistent theory of any sort. We cannot be confident of any account of the thought processes of the early presocratics, but it seems plausible to me that after generating the world with the earth at the center, Anaximander simply saw no reason for it to move from there. He did not think that it is *held* in place by a balance of forces that tend to pull it in all directions at once, or that tend to push it to where it is, but simply that it *stays* in its place because once it has been formed there, there is, as Aristotle says, no reason for it to go anywhere else. Such a view makes no reference to forces or even to motion, and so is not at home in a dynamical or even a kinematic theory.

    In conclusion, I agree with Furley that it is interesting and important to explore the contrast between the Closed World and the Infinite Universe and to investigate the history of those worldviews. I also agree that the Closed World

---

52. Furley (1989, 17–20) holds that Aristotle is really describing Plato's view in *Phaedo* 108–109, which Furley suggests Aristotle takes together with dynamical considerations advanced in the *Timaeus* to imply a centrifocal dynamics. No wonder Furley finds it so difficult to attribute the whole theory to Anaximander! But it is wrong to bring in the *Timaeus* even to understand how Aristotle is treating Plato, since Aristotle expressly complains that the theory in question does not employ dynamical considerations (*Cael.* 2.13 295b16-25, quoted by Furley 1989, 18–19).

53. Furley (1989), 18–19.

model did not come into existence fully formed like Athena from the head of Zeus; some of its elements were stated in isolation before Aristotle grasped the entire picture and set it out with all its interconnections. But I disagree with him on the importance and even on the existence of theories of motion at so early a date as Anaximander, and I have more difficulty than he does in placing Anaximander in either the Closed World or the Infinite Universe camp.

Chapter 4

The Philolaic Method:
The Pythagoreanism Behind the *Philebus*

Carl Huffman

As long ago as 1855 it was recognized as "a hackneyed tradition that the Platonic philosophy contains both a Socratic and a Pythagorean element . . . so that Plato may be styled a Pythagoreanizing Socrates, and Platonism a kind of amalgam of two successive masters."[1] It is with Plato's Pythagoreanizing that I am concerned in this paper and in particular with the influence of Pythagoreanism on the *Philebus*. Unfortunately, what is meant by Pythagoreanism is often left so vague that any time Plato mentions "number" or "wise men" we are told that the passage is influenced by Pythagoreans (which Pythagoreans also being left vague). It is less commonly recognized that Plato refers to Pythagoras only once by name in the dialogues. In Book 10 of the *Republic* (600a9-b5) Pythagoras is said to have been a leader of education in private life, loved by his pupils for his company, and to have left behind a Pythagorean way (*hodos*) or manner (*tropos*) of life (*biou*) that made his followers stand out even in Plato's day, some 100 years after Pythagoras's death. Those followers, the Pythagoreans, are, as a group, also only mentioned once by name in Plato, in an earlier book of the *Republic* (Book 7, 530d). Philolaus, the most important Pythagorean of the fifth century, is discussed in the *Phaedo* (61d7); Archytas, the most important Pythagorean of the fourth century, although never mentioned by name in the dialogues, may be quoted at *Republic* 530d7-9, and he does appear several times in the *Seventh Letter* (e.g., 338c, 339a, 350a).[2] However, it is worth noting that neither Philolaus nor Archytas is called a Pythagorean by Plato, perhaps suggesting that for him this label did not have the magical overtones it has for many modern commentators and that neither Archytas's nor Philolaus's work could be defined properly by it. This, at any rate, is the extent of the explicit references to the Pythagoreans in the dialogues and, while they have their intriguing aspects, they tell us regrettably little about Pythagorean philosophy or its influence on Plato.

---

1. Thompson (1882), 10 (from a lecture delivered in 1855).
2. For *Republic* 530d7-9 as a quotation from Archytas see Huffman (1985) and on the presentation of Archytas in the *Seventh Letter* see Lloyd (1990). On Philolaus's role in the *Phaedo* see Huffman (1993), 1–2, 328–332, 406–410, and Sedley (1995).

There are a number of other passages in the dialogues in which Plato may be referring to the Pythagoreans even though he does not mention them by name (e.g., *Gorgias* 508a, *Republic* 583b, *Statesman* 285a). The most important passage of this sort is *Philebus* 16b4ff. This passage and the Pythagoreanism behind it will be the focus of this chapter. In an attempt to address certain one/many problems that have arisen in the discussion (15b1ff.), Socrates proposes that they use the method of which he has always been a lover, a method that is not difficult to explain but very difficult to use. He then begins to describe the method as follows:

> As a gift, so it appears to me, it was hurled down from the gods to man along with a dazzling fire on account of some Prometheus. And the men before our time, since they were better than we are and lived closer to the gods, handed down this report about the things that are in each case said to be, that they are from one and many and that they have limit and unlimited in themselves by nature.

A series of questions arise about this passage. Are "the men before our time" to whom Plato refers Pythagoreans? Is Prometheus a reference to Pythagoras himself? What is Plato and what is Pythagorean in the description of the method that follows (16b4-20a8)? Is he just borrowing some Pythagorean ontological concepts (limit and unlimited) or is he also, as he explicitly says, borrowing a Pythagorean method? Finally, to what extent does Pythagorean influence extend outside this passage (16b4-20a8) to the rest of the *Philebus*?

It is important to stress that what I am dealing with here is a question in the history of philosophy. What we can hope to learn from answering these questions is something about the way in which Plato used his predecessors' work and in particular how he used the work of one particular group of predecessors, the Pythagoreans. We are in a better position to answer this question thanks to recent work on Pythagoreanism that has better defined the nature of the philosophy of Pythagoras himself and that has produced a consensus that we have some genuine early Pythagorean texts, a core of the Fragments of Philolaus of Croton.[3] One of the central problems in previous attempts to identify Pythagorean influence on Plato was precisely a lack of a clear idea of what Pythagoreanism was and in particular the lack of any texts to use as controls on

---

3. Burkert (1972) and Huffman (1993, see 17–36 on the issue of authenticity). No argument against the authenticity of the Philolaus fragments has been made against the case for authenticity developed in these two works. Authenticity has been accepted in Kahn (1993), Barnes (1982), Schofield in KRS (1983), Nussbaum (1979).

what was said about Pythagoreanism.[4] In the absence of these texts, the only reasonably reliable control has been Aristotle's account of Pythagoreanism, but even as valuable as that account is, it has to yield to the authority of the texts upon which it is largely based, the fragments of Philolaus.[5] These historical questions are of great interest, but it should be recognized that they are not the magic key to solving the riddles of Plato's metaphysics in the *Philebus*. I will argue that at *Philebus* 16b4-20a8 Plato is borrowing not just Philolaus's basic metaphysical principles, limiters and unlimiteds, but also his central insight that there is no knowledge without number and, perhaps most interestingly of all, a philosophical method that can be detected in the Fragments of Philolaus. Nonetheless, Plato's use of these borrowings is largely limited to this small passage in the *Philebus* and even in this passage serves Platonic and not Pythagorean ends. It may be that the solution of the historical questions will have some implications for understanding the metaphysics of Plato's *Philebus* but it is the historical questions and not the implications that are the main focus of this chapter.

Let us return to the questions raised above about *Philebus* 16a ff. With regard to the first question, it is certainly the standard view that Plato is referring to the Pythagoreans when he talks about "the men before our time" who say that things "have limit and unlimited in themselves by nature." This is the view of both of the standard philosophical commentaries on the *Philebus* in English (Gosling [1975], 83, Hackforth [1954], 21) and of many other commentators (e.g. Taylor [1956], 33, Thompson [1882], 10, Sayre [1983], 292 n.6). The evi-

---

4. The last attempt to make some use of the Fragments of Philolaus for understanding the *Philebus* was Thompson (1882). Between the time that his lecture was first delivered in 1855 and its publication in 1882 Thompson notes that scholarship had come to regard the fragments as at least doubtful and from this time until Burkert's work that cloud of doubt has prevented their use in understanding *Philebus* 16b4-20a8. The problem with Thompson's own use of Philolaus in his original lecture is that, at his time, the standard approach was either to accept all of the fragments of Philolaus as genuine or none. As a result he uses spurious fragments alongside genuine ones and this undercuts his analysis (see page 15 where he appeals to the genuine Fragment 4 alongside the spurious Fragment 11).

5. For example, Sayre, in his fine book (1983), appeals to the Pythagoreans many times but they are almost always the Pythagoreans as presented by Aristotle, largely as presented in Book I of the *Metaphysics*. Philolaus is mentioned once (109) in an inconsequential context. In note 40 on page 278 Sayre seems to distance himself from historical questions about the influence of the Pythagoreans on Plato; instead he treats Pythagorean metaphysics as a *style* of metaphysics, independent of the extent to which this metaphysics can be shown to have been actually adopted by any historical Pythagoreans. For Philolaus as Aristotle's source see note 12 below.

dence of both Aristotle's account of Pythagoreanism and the earliest primary texts for Pythagoreanism that have survived, the fragments of the book of Philolaus of Croton, written in the second half of the fifth century, show that these scholars are undoubtedly correct. In his survey of his predecessors in Book I of the *Metaphysics*, Aristotle assigns precisely this pair of first principles, limit and unlimited (*peratos kai apeirou* 990a9 cf. 986a19-20, 987a10) to the Pythagoreans of the fifth century, long before Plato (985b24ff), and makes clear that, insofar as he adopted such principles, Plato was the follower and not the leader (987a29). Moreover, Fragment 1 of Philolaus, which is likely to have begun his book, states in more archaic language exactly the thesis that Plato assigns to the men of old:

> Nature in the world-order was fitted together both out of things that are unlimited and out of things that are limiting, both the world order as a whole and all the things in it.

Some, notably Erich Frank (1923, 302–309), have wanted to see these first principles as a creation of Plato. Indeed, there would be nothing impossible in Plato presenting his own views as the work of unnamed wise men. However, the evidence of Aristotle quoted above makes it clear that it was the Pythagoreans who first posited limiters and unlimiteds as first principles and Fragment 1 of Philolaus puts the nail in the coffin of the view that limit and unlimited are metaphysical principles invented by Plato.[6]

The majority of scholars have not only accepted that Plato is referring to the Pythagoreans in this passage of the *Philebus* but have also been quick to assume that Plato was referring to Pythagoras himself when he describes the metaphysical system as a gift of the gods "hurled down by some Prometheus along with a dazzling fire" (16c5). Who else but Pythagoras could this Prometheus be? This is the interpretation of both Hackforth (1954, 21) and Gosling (1975, 83 and 165). However, I have argued elsewhere that close read-

---

6. Hampton, in her very valuable book on the *Philebus* (1990), treats 16aff as if it were essentially the work of Plato and has nothing to say about its Pythagorean origins. This is evidently the result of her belief that "reliance on sources outside the Platonic corpus as an interpretive key is a risky practice" (25). I would agree with this point in principle, that we should not expect to find the key to interpreting Plato in the fragments of Philolaus, but to ignore a reference to the Pythagoreans here is to throw out the baby with the bath water. It is undeniable that Plato assigns the metaphysics of limit and unlimited to men of old and, when we have clear independent evidence (Aristotle and Philolaus) that there were indeed men of old who adopted these principles, surely we must admit that Plato is at least nodding in the direction of the Pythagoreans. Hampton recognizes that Plato is alluding to Pythagoreans at *Republic* 583b (55) and *Statesman* 285a (76).

ing of Plato shows that he is not referring to Pythagoras here.[7] The modern tendency to see Pythagoras lurking behind the text is in part a result of the influence of the later Pythagorean tradition that did elevate Pythagoras to a semi-divine "Promethean" figure from whom all true philosophy was handed down to mortals, a tradition which still has an undue influence on modern scholars.[8] Plato's reference to Pythagoras in the *Republic* passage cited at the beginning of this chapter, on the other hand, in no way portrays him as a divine figure but rather as an influential private teacher. Moreover, the *Republic* passage emphasizes the way of life that he left to his followers with no hint that he was the founder of a major metaphysical system. Indeed, in the *Philebus*, the system hurled down from the gods is said to be the basis of all progress in the arts (*technai* 16c2), while in the *Republic* it is Thales and not Pythagoras that is associated with *technai* (600a5).[9] The emphasis on *technai* in the *Philebus* also explains the reference to Prometheus. He is not a cover for Pythagoras or for any other philosopher but rather just Prometheus and is introduced in his standard role as the patron saint of all *technai* (see, e.g., *Prometheus Bound* 252–254).[10] Since Prometheus is not usually associated with a philosophical method, Socrates is playfully suggesting that the Pythagoreans must have received their method from "some Prometheus," a revised Prometheus who gave philosophical method along with fire.[11] There is in fact evidence in the later tradition that this passage of the *Philebus* was more closely associated with Philolaus than Pythagoras which is remarkable given the deification of Pythagoras in that tradition (Proclus *Plat. Th.* I Ch. 5, Syrianus *Met.* 10.2).

Thus, while Plato is not referring to Pythagoras under the mask of Prometheus, it seems beyond doubt that he does mean us to think of the Pythagoreans when he says that he is using a method derived from "the men before our time," that is, Aristotle's Pythagoreans of the fifth century and in

---

7. "Limite et Illimité chez les premiers philosophes grecs," in Dixsaut (1999).
8. See O'Meara (1989) and Burkert (1972) for a good account of the later tradition about Pythagoras.
9. Burkert's work (1972) has shown that the earliest evidence makes clear that Pythagoras was not primarily a mathematician involved with the *technai* nor part of the tradition of Presocratic cosmology but rather a charismatic founder of a way of life much as he is portrayed in *Republic* 600a.
10. Hampton (1990, 24) also draws attention to the appropriateness of the reference to Prometheus in this context.
11. If we were to assume that Prometheus was Pythagoras, Plato would be attributing to him not just the philosophical method he goes on to describe but also the gift of fire to humans, since he says that the method was a gift hurled down from the gods along with (ἅμα) a dazzling fire. This would go further than even Neopythagorean hagiography.

particular Philolaus, who is Aristotle's primary source.[12] But this still leaves the three related questions that I raised above about the extent of Plato's borrowing from the Pythagoreans. In order to answer these questions we will need first to look carefully at the evidence that is provided by the text of the *Philebus* and then turn to the fragments of Philolaus. My basic point about the evidence provided by a close reading of the text of the *Philebus* is that Plato's borrowing from the Pythagoreans is largely limited to the passage at 16a-20b. Even within that passage he is not merely parroting Philolaus or mechanically adopting his principles but rather translating Philolaus's metaphysical system and philosophical method into the language of his own philosophical concerns. The first entrance of the Pythagoreans into the *Philebus* is clearly marked by the dramatic story at 16a of "the men before our time" who received the gift hurled down from the gods. There is no hint that they are lurking in the few pages that precede this passage in the *Philebus*. However, in order to understand the way the Pythagorean system is presented by Plato in the passage at 16a-20b, it is necessary to look at the context in which "the Pythagoreans" are introduced. Immediately before "the men of old" passage, Plato has raised a series of one/ many problems and in particular one/many problems relevant to the forms (15b1–8). This latter passage has been the subject of heated controversy (e.g., Hahn [1978], Dancy [1984]) and is important for understanding the development of Plato's metaphysics, but it does precisely deal with Platonic metaphysics and shows no trace of Pythagorean influence. In particular the passage involves the Platonic contrast between the one unchanging form (e.g., man, ox, beauty) and the many perishable things in which it is found and thus the problem of separation between forms and sensibles. Hahn says that one of the central problems that Plato poses in these lines is to show "how the Forms, ontologically distinct from changing phenomena, are yet related to those phenomena" (169). But it is precisely this problem of separation that the Pythagoreans did not have according to Aristotle, since the Pythagoreans recognize no reality other than sensible reality (e.g., *Metaph.* 987b15ff, 989b34), so that the whole passage can be seen as peculiarly Platonic and not Pythagorean.

---

12. For Philolaus as Aristotle's primary source see Huffman (1993, 28–31). I have consciously adopted the translation "men before our time" for Plato's *hoi palaioi* (Gosling's "our forefathers" is also good) rather than "men of old" (Hackforth). While *hoi palaioi* can certainly refer to people of great antiquity (in which case Philolaus and other Pythagoreans of the fifth century would not seem to fit Plato's description very well), it also can refer to people a generation or two ago in contrast to people of the recent past. See [Demosthenes] *Erotic Essay* 44–47 where the author, writing in the mid fourth century, refers to the activities of Pericles and Alcibiades at the end of the fifth century as *palaia* in contrast to his discussions of Timotheus and Archytas.

Nonetheless "the gift from the gods" is introduced to help deal with such one/many problems which Plato suggests to be "an indestructible and unchanging feature of our statements" (15d6 tr. Gosling), a feature that is often abused by young men to the confusion of those around them. It is crucial to recognize three things about Plato's presentation of "the gift from the gods." First it is introduced as a method (*hodos* 16b5) and not just as a metaphysical thesis. So, according to Plato, as Pythagoras was famous for introducing a "way of life," the later Pythagoreans were famous for introducing a "way of inquiry." Second, it is said to have been handed down by "the men of old." Third, it is said to be a method of which Socrates has always been a lover (*erastēs* 16b6). This third point cannot be literally true. There is no evidence either for the historical Socrates or for the Socrates of earlier Platonic dialogues that he adopted limit and unlimited as basic principles or that he was searching for numbers in the way the method calls for. Plato is telling us not that he, Plato, or Socrates himself has been secretly practicing this Pythagorean method all along but rather that he is here equating the Pythagorean method with one of his own. Thus we should expect what follows to be a method stated in both Platonic and Pythagorean terms.

The combination of Platonic and Pythagorean terminology can be seen in the initial statement of the metaphysical underpinnings of the method. The "men of old" are said to have handed down the report that "the things that are said to be in each case are from a one and a many, having limit and unlimited in themselves by nature" (16c9-10).[13] The assertion that things are "from a one and a many" is clearly a Platonic formulation designed to connect the method of "the men of old" with the one/many problems that Plato raised shortly before, whereas the description of things "having limit and unlimited in themselves by nature" is Pythagorean and very reminiscent of Fragment 1 of Philolaus. On the other hand, the contrast between one and many never appears in the fragments of Philolaus that have survived. The one does appear, but, in Philolaus, the one is not a basic principle but rather a product of the combination of limit and unlimited (fr. 5, fr. 7 cf. Huffman [1993], 177–193,

---

13. I translate ἀεί as "in each case." This is close to Gosling's translation "from time to time." The point is that each time we consider something as existing we have to assume that it has limit and unlimited in it by nature. There is, strikingly, a parallel for this use of ἀεί in Fragment 2 of Philolaus (Huffman [1993], 109). Further, since this statement is explicitly assigned to the "men of old," Gosling (84) is right to emphasize that it is accordingly impossible to interpret the passage as talking about "those things said to exist eternally" (that is, forms—Striker [1970], 18–22) since the Pythagoreans did not employ eternal forms or discuss an eternal being separate from the sensible world (cf. Philolaus Fragment 6 and Huffman [1993], 124–129).

202–215).[14] Thus Plato presents us with a Pythagorean method but also with a translation into Platonic terms to show how it can be a method that Socrates has always practiced. I will return to a more detailed discussion of Plato's presentation of this method and its relation to Philolaus shortly, but first I want to examine what happens to this method in the succeeding passages of the *Philebus* in order to define more precisely the scope of Pythagorean influence.

After describing the method and giving two examples of it, Socrates is taxed by his interlocutors to explain its relevance to the central question of the dialogue, whether the life of pleasure or the life of intelligence should be chosen (18d6 ff). It is suggested that the natural procedure, in light of the method's claim that we only have knowledge insofar as we know the precise number of each thing, would be to determine the complete number of forms both of pleasure and of intelligence (19b). However, this is not done at this point (20c4); instead, Socrates develops the argument that it is the life that is a mixture of pleasure and intelligence that is the good life and that what they need to do is determine whether it is pleasure or intelligence that should win the second prize as what is more closely related to what makes the mixed life desirable and good (22e). Socrates says that in order to answer this question they will need "different equipment" (*allēs mēchanēs*) and "other weapons" (*bela . . . hetera*) than in their previous argument, although he adds that perhaps some will be the same (23b6-9). The emphasis here is clearly on the idea that a new approach is being presented, while conceding that it has some limited contact with their

---

14. Aristotle does talk in several passages as if the Pythagoreans treated "the one" as equivalent to limit (e.g., *Metaph.* 987a16). However, these passages are found in contexts in which Aristotle is comparing Platonic and Pythagorean metaphysics closely. I think that this leads Aristotle to interchange terminology in an unhistorical way in all likelihood under the influence of precisely this passage of the *Philebus* where Plato translates the Pythagorean limit and unlimited as one and many (Huffman [1993], 207). Schibli (1996) argues that, even though the one is derived from limit and unlimited in Philolaus, we can still regard it as a principle of limit insofar as it has limit in itself. After it is created from a combination of limit and unlimited it becomes "the source for everything else in the cosmos" (127). But there is no direct evidence for this idea in Philolaus himself and, on this interpretation, it is surprising that Philolaus talks so much about limiters and unlimiteds and so little about the one. Schibli's interpretation is mainly an attempt to save Aristotle's evidence, but even here there are problems. If the one is "the source for everything else in the cosmos" it should be equated not just with the principle of limit, as Aristotle does, but also with the unlimited, as Aristotle does not. It still seems more reasonable to me to explain the divergences between Aristotle's presentation of Pythagoreanism and what we find in Philolaus as a result of Aristotle's formulation of Pythagorean ideas in his own terms under the influence of his comparison of them with Plato's metaphysics.

earlier discussion. What follows in fact has some terminological connections with the earlier method of the men of old, but beyond that a close reading shows that almost every feature of "the four kinds" that Plato describes is marked as an innovation of his own.

Socrates begins by suggesting that they take "some of the things we discussed just now" (*hatta tōn nundē logōn*) and summarizes what he wants to borrow in the assertion that "part of the things that are is unlimited and part limit." This is clearly a reference to the teaching handed down by the men of old, but Socrates quickly adds a third class that is a combination of these two. It is not quite clear whether Socrates is presenting this third class as something new or whether he regards it as implicit in the earlier method. I would argue that the latter is the case, in light of the fact that Philolaus clearly recognizes all three classes in Fragment 2. He talks of some things that limit, others that are manifestly unlimited and still others that "from both limiting and unlimited (constituents) both limit and do not limit."[15] But certainty is not possible here. What is clear is that, from this point on, what Plato introduces is labeled as his own innovation.

First, there is the introduction of the fourth class, the cause of the mixture. Plato marks this as an innovation at 23d ff by his emphasis on how ridiculous he has been in his classifications so far and his need of a fourth class. Next, Plato turns to the class of the unlimited and makes crystal clear that the definition that he is going to give of it is not something pat handed down by the tradition but rather something "difficult and controversial" (24a6). The unlimited is then defined in terms of what admits of the more and less. It should be noted that it is precisely on the nature of the unlimited that Aristotle says Plato differed from the Pythagoreans, "but is it peculiar to him [Plato] to posit a duality instead of a single unlimited and to make the unlimited consist of the great and the small?" (*Metaph.* 987b26).[16] Sayre quite plausibly argues that the more and the less here in the *Philebus* is what Aristotle refers to as the Great and the Small.[17] Finally, when he turns to the definition of the class of the limit and the class of the mixture, which are treated together, once again Plato makes clear that he is not recounting an earlier definition but developing a new one of his own by calling on some god to come to their aid and listen to their prayers (25b8-9).[18] Thus, Plato's presentation of the four kinds clearly suggests that they are mostly of his own creation. The terms "limit" and "unlimited" belong to the Pythagoreans and perhaps the concept of the mixed class, but the definitions of these

15. τὰ δ' ἐκ περαινόντων τε καὶ ἀπείρων περαίνοντι τε καὶ οὐ περαίνοντι. See Huffman (1993), 101–113.
16. Hackforth, 42.
17. Sayre (1983), esp. 133–155. But see Hampton (1988).
18. Hackforth, 46 n.1.

three classes as well as the fourth class, the cause of the mixture, are marked as Plato's own. Therefore, if we are looking for Pythagorean influence on Plato and some sort of direct account of Pythagorean doctrine by him, the structure of the *Philebus* suggests that it will largely be found in the "men of old" passage at 16a-20b.

It is time to look in more detail at what Plato presents as the Pythagorean method. We have already seen that the metaphysical underpinnings of the method are stated in both Platonic and Pythagorean terms: "the things that are in each case said to be are from a one and a many and have limit and unlimited in themselves by nature." The first crucial feature of the method, as Plato goes on to describe it, is that it is not enough for someone to recognize that each thing has a one and a many, a limit and an unlimited in it, but that philosophical argument as opposed to sophistic argument requires us to see the complete number of each thing between the indeterminate and the one.[19] Plato makes quite clear that this search for the number of each thing is at the core of the ancient method that the Pythagoreans received from the gods by contrasting it with the practice of the wise men of the present day who proceed either too quickly or too slowly from the one to the many (16e3).[20]

In order to make his meaning clearer Socrates goes on to give two examples of what he means, both of them having to do with vocal sound (*phonē*). The first example has to do with the art of music. The musician must recognize not just that sound is both one thing and at the same time an unlimited or even that sounds can be divided into those of high and low pitch. To be wise in music one must recognize

> the number and nature of the intervals formed by high pitch and low pitch in sound and the notes that bound those intervals, and all the systems of notes that result from them, the systems which we have learnt, conformably to the teaching of the men of old days who discerned them, to call scales (*harmonias*) . . . [and] certain corresponding features of the performer's bodily movements, features that must, so we are told, be numerically determined and be called figures and measures. (17c11-d7 tr. Hackforth)

The bottom line once again is that true wisdom comes from seeking the number (*arithmon*—17e5) in things. It is striking that Plato twice emphasizes that what he is reporting in this passage is what he has been "told" or what he has learned from others. This is in clear contrast with the later description of the

---

19. τὸν ἀριθμὸν αὐτοῦ πάντα κατίδῃ τὸν μεταξὺ τοῦ ἀπείρου τε καὶ τοῦ ἑνός.

20. Taylor (1956, 33) oddly argues that Plato is criticizing the Pythagoreans for jumping from the one to the many, but I don't see how this can be squared with Plato's text.

four kinds in which, as was noted earlier in this chapter, he gives constant indications that he is developing something novel.

Plato's second example of the method in action again applies to sound, but this time the art involved is not music but rather the art of letters, the invention of the alphabet, here assigned to the Egyptian God Theuth. The God establishes the art by determining the precise number of letters that constitute the alphabet out of the indeterminate variety of vocal sounds, just as earlier a precise set of musical sounds were picked out of the indeterminate range of pitches to constitute a scale. However, what Plato emphasizes in this second example is Theuth's recognition that "none of us would ever learn about one of them [i.e., the letters] in isolation from the rest" and his conclusion that "this constituted a single bond that somehow made them a single unit" (18c7-d2 tr. Gosling). The crucial feature here is "the bond" (*desmos*) which unites the elements of the alphabet or the scale and gives them their unity and which therefore must ultimately determine their number. The bond consists precisely in the fact that each of the elements is part of a system and is required to make that system intelligible.

This marks the end of Socrates's description of the method of the men of old. There have been numerous attempts to further explicate this method, either as "a Pythagorean method" or as a reference to Platonic method, most commonly the process of collection and division.[21] Part of the difficulty in interpreting the passage, and this has not been given its full weight by scholars, is that, as we have seen, Plato seems to be presenting the method both in Pythagorean and in Platonic terms. A full account of the resulting method would have to take account of both the Platonic and the Pythagorean strand. However, since my purpose here is to focus on the historical question of what Plato got from the Pythagoreans, I will limit myself to a comparison of the main outlines of the method described by Plato with what we find in the Fragments of Philolaus.

The central features of Plato's description of the method of the men of old at *Philebus* 16a-20b bear a striking resemblance to what is found in the Fragments of Philolaus. We have already noted that Philolaus began his book

---

21. Gosling, (1975, 153–181) presents a "Pythagorean" interpretation that is very ingenious and has many plausible features but that is based mostly on conjecture rather than on direct evidence for fifth-century Pythagoreanism. Also see his account of previous interpretations. Sayre (1983) relies heavily on Aristotle's account of the relation between Plato and the Pythagoreans; this produces valuable results but inevitably obscures the precise nature of Pythagorean influence because of the distortions introduced by Aristotle's own purposes. Hampton (1990, 23ff) eschews the Pythagoreans completely to give an explanation solely in Platonic terms. My goal is to try to clarify the nature of the Pythagorean component in the method Plato presents.

with the assertion that "Nature in the cosmos was fitted together out of things which are unlimited and out of things which are limiting" (fr.1). This corresponds closely to Plato's first assertion about the method, that the things that are said to be "have limit and unlimited in themselves by nature." But this is just the beginning. Plato's insistence on grasping the precise number between the one and the unlimited as the basis for all "inquiring, learning, and teaching" (16e3-4) appears to be based on Philolaus's assertion in Fragment 4 that: "Indeed all the things that are known have number. For it is not possible that anything whatsoever be understood or known without this." Of course there are puzzles as to exactly how he thinks that numbers solve epistemological questions (Huffman, 1993, 172–201), but it is clear that for Philolaus, just as in Plato's description in the *Philebus*, it is number that makes us "wise" (17b6).

Next, one of the two examples that Plato uses to illustrate the method, the construction of musical scales, is precisely the example that Philolaus uses to illustrate the combination of his limiters and unlimiteds.

> But since these beginnings [i.e., limiters and unlimiteds] preexisted and were neither alike nor even related, it would have been impossible for them to be ordered, if a harmony (*harmonia*) had not come upon them . . . But the magnitude of harmonia is the fourth and the fifth. The fifth is greater than the fourth by the ratio 9:8 . . . Thus the harmonia is five 9:8 ratios and two dieses [smaller semitones]. The fifth is three 9:8 ratios and two dieses, and the fourth two 9:8 ratios and a diesis. (fr. 6 and 6a)

Philolaus is here illustrating the construction of the world out of limiters and unlimiteds by constructing the diatonic scale that Plato will also use in the *Timaeus*.[22] It seems very plausible that Plato is referring to Philolaus's insistence on the term *harmonia* in Fragment 6, when he talks of "those of old" who handed down to us the tradition of calling the arrangements of intervals *harmoniai* (17d2-3).

Plato's second example of the method, Theuth's invention of letters, finds no parallel in what survives of Philolaus. However, the main lesson that Plato derives from that example, that there is a common bond between the letters that constitutes the unity of the system comprised by the alphabet, is again to be found in Philolaus Fragment 6. In that fragment Philolaus argues that limiters and unlimiteds are not in themselves sufficient to explain the world, that there must be a bond that holds them together and this bond is the

---

22. For the connections to the *Timaeus* see Huffman (1993), 149ff, and for further commentary on fragments 6 and 6a see 123–165.

harmonia, the mathematical structure that we have seen him illustrate with the diatonic scale above, p. 76.

> But since these beginnings [limiters and unlimiteds] preexisted and were neither alike nor even related, it would not have been possible for them to be ordered, if a harmony had not come upon them, in whatever way it came to be. Like things and related things did not in addition require an harmony, but things that are unlike and not even related . . . , it is necessary that such things be bonded together (*sunkekleisthai*) by harmony, if they are going to be held in an order (*en kosmōi katechesthai*).

The language is not as close to Plato here as it is in the previous three examples in that instead of Plato's term *desmos* we find the verb *katakleiō* (literally "shut in"). Nonetheless, the central idea that limit and unlimited are not adequate explanatory tools and that what is needed is a numerically determined system (*harmonia*) which is described in the language of "bonding" constitutes a clear connection to Plato.[23]

These four points of contact between the Fragments of Philolaus and Plato's account of the method of the men of old in the *Philebus* constitute a strong *prima facie* case that Plato had Philolaus in mind when writing this passage of the *Philebus*. But up to this point we have seen nothing explicitly about a method in Philolaus. Indeed, Philolaus nowhere explicitly talks of a method that he follows. Nonetheless Fragment 6 clearly sets out the principles for a method of inquiry and explanation, and traces of this same method can be found in a number of other places in Philolaus. I have given a detailed account of this method elsewhere (Huffman, 1993, 78–92) but, in order to reinforce the connection between Plato and Philolaus, I will here rehearse the main features of this "Philolaic method" and conclude by showing its connections to Plato.

It is in Fragment 6 that Philolaus turns reflective and both identifies the limitations of human knowledge and sets out a method of inquiry that he follows with regard to the cosmos as a whole and which other fragments show that he followed with regard to each aspect of the cosmos. The first part of the fragment reads as follows:

> Concerning nature (*phuseōs*) and harmony (*harmonias*) the situation is this: the being (*estō*) of things which is eternal, and nature in itself (*auta ha phusis*) admit of divine and not human knowledge, except that it was impossible for any of the things that are and are known by us to have come to be, if the being of the things from which the world order came together, both the limiting things and

---

23. For the role of harmonia as a bond in Philolaus see Huffman (1993), 124–145.

the unlimited things, did not preexist (*huparchousas*). But since
these beginnings preexisted (*archai huparchon*) and were neither
alike nor even related . . .

The fragment identifies two concepts for consideration: nature and harmony
(fitting together). Philolaus first focuses on nature and begins by specifying
what sort of nature he is talking about. He is concerned with "nature itself"
(*auta ha phusis*) and this expression is paired with and, I think, partially explained by the phrase "the being of things" (*ha estō tōn pragmatōn*). It seems
that Philolaus is referring to ultimate reality here and this is confirmed by the
fact that he describes it as eternal (*aidios*). Thus, he is talking about the being
that was the focus of Parmenides' discussion. However, he does not seem to
think there are as many signposts on that road as Parmenides supposed, since
he says that it admits only of divine and not of human knowledge.

Philolaus's skepticism or epistemic modesty is of a peculiar sort. Other
fragments (e.g., Fragment 4) show that he did think that human beings could
have knowledge and, as we have seen, that he tied human knowledge to the concept of number. Those fragments seem to suggest that humans can gain knowledge of the cosmos and the things in it by grasping the number according to
which they are put together. Thus there are plenty of things that humans can
know and know with the clarity and certainty of mathematical relationships.
However, in Fragment 6 Philolaus denies humans clear knowledge (*gnōsis*) of
the reality that underlies the phenomenal world, or perhaps its is better to say,
the reality from which the phenomenal world came to be. Philolaus's restrictions on human knowledge are quite different from those of Xenophanes. As
Lesher (1992, 149–186) has argued, Xenophanes's concerns about human
knowledge focus on knowledge of the natural world and are based on the relatively limited circle of human experience which keeps us from ever going beyond unconfirmed belief based on that limited experience. Philolaus seems to
have no modesty about knowledge of this sort. It was what Parmenides claimed
to know that bothered him.

Yet, even here Philolaus is not as bashful as he appears. He in fact goes
on to make one exception to his ban on human knowledge of ultimate reality.
This exception is based on what Philolaus calls "the things that are and are
known by us" which I again take to be the cosmos and its parts. His point is
that it would have been impossible for any of these things to have come to be,
if the being of the things from which they arose did not preexist. The cosmos
that we know cannot have come from nothing. We cannot know everything
about the nature of what it came from, that knowledge is reserved for the
gods, but there are certain minimal conditions that must have preexisted, that
must characterize ultimate reality in order for the world we know to have
come to be at all. And what are these minimum conditions? Both things that

are unlimited and things that limit must have preexisted for the world to have arisen. What is striking here is that he is so circumspect about postulating specific elements that must be supposed to have preexisted. He does not privilege a specific set of elements such as the earth, air, fire, and water of Empedocles. He instead postulates two types of elements that must have preexisted—limiters and unlimiteds—and argues that we can go no further in specifying their nature or number.

These principles that must be assumed in order to explain the cosmos he then calls *archai:* "beginnings" or "starting points" and the term is clearly closely connected with the verb *huparchein* which is used to describe the limiters and unlimiteds as preexisting. Philolaus then goes on to make one further point:

> But since these beginnings preexisted and were neither alike nor even related, it would have been impossible for them to be ordered, if a harmony had not come upon them, in whatever way it came to be. Like things and related things did not in addition require any harmony but things that are unlike and not even related . . . , it is necessary that such things be bonded together by harmony, if they are going to be held in an order.

The *archai* specified so far are not in fact sufficient to explain the cosmos. While likes may naturally bond with likes, Philolaus argues that limiters and unlimiteds are unlike and thus will not of their own accord combine to form an order. Thus, since the world does have an order, we have to suppose that an ordering principle did supervene on the limiters and unlimiteds and this principle is harmonia. It is this that serves as the bond, which, as we have seen, Plato emphasizes in his account and which holds limiters and unlimiteds together in an order or cosmos. Once again Philolaus recognizes that human knowledge of the origin of this principle is limited and refers to it as supervening "in whatever way it came to be." Then, Philolaus at long last gives an example of what he is talking about: the diatonic scale. Harmony, the bond that fits things together, turns out to be the whole number ratios that determine the fixed points, or limiters, on the continuum of sound or the unlimited.

I want to argue that Philolaus has formulated a method of investigation here with regard to the cosmos as a whole that he will go on to apply to specific areas of the cosmos and that can be labeled the Philolaic method. The first step is to identify the minimum number of principles that must be posited in order to explain the phenomena as we know them. These are the *archai* or starting points. In the case of the cosmos as a whole these starting points are quite schematic, limiting things and unlimited things. However, Fragment 1 of Philolaus asserts that his central thesis applies not just to the cosmos as a whole but also to "all the things in it" and this in turn suggests that his method of inquiry can be applied to everything in the cosmos, that is, each thing in the cosmos will also have a set of *archai* necessary to explain it and these starting points will include both limiters and unlimiteds. After identifying the relevant set of *archai* for any given area, the second step in the method would be to identify the harmony that holds them together, the bond. There are no other fragments in which this method can be seen to be explicitly applied in its entirety. However, one of the striking things about the remaining fragments and testimonia of Philolaus is the regularity with which things called *archai* turn up. It is hard not to see these lists of *archai* as the result of what I labeled in my book Philolaus's method of *archai* and what I am here calling the Philolaic method.

In Fragment 13 the subject of inquiry is the psychic faculties of a human being.

> The head [is the seat] of intellect, the heart of life and sensation, the navel of rooting and first growth, the genitals of the sowing of seed and generation. The brain [contains] the origin (*archan*) of man, the heart the origin of animals, the navel the origin of plants, the genitals the origin of all (living things). For all things both flourish and grow from seed.

The author of the *Theologumena Arithmeticae*, who preserves this fragment for us, introduces it by saying that "there are four *archai* of the rational animal, just as Philolaus says" and, however skeptical we may be of the *Theologumena* as a reliable source, this is not a bad summary of the content of Fragment 13. Philolaus has identified a set of four starting points (the word is *archē* as in Fragment 6) necessary to explain the psychic abilities of a human being or of animate life as a whole. These *archai* seem to be arrived at in the same way as in Fragment 6, for they are what must preexist in order to explain the cosmos as we know it, in this case what must preexist in order to explain each level of life. What binds all life together is that it originates "from" a seed and hence the genitals are said to be the origin of all life. The language here emphasizes the same notion of *archē* as a starting point that was emphasized in Fragment 6. Next, the navel seen as a root, the heart as the seat of sensation, and finally the brain as the seat of intellect are presented as the *archai* that we must posit in order to explain plants, animals, and human beings, respectively. It is striking that, once we have turned to a specific aspect of the world, the *archai* are now much more specific: the brain, the heart, the navel, and the genitals. Yet, there are plenty of obscurities. Are these meant to be limiters or unlimiteds? Where does harmonia come in?

It might seem most reasonable to in fact regard the genitals, navel, heart, and brain as each involving both limiters and unlimiteds. The body itself can be seen as the unlimited continuum on which these specific organs are picked out. Moreover, each organ is a combination both of "unlimiteds" (i.e., materials and qualities of which they are composed, e.g., blood, hot, etc.) and also of structural features (limiters) that determine their function. What then of harmony? If harmony always involves number, at least part of the answer seems clear. The only place number appears is in the specification of precisely four *archai* for the rational animal, but we must be cautious since the actual words of Philolaus do not include the number four but occur rather in the context in the *Theologumena Arithmeticae*. Other difficulties arise because Fragment 6 seems to suggest that the numbers that were involved in harmony's binding together of limiters and unlimiteds were relations of numbers such as the whole number ratios in the diatonic scale, rather than just an enumeration of the relevant *archai* (four in this case). Thus, the evidence provided by Fragment 13 is clearly strong enough to suggest that Philolaus is here, as in Fragment 6, searching for a set of *archai* necessary to explain a certain domain of phenomena but whether and how this involves limiters and unlimiteds and harmonia must remain conjectural.

Much the same thing seems to be true of Philolaus's medical theory. But, here we have the added problem that there are no fragments and we must rely solely on secondhand reports. Testimonium A27 which comes from the medical papyrus known as the *Anonymus Londinensis*, which is in turn based on the history of medicine written by Aristotle's pupil Meno, begins the account of Philolaus's theory of disease as follows: "He says that diseases arise through bile and blood and phlegm, and that these are the origin (*archēn*) of diseases." The second half of this sentence is rather redundant if we take *archē* to be the word of the author of the papyrus, but makes sense if we see it as a report of the actual word Philolaus used to describe bile, blood, and phlegm. This suggestion is supported by the fact that, although *archē* is not a common term in the papyrus (it is used only once outside the section on Philolaus), after going on to discuss some of the details of Philolaus's theory of disease the section concludes by using the term *archai* again: "It is these then that he postulates as the origins (*archas*) of diseases." Thus, I submit, Philolaus is using the Pythagorean method here as well. It is admittedly unclear exactly how we are to understand bile, blood, and phlegm in terms of limiters and unlimiteds and even more problematic where harmony with its attendant numbers come in, since no numerical relations are mentioned in the passage. There is no time here to speculate on these questions, but it remains striking that once again as in Fragments 6 and 13 we have a set of *archai* postulated in order to explain a given domain.

I will deal with one last important appearance of *archē* in the fragments even more briefly. In Testimonium A7a, which should really be regarded as a fragment, since it seems to quote Philolaus, he is reported to have said that "Geometry [is] the source (*archē*) and mother city of the rest" of the mathematical sciences. Just as he came up with a set of *archai* and a hierarchical structure for the psychic faculties of a rational being so he here posits geometry as the *archē* of the rest of the sciences and thus implies a similar hierarchical structure. The striking image of geometry as the "mother city" that sends out the other sciences as colonies continues Philolaus's emphasis on the *archē* as the starting point for explanation.

Obviously much time could be spent speculating on the details of the method I am ascribing to Philolaus (see Huffman [1993], 78–92) but what I hope to have made plausible is that there is a pattern here in the fragments of Philolaus that suggests a conscious method of inquiry and explanation. But how does this method compare to what we have seen Plato describe in the *Philebus*? First, it must be granted that there are some obvious points of dissimilarity, particularly in terminology. Plato never uses the word *archai* in describing the method, although it is a central term for Philolaus. Philolaus in turn never explicitly describes what he is doing as a *hodos*. But, on the other hand, we have already seen that there are a number of other similarities between the *Philebus* and Philolaus that make a strong case for a connection. Moreover, looked at schematically, I would argue that there is also a compelling similarity between the method of Philolaus as I have described it and the method of the men of old that Plato presents. In simplest terms Plato calls on us to follow three steps: 1) to recognize that all the things that are have limit and unlimited in them; 2) to try to determine the limited number of principles relevant to knowledge in each domain (e.g., notes in scales and letters in an alphabet); and 3) to find that bond that unites these principles into an ordered system. But these are exactly the three steps that Philolaus follows in Fragment 6 and evidently followed in other areas of inquiry: 1) it is Philolaus's central thesis that the cosmos and all things in it are composed of limiters and unlimiteds; 2) in each area of inquiry Philolaus seeks to determine a limited number of principles that are necessary to explain that domain (e.g., the notes in the diatonic scale for the cosmos as a whole; blood, bile, and phlegm for disease); and 3) Philolaus recognizes that these elements must be held together by a harmonia in order to constitute a system or cosmos (the only clear example here is the diatonic scale in fr. 6). Thus, it is not just the concepts of limit and unlimited that Plato is borrowing from Philolaus, but an entire approach to explaining reality. Having said this much, it must be recognized that, although the Fragments of Philolaus allow us to be much more precise about the Pythagorean background of this passage of the *Philebus* than has been possible up to now, Philolaus's work remains fragmentary and controversial so that it is impossible to push the comparison between Philolaus and Plato much further. Moreover, for Plato the Pythagorean method is from the distant past. Philolaus's book was probably written more than 75 years before Plato wrote the *Philebus*. Accordingly, as I have argued, Plato is not adopting an antiquated system wholesale but taking the central insights of that system and recasting them in terms of his own earlier work. I have not been able to consider all the ways in which he reformulates that system here, although I suspect that the whole passage may have less far-reaching significance for Plato's metaphysics than is commonly supposed and may have more to do with the specific task at hand, namely, suggesting how pleasure and intelligence can be both one and many. Thus, even if we had a more detailed understanding of Philolaus's method I doubt that it would be the key that solves the problems of the *Philebus*. Nonetheless, it is surely an important aid to understanding Plato to come to understand the method of "the men of old" that he is modifying for his own purposes. It remains a tribute to Philolaus that Plato found his method worth resurrecting. Indeed, it is hard to think of any Presocratic method that is articulated as clearly or applied as consistently as the Philolaic method.

Chapter 5

Zeno Moves!

Wallace I. Matson

MAJORITY AND MINORITY

One of the most received of opinions among historians of philosophy has long been that Parmenides, Zeno, and Melissus denied motion, that is to say, claimed to have shown that motion, and indeed all change, variegation, and particularity, are contrary to reason and therefore mere illusions. The crucial contention is that the "On Truth" part of Parmenides's poem, in which the referent of *esti* is said to be motionless,[1] is put forward as entirely true, whereas "On Opinion" which speaks of the wandering moon, the male being led to the female, and so on, was intended and regarded by its author as nothing but a compendium of false beliefs of mere mortals. I shall refer to holders of this view as the Majority.

While the Majority is large,[2] it has never been total. Simplicius, to whom we owe the preservation of most of the Parmenidean text, held the contrast of the poem's sections to be between the intelligible world, of which there is certain knowledge, and the sensible world, which *d'après* Plato is of a lower grade of reality and knowability, but not on that account utterly illusory. This view of Parmenides as having made the fundamental philosophical distinction between the domains of *a priori* knowledge on the one hand, and of uncertain, merely empirical cognition on the other, was continued in the nineteenth century by Paul Tannery, who equated *to eon* with Cartesian extension—which after all was a homogeneous, unchanging plenum, an object of clear and distinct ideas—and in the twentieth by (among others)

---

1. *akinēton*, B8, 26. This chapter is a revision of Matson (1988), in turn a revision of a paper entitled "Eleatic Motions," presented to the Society for Ancient Greek Philosophy, December 28, 1982.
2. As far as the English-speaking world is concerned, at the present time it still includes most scholars of Presocratic philosophy, the articles in all encyclopedias that I know of, and all college textbooks with (to my knowledge) the exception of my own (Matson [1987]). But the situation seems to be radically different in Italy: Casertano reported in 1978 (107) that the true/false contraposition of Aletheia/ Doxa was "rejected unanimously by almost all scholars."

Giorgio de Santillana, more recently by Giovanni Casertano, who in his magisterial book interpreted it as "the world, reality considered in its unity and totality" (1978, 94), and Matson (1980). To Minority exegetes *to eon* is *at least* space, which is motionless and indivisible, but within which divisible things move.

The purpose of this chapter is to counter the objection to this interpretation based on the alleged fact that Zeno of Elea defended his master by producing arguments "against motion."[3] I shall offer support to Tannery's interpretation of the fragments and testimonies concerning Zeno, according to which Parmenides's disciple did not purport to prove the impossibility of motion, but rather showed that the *opponents* of Parmenides were in the ridiculous position of being logically committed to denying motion. I shall try to show also that neither does Melissus of Samos pose a threat to the Minority position.

RECEIVED OPINION

"Everybody knows" that Zeno, in defense of his master's denial of motion, developed four "paradoxes," arguments purporting to show that the very concept of motion is self-contradictory—if something moves, then it does not move—and that, in consequence, Parmenides was right when he insisted that motion cannot really occur, our conviction that things do move being mere illusion.[4] Philosophers of mathematics from Aristotle to the present day have exercised their ingenuity in indecisive attempts to "solve" these "paradoxes," that is, to expose the alleged fallacy in Zeno's reasoning and thus show that motion is logically all right.

Plato, as we shall see, did not regard Zeno in this light, but Aristotle—the first with a "solution"—seems to have done so, and the rest of the ancients after him. It remained for Paul Tannery to rediscover the true intent of Zeno's arguments and their relation to the defense of Parmenides.

---

3. For instance, van der Waerden *apud* Guthrie (1965, 84): The Tannery view "credits [Zeno] with the following train of thought: 'On the hypothesis of plurality motion is impossible. Since however motion evidently can occur, plurality must be rejected.' " Guthrie takes this as a patent *reductio* of Tannery's exegesis. On the contrary (so I shall argue) that is precisely how the famously clever Zeno did think.

4. Some recent writers taking this for granted are Sherry (1988, 73); Shwayder (1955, 450); Smith (1985, 1); Shamsi (1994, 66); Vlastos (1966a, 1966b, 1967, 1975, passim); Bolotin (1993, 323); Kerferd (1965, 132); Owen (1958, 213); Guthrie (1965, passim); and Booth (1957b, 91).

PLATO'S ACCOUNT OF ZENO

Our earliest, fullest, and solidest information about Zeno of Elea comes from Plato's portrait of him in the dialogue *Parmenides*.[5] We are told that Zeno, intimately attached to Parmenides, while still a young man wrote a book for the purpose of defending the Master's teaching that One Is (*hen esti*) against unspecified persons who "tried to make fun of it." His strategy in the book was to show that "the hypothesis that 'many are' would suffer even more ridiculous consequences if followed out far enough." The first argument in the book was this: "If things are many, the same thing is like and unlike; but it is impossible for the same to be like and unlike; therefore the things are not many."[6]

Who were the people who ridiculed the Master and whom Zeno intended to "pay back with something left over" (128D)? Were they plain men?[7] Or were

---

5. 127A-128E. The reliability of the account, questioned by Solmsen, was vindicated by Vlastos (1975), who, however, made one major concession—unnecessarily, as we shall see.

6. 127E. Diels and Kranz (DK) do not print the sentence just quoted as a fragment or even as a testimonium, although they print 127A-D (immediately before it) and 128B-E (closely following); why, I do not know, since Plato has Zeno say explicitly that the sentence paraphrases his book correctly. Solmsen 1974 (370 n.9) accepts "If things are many, the same thing is like and unlike" as genuinely Zenonian, but rejects the rest on the grounds that it "has no parallel in the fragments." I daresay he is right about this; if he is, then it may have been a feature of Zeno's style of *reductio* to suppress the denial of the consequent and statement of the conclusion. That would go a long way toward explaining how it came about that even ancient writers took him to be arguing "against" motion.

7. The very idea of a *reductio ad absurdum* aimed at refuting "ordinary opinions" is dubious. *Reductio* requires a premise to be reduced; and plain men do not deal in premises. On the few occasions in the history of philosophy when attempts have been made to do this sort of thing, the philosophers have found themselves obliged to begin by *supplying* their putative plain men with premises for the purpose. There has been an air of absurdity about the theses thus manufactured: Hume (1896, 210f; 1902, 152), for example, alleged that plain men hold that "perceptions are their only objects," a view that he proceeded to demolish by arguing that "the slightest philosophy"—viz. pressing one eyeball—shows it to be false. It is doubtful, however, whether a plain man would have any notion of what an utterance such as "perceptions are my only objects" might mean. If told that what is involved is this: "When you press one eyeball, you see two 'tables,' but you know there aren't really two tables out there, so what you see can not be even one real table," it is unlikely that he will be convinced. Only philosophers having been so incautious as to assert explicitly that what is given in the visual field—*any* visual field—is identical with what is seen would find themselves embarrassed. Returning to Zeno: The plain man's appropriate response to "If things are many, then they must be both like and unlike" would be "Certainly. Like this and unlike that." Only someone consciously committed to an oversimplified doctrine of noncontradiction—that is to say, a philosopher—might sweat over this *aporia*.

they ancestors of those who today like to call themselves "professional philosophers?" Some evidence bearing on this question can be elicited from the dialogue, if we pay attention to the *mise en scène*.

Zeno began his reading (so Plato says) to an audience of three: Socrates and two other unnamed persons. They were later joined by Parmenides, Pythodorus, who afterwards became a general but at the time was a paying student of Zeno,[8] and Aristoteles, who became one of the Thirty Tyrants. Not counting Parmenides, then, the audience of five was made up of two persons who had special interest in philosophy, and three others whose reasons for being there we do not know. Pythodorus had heard a previous reading of the book. The tininess and (at least partial) specialization of the audience reminds us of philosophical meetings in our own day where a few people turn out to hear a not very well known visitor hold forth on a technical topic.

Now of course the *Parmenides* is a work of fiction. Precisely for that reason Plato had to make it conform to probability.[9] What Plato chose to say about this meeting, which perhaps never occurred, thus tells us all the more about what Plato conceived as having been Zeno's situation and aim in his own time. And if Plato was misinformed about these matters, then we know virtually nothing about Zeno.[10]

The setting is thus in keeping with a view of the intended audience for Zeno's book as consisting of people with a special interest in rather esoteric philosophical matters, not a representative sample of ordinary Athenians. This impression is reinforced if we turn our attention to the argument that Plato purports to extract from Zeno's book. Would plain men make fun of someone who assured them that things are not many, only one? Perhaps. But would they then be thrown into confusion and consternation if someone rebutted by saying: "You say there are many? Then there are shoes and ships? Then the shoes are like each other and unlike the ships? Then shoes are both like and unlike? *Now* who's being absurd? The joke is on *you!*" There is no reason to suppose that a fifth-century plain Athenian would have been discomfited by this kind of hectoring.

---

8. [Plato] *Alcibiades I*, 119A.
9. The force of this consideration is not diminished by the fact (as I take it to be, following Allen 1997 [69–72]) that Plato was concerned to stress the fictitiousness of the conversation. "Dialogues of the Dead" and the like become pointless if their *personae* fail to speak in character. That Plato endeavored to paint the Eleatics realistically, and, consequently, to represent accurately their mission and to whom it was directed, is evidenced further by his mentioning that Zeno had been Parmenides's *paidika*, a detail that five centuries later aroused the prudish wrath of Athenaeus (DK 29A11).
10. As Solmsen 1974 (379f) observes, Simplicius's account of Zeno is probably derived almost entirely from Plato's.

The argument that Plato sketched, and said to be in substance the first in Zeno's book, is of the type he ascribed to Zeno, which quickly became a philosophical favorite: *reductio ad absurdum*. If many are (this is the premise of the opponents who are to be made to appear even more ridiculous than Parmenides), then these many will be both like and unlike—which is supposed to be absurd. There is no suggestion, of course, that the same or any other "absurd" inference could be drawn from the Parmenidean premise that One Is.

Fragments 1 to 3 of Zeno's writings, preserved by Simplicius and assigned by Diels and Kranz (hereafter DK) to *On Nature*, seem clearly to be taken from the book referred to by Plato, for all of them purport to deduce contradictions from the hypothesis Many Are. Like Plato's exemplar they have bite only for the philosophical sophisticate who has already given some consideration to problems that arise when contemplating the carrying of processes to infinity. No one without such a background would comprehend what was being asserted and denied in this kind of discourse, much less assent to it or reject it. And to repeat, the arguments are based on the premise of Many, not on the Parmenidean premise.

ZENO'S BOOK

Proclus said (DK 29A15) that Zeno's book contained forty arguments. Whatever their number, some questions we face are: whether the arguments about[11] motion were in the same book as those about One vs. Many, the book cited by Plato; whether those arguments were *reductiones ad absurdum* of the opponents' premises; and if so what those premises were and what the absurd consequences were supposed to be.

IN WHAT BOOK DID ZENO PUBLISH HIS ARGUMENTS ABOUT MOTION?

All of Zeno's arguments, and therefore the arguments about motion,[12] must have been in the book referred to by Plato, if Zeno wrote only one book. And the impression we get from Plato's account is that he did write only one book. Nothing is said or hinted of any writing by Zeno beyond the one under consideration—and this at a dramatic date when Zeno, said explicitly to be about forty years of age, had already had plenty of time to follow up the treatise of his youth if he had seen fit to do so. This is one reason for reluctance to credit the

---

11. *Sic*: *logoi peri kinēseōs*, Aristotle, *Physics* VI 9, 239b10. The question-begging phrase "arguments against motion" found in Guthrie (1965, 82 et passim) and so many other discussions has no Aristotelian warrant.
12. Unless they were delivered and transmitted only orally, a possibility that surely we can ignore.

testimony derived from Hesychius that Zeno wrote four books: *Wrangles* (*Erides*), *Against the Philosophers*, *On Nature*, and *Examination of Empedocles's Philosophy* (DK 29A2). Another is that this (sole) notice of more than one Zenonian book is very late, nearly a millennium after Zeno's time. It has been plausibly suggested that the first three titles refer to the same book.

We can leave out of consideration the putative book on Empedocles, which if it existed would hardly have been the venue for the arguments about motion. If there were in addition two other books besides the one mentioned by Plato, and if the motion arguments were in one of them, we could then not be certain that what Plato says about Zeno's method and purpose would apply to the motion arguments. These arguments then, if published in other books, might have been of form other than *reductio*; they might have been directed against some other thesis than that Many Are; they might not have argued on the basis of that thesis; and they might not even have been intended to support the views of Parmenides. All these possibilities strike me as unlikely, but I do not see how to rule them out *a priori*.

WHERE, ON THE MAJORITY VIEW, THE ARGUMENTS ABOUT MOTION MUST HAVE BEEN PUBLISHED.

These are problems, however, that beset only the Majority; for if—but only if— their interpretation of the motion arguments is correct, then those arguments must have been published elsewhere.

The Majority view of the four arguments about motion is that each of them purports to derive a contradiction, or at least an unacceptable absurdity, simply from the assumption that motion occurs, thereby showing that motion cannot occur, inasmuch as nothing self-contradictory (or otherwise unacceptably absurd) can really be. If then we believe that things move, we are victims of illusion. Support is thus afforded to the doctrine of Parmenides (according to the Majority) that What Is is immobile in the bonds of mighty chains; mares drawing carts containing knowing men through cities and gates high in the air, and so forth, are merely mortal Doxa in which there is no truth at all.

If this Majority account is correct, and if Plato accurately described *a* book by Zeno, then the motion arguments must have been published in some book other than that one. For those arguments, on the Majority reading of their content and intent, do not at all fit the specifications of Zeno's book as set out by Plato.

Plato's discussion of the book occupies one and one-fifth Stephanus pages: 127D6 to 128E6. Of this, 127E10 to 128D3—sixty percent[13]—is devoted entirely to asserting, and hammering in with repetition and variation, a single (alleged)

---

13. Approximately the same amount of space as given to the death of Socrates (*Phaedo* 117C-118A).

fact about the book: that its *sole* purpose was to defend Parmenides's monism, his teaching that The All is One (*hen einai to pan*). But, the Majority say, the "paradoxes" defend Parmenides's "immobilism."[14] And although proving monism might establish immobilism *per corollarium*, the inference cannot go the other way; immobilism, a "frozen" world, is obviously compatible with pluralism.[15]

The rest of the passage on Zeno's book describes his argumentative strategy: showing that "the hypothesis that 'many are' would suffer even more ridiculous consequences [than those alleged to follow from Parmenides's teaching] if followed out far enough."

Now, what were the doctrines of Parmenides that people made fun of him for? This dialogue mentions only Monism, "One Is." For the sake of argument, however, let us assume, with the Majority, that "Nothing Moves" was another, arousing additional merriment among the vulgar. The "paradoxes," as the Majority read them, are arguments proving this much-ridiculed thesis. How could this then be described as a turning of the tables on Parmenides's opponents, "paying them back in the same coin with something to spare?" If they laughed when Parmenides (supposedly) declared that nothing moves, why would they sober up when Zeno told them the same thing? Because they were forced by his (though not Parmenides's) irrefutable logic? We are talking about a time when philosophical argument was something quite new—Parmenides's poem is in

---

14. Vlastos, adamant in the conviction that the "paradoxes" are "against motion," came to the painful conclusion that Plato did indeed grossly misdescribe the book. In his horror at the deception he wrote of "the junk heap to which [this testimony—Plato's!] belongs" (1975, 149). That the immobilism thesis should lead the greatest Plato scholar of his generation to express himself thus, in a paper otherwise devoted to defending Plato's veracity, constitutes, in a way, a *reductio* of the thesis, though too saddening to be called *ad absurdum*.

Owen (1958, 201), conceding that the "paradoxes," if intended to refute motion (not plurality), must have come from a book other than that mentioned by Plato, and thinking the existence of such a book unlikely, attempts an escape through the horns of the dilemma, maintaining that "they play an essential part in the attack on plurality." He does not, however, specify what that part is. (Nor could he: see next note.)

15. Or if not, some argument is called for. I have found only this (Guthrie, 1965, 97): "It has rightly been pointed out [citing Ross, 1951, 83] that Zeno's arguments against motion are themselves arguments against plurality no less than those which attack it directly" because "[t]he apparent fact of motion, involving the occupation of different places at different times, is a *prima facie* evidence of plurality and therefore Zeno tries to deprive pluralism of this support by proving the nonexistence of motion." Besides involving an illicit conversion, this ascribes to Zeno the following curious train of thought: "I'll convince the Pluralists that nothing moves. Then they will be less likely to continue believing in Pluralism."

fact the earliest surviving specimen; it is out of the question that plain men (Zeno's opponents, according to the Majority) could be induced by this means to give up believing that, as Guthrie (100) put it, "rabbits run," or even to feel shamefaced about persisting in that belief.

In sum: Those who believe that Zeno's "paradoxes" attempt to prove the impossibility of motion, in support of Parmenides's (alleged) teaching, must either reject Plato's testimony as—let us not mince words—a lie, or they must conjecture that those arguments were published elsewhere than in the book Plato discusses. Either way, Plato's support for the contention that "Zeno rejected motion, therefore Parmenides did" vanishes. With Plato subtracted, what is left? At most, a vague tradition.[16]

THE TANNERY INTERPRETATION

So much for the negative argument. We turn now to a positive account of the relation of Zeno to Parmenides, one that leaves Plato's testimony entirely intact. In its terms, Plato knew of, albeit not mentioning in the dialogue, the presence of the arguments about motion in Zeno's book.[17] He took them, like all the arguments in that book, as intended to refute the thesis that Many Are by showing that thesis to lead to consequences even more absurd than those drawn from Parmenides's poem by his opponents.

According to Paul Tannery 1887 (chapter 10), nothing was further from Zeno's thought than the denial of motion. On the contrary, "Motion cannot occur" was precisely the super-ridiculous consequence that Zeno accused the ridiculers of Parmenides of being logically committed to. The people making fun of Parmenides were not plain men, partisans of common sense, but a particular school of philosophers: Pythagoreans. And their doctrines, from which were derived the premises of the Zenonian *reductiones*, were not common sense beliefs but the explicit doctrine that What Is—the real world—is an aggregate of units: pluralism, "Many Are."

THE ARROW AND THE RACECOURSE

Tannery thought that the argument known as The Arrow went this way: If the world is made up of unit places, then a given stretch of the world must be composed of either a finite or an infinite number of them. Let us suppose first that

---

16. To which, by the way, Aristotle has not been shown to have subscribed. In more than one place (188a20, 318b7, 330b15, 648a25, 984b25, 986b27) he takes the Doxa seriously, and as seriously meant, as a 'physiological' account. The Philosopher's understanding and views of the Eleatics need further study.

17. Plato knew of the Arrow at least; *Phaedrus* 261d. Owen (1958, 201) points also to *Parmenides* 152b-e as an "application" of The Arrow.

the number is finite. Then a line segment will consist of a finite number of atomic places lined up one after the other, the places being atomic in the sense that there are no lesser places that compose them or into which a single place is divisible. Then, said Tannery's Zeno, "the flying arrow is at rest." For motion must consist in the successive occupation of each of the places in the line; there cannot consistently be said to be motion *between* one such place and the next. This conclusion—that motion turns out to be really a succession of states of rest, and nothing else—may not be a self-contradictory proposition, but it certainly seems "ridiculous."

The Racecourse, according to Tannery, extracts an actual contradiction from the assumption of finite unit places, if Aristotle's sketchy summary of the argument is filled out—quite legitimately—with the assumptions that the units involved (the *onkoi*) are minimal places; that time is analogously composed of atomic instants, which are before and after each other, but within which there is no before and after; and that motion consists in the successive occupation of adjacent places. There would then be a maximum velocity—namely, one atomic place per atomic instant; for to move faster would entail "skipping" places—there would be spatial minima where the moving body *never* (i.e., at no instant) was. Given these assumptions, if two files of bodies moved in opposite directions at maximum speed past a row of stationary bodies—that is, each moving body distanced itself from each stationary body by one spatial minimum per instant—then each body in each moving file would pass *two* bodies in the other moving file in the same time in which it passed one stationary body. So it would be "skipping" spatial minima after all, contrary to hypothesis.

Vlastos (1966a) combined Fragment 4 (from Diogenes Laertius), "What moves moves neither in the place where it is nor where it is not," with Aristotle's account to give a slightly different version of The Arrow, according to which the reason why the arrow cannot move in the place where it is, is that this is "a place equal to itself" (*kata to ison*), and whatever is in a place "equal to itself" is at rest. This version is reminiscent of Zeno's argument against place: "If place is something, what will it be in?" (DK 29A24; Aristotle *Phys.* 210b22). Aristotle thought this argument, clearly of the vicious regress type, was "not difficult to solve." He held commonsensically that "place" is "like, 'in the Agora, in the Lyceum'" (*Categories* 2a1). The Agora is in Athens, Athens is in Greece, which is in Europe, which is . . . A regress, maybe even infinite, but benign.

But one can hardly doubt that Zeno would have been capable of formulating this rejoinder for himself. And that in turn seems a reason to believe, again, that he was arguing not against "common sense" but against holders of a more refined and philosophical conception of place. And what might that conception have been? Place as *precisely* where the thing is; place as an absolutely tight skin of zero thickness around the thing. Against that kind of conception the argument of Zeno is effective.

What could Zeno have had against places? Obviously, their plurality; more specifically, the view that the cosmos is the totality (aggregate) of places.[18] As Kant has taught us, space—the concept that, according to the Minority, Parmenides was struggling to express—is a given manifold, not a congeries of lesser spaces, let alone places.

To return to the Vlastos version of The Arrow: If we think of Place as an absolutely tight skin around the thing of which it is the place, and also as immobile—and of course no Greek ever contemplated the motion of a Place, any more than a modern set theorist allows the generation or destruction of a Set—then it is not an arbitrary and unconvincing assertion that nothing can move (either in an instant or over any stretch of time you please) in the place where it is. And even more obviously, not in the place where it is not. So, since (according to the Place theorist) a thing must always—at each instant and throughout every stretch of time—be in a definite place, it cannot move. *But that is absurd!* Indeed it is! Zeno retorts. Which shows that the assumption leading to the absurdity—namely, that the cosmos is an aggregate of Places—is false.

Here are two instances—we shall find others—where it turns out that an argument allegedly "against" motion is really directed against plurality—as we should have known all along, since Plato told us so.

Suppose that Zeno's argument of The Arrow was, as the Majority claim, a straightforward refutation of the plain man's belief in motion. And suppose that the Vlastos reconstruction is correct. Then the crucial premise is that a thing cannot move in the place where it is, which to common sense is an altogether implausible claim: why cannot a dervish rotate in the marketplace? Zeno could hardly have paid back the jeerers at the Master in their own coin by producing an argument with a premise that none of them would accept; nor, being no fool, would he have tried to do so.

Some have objected to Tannery's ingenious reconstruction of The Racecourse on the grounds that it depends on the supplying of additional premises with no textual support. There is no evidence, we are told, that any Pythagoreans ever held time to be composed of minimal instants, or even that space (or place) was composed of minimal extensions; both of which assumptions are needed in order to make this version of the argument work. That is true, no doubt, though in the unsatisfactory state of our knowledge about Pythagoreanism, absence of evidence about a particular tenet can hardly afford a daunting consideration against Tannery. In any case, his interpretation does not stand or fall with the identification of Parmenides's opponents as actual card-carrying Pythagoreans.

---

18. As is well known, though sometimes forgotten by translators, *topos* means place, not space in anything like the modern cosmological sense—a notion for which indeed the Greeks had no word. See De Santillana (1961, 95).

The main consideration in favor of the Tannery version is that on it Zeno turns out to have been a dialectician of great skill, in keeping with the reputation that antiquity unanimously assigned to him; whereas on the unsupplemented Aristotelian account the so-called argument could have amounted to nothing but the well-nigh incredible blunder of supposing that it takes as long to pass a body moving in the opposite direction as to pass a stationary body—an assumption that even Meno's slave boy would have rejected with scorn.[19]

THE ONE VERSUS THE MANY

Before going on to the Dichotomy and the Achilles, let us ask what is at issue between those who hold that One Is and those who say Many Are.

To a philosopher brought up in our times the fifth-century dispute between Monists and Pluralists may look like a primitive instance of metaphysics in the bad sense, happily obviated once and for all by Aristotle's remark that "'one' is said in various ways," *to on legetai pollachōs*. Pluralists must admit that the universe is one *whole*, while Monists must agree that the one whole has many *parts*. Anybody but a fanatic from Elea would admit that one mile is divisible into 5,280 feet.

Well, let us assume that the whole we are talking about is extended, and that by division we mean a process of making separation possible—that is to say, after a division has been made we can, physically or at least in thought, remove one segment from the other segment; and if the division is done cleanly, everything that was in the whole before division will now be in one or the other of the segments: we could subsequently put them back together, recreating the whole as it was before separation.

Is extension itself—space—divisible in this sense? Obviously not. It makes no sense to talk about scooping out a cubic foot of space and putting it a yard to one side—not even in thought. Space cannot be divided; space is that within which division takes place. Nevertheless (the Pluralist may say) any extended thing in space, whether material object or merely ideal construction, can be divided. Division of material things is a process subject to various physical limitations, but in thought division of things is capable of being carried on to infinity.

The path of a runner in a stadium may be taken as an instance of something fitting the description. It is not exactly a "physical object," but neither is

---

19. Furley's alternative reconstruction of The Racecourse (1974, 364f) requires less supplementation of the Aristotelian text than Tannery's, while attributing to Zeno a less egregious (though still embarrassing) error than did Aristotle. Since, however, it, like Tannery's, is based on the hypothesis of spatial and temporal minima, we need not discuss it separately.

it mere extension: it gets longer as the runner advances; we can speak of the first half as distinct (and therefore separable in thought) from the second half; and so on. And the path contains—to the Pluralist it is nothing but—a set of points,[20] either a finite or infinite number of them, each of which is traversed—passed—by the runner. *E pluribus unum.* The one path is made of many points. There is no issue left for Monist and Pluralist to dispute.

Isn't there? The runner's path—not space itself but a line *in* space—is divisible, in the sense we have specified, at any point, at least in thought; so the Pluralist avers. But he is mistaken: A line is not divisible, even in thought, into two segments together containing all and only what was in the undivided line. Not, at any rate, if a line is thought of as a dense ordered set of points (a Pluralist conception[21]). For suppose it to be divided, and the two resulting segments separated (whether in reality or only in thought). The first of the segments has a last point, the second has a first. Both points were in the uncut line, and they were distinct. (If they were not distinct, then what was one has miraculously become two.) Being distinct points of the uncut line, there were other points—indeed, an infinity of points—between them, which have now been lost, contrary to the conception of "clean" division.

THE DICHOTOMY AND THE ACHILLES

The Dichotomy and the Achilles exhibit in picturesque terms this incoherence in the notion of a line as a set of points. If what is between the runner and the goal, or between Achilles and the tortoise, is a "many," an ordered dense set of points, then the point at which the goal is reached must divide the line into two segments, one of which contains all and only the points before the goal, the other all the rest, including the goal point.[22] On the hypothesis of Many, these constitute two really separable sets, of which the first has a last member and the second has a first member (the goal). The arguments show

---

20. "A line segment is an aggregate of points." Sherry (1988, 59).
21. Zeno DK 29B3, "If Many Are, . . . always . . . there are others between the beings, and again others between *them*, . . . ," is (as far as I know) the earliest (surviving) explicit statement of this notion, and shows that Zeno considered it an entailment of the hypothesis Many Are. This is of course another linkage between the motion arguments and the refutation of Pluralism.
22. It does not matter whether we take the absurdity inferred in the Dichotomy (confusingly named "Race Course" by Vlastos [1966b]; Aristotle refers to it only as "the first [sc. argument about motion]") to be that the runner can never reach the goal (as Vlastos argues, loc. cit.) or (with Tannery, Owen [1958, 207], and others) that he can never get away from the start.

that this condition is unsatisfiable because contradictory: there would have to be two members of the original set of points, between which there were no other points.[23]

Zeno's arguments about dividing a line *are* arguments against a Many; for the difficulty noted does not beset the adherent of One. The Monist need have no fear of the infinity of points (i.e., positions discriminable from each other in principle) that must be traversed by the runner. Achilles the Monist *can* overtake the tortoise; for him there is no awful Void between the last point before he catches up and the point where he does. For him, stationary points are merely markers along the course;[24] they can be put anywhere on it, but they do not constitute it. What *is* the Monistic line? The path of a moving thing, such as a runner!

Why did Zeno include arguments against a "quantum" conception of space and time, and why did they come, in his book, *after* those against a Pluralistic continuum?[25] Vlastos and others object to the Tannery reconstruction of The Arrow and The Racecourse on the ground that there is no evidence for Pythagoreans (or others) having held such views, at least as concerns time. One might add that the untenability of a conception of space (or place) as an aggregate of finite minima was a corollary of the discovery of incommensurable lines, which almost certainly had been made long before Zeno's time. So would not Zeno have been flogging a dead horse?

On the Tannery model, an answer to this question can be advanced. Zeno first presents two arguments against a Many as a dense continuum—which would have been the sophisticated, "professional" conception held by the Pluralists (whoever they were) of the day. A Pluralist who could not force his way past these obstacles might yet see an escape route: he could hold that

---

23. The Dedekind *Schnitt*, boldly affirming the existence of line segments without end points, is said to have cleared this up. Perhaps so. But the *Schnitt* is so counterintuitive that it was not even thought of until the nineteenth century; which is enough to vindicate the plausibility, at least, of Zeno's argument at the time and place of its conception. And that is all that is relevant in our context.

24. Metaphorically speaking, that is. Zeno held that there are no such things as points: "If a thing had no size, it would not exist," DK 29B1.

25. Assuming, with Furley (1974, 360), and pace Booth (1957b, 91), that Aristotle's explicit numerical ordering of the arguments (*Phys.* VI, 9) reproduces Zeno's. This seems a reasonable assumption to make in view of the fact that in mentioning numbers at all, Aristotle is deviating from his usual practice when dealing with several arguments in a continuous passage, which is not to number them but to mark a boundary with "And again it is said" or some such phrase. Anyway, Tannery's case does not stand or fall with this consideration.

regardless of the results of *a priori* mathematical analysis, space and time are quantized *in fact*.[26] But then he would find that way blocked by The Arrow and The Racecourse.

INTERIM SUMMARY

We have seen that according to Plato, who is our fullest, perhaps our only, source of information about Zeno's relation to Parmenides, Zeno at the age of forty had written only one book; that book defended Parmenides's teaching that One Is by arguments showing that the theses of his opponents led to even more ridiculous conclusions. Evidence for any book by Zeno other than the one mentioned by Plato is negligible. It is therefore probable that the four arguments "about motion" were in the book that Plato mentions in defense of Parmenidean Monism. These arguments can be interpreted as defenses of Monism against "professional" Pluralists; as such they would be powerful and convincing. So interpreted they do not conclude that motion is logically impossible; on the contrary they show that this "ridiculous" conclusion follows from Pluralist principles. On this reading, then, Zeno defended the Master not by adducing new arguments "against motion," but rather by showing that his opponents—not Parmenides—were logically committed to "denying motion."

If on the other hand Zeno was straightforwardly trying to exhibit logical difficulties in the plain man's conception of motion—that "rabbits run"—or from premises that Zeno himself accepted as true, then his attempt was a miserable failure; he merely produced four puzzles "not difficult to solve," as Aristotle superciliously remarked.

REBUTTAL OF VLASTOS

Vlastos (1967, 376), defending the Majority interpretation of Zeno, summarizes Tannery's exegesis in six theses, all of which, he claims, are false. I shall defend the first four. The fifth and sixth, which have to do with the influence of Zeno on subsequent developments in mathematics, do not concern us.

---

26. This retreat position held distinguished occupants as late as the eighteenth century. Berkeley pronounced (1710, Sec. 127) that "there is no such thing as the ten thousandth part of an inch," and Hume concurred (1896, Bk. 1, Pt. 2, Sec. 2). Indeed, the notion is still present at the cutting edge of physics: Ray mentions "an idea drawn from superstring physics that space itself is not infinitely divisible, but breaks down at a distance scale of 10 to the minus 35th power meters" (*New York Times*, November 11, 1997, B11).

First Tannery Thesis

"Zeno's arguments were not directed against the commonsense belief in plurality and motion." Vlastos says this is contrary to "unanimous opinion of antiquity that Zeno was a faithful Eleatic. . . . As such he could not but reject *all* current professions of plurality and motion–starting with those of the man in the street."

This enthymematic argument is sound if, but only if, its suppressed premise is true—namely, that Parmenides himself rejected all current professions of plurality and motion, starting with those of the man in the street. And that is precisely the point at issue between Majority and Minority readings of Parmenides' poem. The senior Eleatic indeed held (so the Minority maintain) that Being, *to eon*, that which *esti sensu stricto*,[27] of which alone we know the well-rounded truth, admits of no plurality and no movement; but that Being is space, not the things in space. Things in space are not knowable with the certainty that space itself is knowable in geometry, the new science of the time; but that does not mean, nor did Parmenides imply, that they are mere illusion.[28] As Simplicius put it, "Obviously Parmenides was not unaware of the fact that he himself was generated, no more than that he had two feet when he said that Being is one" (*Commentary on De Caelo*, 559, 27).

Vlastos's argument is two-edged. Granted that Zeno was a faithful disciple of Parmenides, any independent evidence in favor of the Tannery interpretation *strengthens* the Minority claim as to Parmenides. And such evidence abounds: The emphatic testimony of Plato that all of Zeno's arguments were polemics against Pluralism—testimony that Vlastos found himself forced to "consign to the junk heap"—as well as all the circumstantial evidence that the arguments are profound and effective against technical mathematico-philosophical Pluralism, though if considered as telling against the common notion that we can go from here to there, they are junk indeed.[29]

---

27. See Loenen (1959), 11 et passim.
28. For supporting argument see Casertano (1978) passim, De Santillana (1961, Ch. 6; 1963, passim), and Matson (1980).
29. Two and a half millennia of playing with paradoxes—that all opinions are true, that nothing is known, that matter does not exist, that we make up space and time, and truth too, that we can't see trees, that nobody deserves anything, that there are no beliefs, and so forth—have so raised the threshold of shock among "professional" philosophers that discussants of the Eleatics seem not in the least astonished by someone's "proving" that "rabbits don't run," not noticing that Nothing Moves (which amounts to Nothing Happens) and its immediate and obvious corollaries, There Are No Arguments, There are No Arguers, You Don't Exist, *I* Don't Exist, is more paradoxical by several orders of magnitude than any on the short list above: indeed, a philosophical black hole, sucking in not only all of reality but appearance along with it. But attitudes during the first century of the endeavor *must* have been different: "Achilles can't catch the tortoise" *couldn't* have been anybody's actual—or even "Pickwickian"—belief, it could only have been the *absurdum* that something *reducebatur ad.*

Second Tannery Thesis

The Pythagorean doctrine against which Zeno's arguments were aimed was "that all objects are made up of elements which were expected to combine somehow the properties of the arithmetical unit, the geometrical point, and the physical atom."

Vlastos says this is "probably false," on the ground that evidence is lacking that *early*—Vlastos's emphasis—Pythagoreans held it.

The question of course cannot be resolved with certainty. However, Tannery was not (or at any rate we, in this chapter, are not) concerned primarily with the historical identity of Zeno's opponents, the ridiculers of Parmenides, nor with what in detail they held, but with what Zeno's arguments were. The answer to the historical question might help in answering the exegetical question, but it is not indispensable for the purpose. Indeed, it can be the other way around: if we see clearly what Zeno's arguments were, we may be in a position to make, quite legitimately, inferences as to what doctrines he was polemicizing against.

Third Tannery Thesis

"These Pythagoreans thought that time and motion were similarly discontinuous."

Vlastos condemns this view as "pure conjecture and most implausible," on the ground that "so abstruse a theory as the quantization of time and motion could not have been seriously entertained until well after the much less daring speculation of the atomic constitution of matter had become thoroughly assimilated by the philosophical imagination—that is, well after Zeno."

It is hard to know what to say in reply to this contention, for the "quantum theory" impresses *me* as quite naive, indeed as what a priori would most likely be the *first* conception to suggest itself once the question of the structure of space (or "place") and time had been raised—and (as I mentioned earlier) destined to be sunk without a trace by the discovery of incommensurable lines. I have no idea how to argue with someone whose intuition of naiveté is different from mine.

Vlastos, however, seems to make an implicit appeal to a supposititious law of intellectual development according to which the more "daring" a speculation is the later it must be. To such a "law" there are, in early Greek philosophy, a host of (what appear to me to be) counterexamples, beginning with Anaximander's unsupported earth (*followed* by Anaximenes's pneumatic float and Xenophanes's "going all the way down") and theory of cosmic and organic evolution (*followed* by the steady-state universes of Heraclitus and Aristotle).

Again, in any event the question who actually held the quantum theory, and when, is peripheral to the Tannery interpretation. It may be the case that no one did, that (as I speculated earlier) it was invented by Zeno himself as a proleptic precaution.

Fourth Tannery Thesis

Zeno's arguments as Tannery interpreted them were "clear, forceful, irrefutable—even those in which nothing but simple paralogisms had been commonly seen."

Vlastos agrees that Tannery's reconstructions have this character, but he raises the objection that an opponent of Zeno who accepted the discontinuity premise of the third and fourth arguments would reject the infinite divisibility of the first and second; so what could have been Zeno's point in offering both kinds of arguments?

I have tried to answer this question already, by pointing out that Zeno's four arguments as an ensemble constitute a dilemma to confute anyone holding *any conceivable* Pluralistic view. And I hope I will not be thought to be appealing *ad misericordiam* in reminding the reader of the Principle of Charity, which implies that if according to one reading arguments are "clear, forceful, irrefutable," while according to another they are "nothing but simple paralogisms," then the former reading is to be preferred, at least *prima facie*. A *secunda facies* negating this preference could only be a conclusive proof that Parmenides really did deny that rabbits run, and that is, to say it yet again, the central point in contention. If the Majority, who hold this, are right, then yes, Zeno's arguments are paralogisms; but this proposition cannot be converted. It certainly will not do to say that *since* Zeno advanced paralogisms ("proving" that rabbits don't run), *therefore* Parmenides too denied that rabbits run. And that, again, is what this chapter is concerned primarily with demonstrating.

Since Vlastos's demurrers constitute the most serious challenge (that I know of) to the Tannery interpretation, its survival of these objections (if it is judged to have done so) would seem to amount to its virtual establishment. Which in turn amounts to vindication of the Minority position with regard to Parmenides.

THE MILLET SEED

Zeno is reported (DK 29A29) to have engaged in the following little dialogue with the sophist Protagoras:[30]

> "Tell me, Protagoras, does one falling millet-seed make a noise, or the ten-thousandth of a seed?"—No.—"But does a bushel of millet make a noise when it falls or not?"—It does.—"Well, isn't there a

---

30. Probably it is no accident that Protagoras, guilty (at least by association, *Theaetetus* 152f) of Heracliteanism, is the straight man. See below, at "Who were Melissus's opponents?"

ratio (*logos*) of the bushel of millet to the single millet-seed and to the ten-thousandth part of it?"—Yes.—"Well, won't the ratios of the noises to each other be the same? For as the noise-makers, so the noises; this being so, if the bushel of millet makes a noise, so does the single seed and so does the ten-thousandth of the seed."

All commentaries (that I have seen) refer to this as an "argument," but if it is, it is an enthymeme lacking a conclusion (at least). What is its point? Aristotle (*Phys.* 250a19) treats it as a puzzle for physics, solved by his "principle" that while movement is generally proportional to force, very small forces may produce no motion at all. Vlastos (1967; Booth [1957b], 8 concurs) interprets it as an attack on the trustworthiness of the senses—there has to be a noise, but we don't hear it[31]—which "could scarcely have come except from someone who was prejudiced against them to begin with—as the Eleatics, and only they, are known to have been at the time."

Perhaps no one can claim certainty as to what Zeno's point was. However, a natural line of interpretation would take the testimonium as a counterexample to the core contention of Pluralism, that every whole is the sum of its independent parts. Thus the Pluralist must suppose the thud of the falling bushel to be the sum of the microthuds of the individual falling seeds, and they in turn of the nanothuds of their ten-thousandth parts. But there are no such microthuds. So, *modo tollente*, another blow is struck against division and separation.

And how do we know there are no microthuds? Because we don't hear them!

THE PROBLEM OF MELISSUS

An Eleatic only by courtesy, Melissus of Samos attributed to Being (*to eon*) three properties that Parmenides did not explicitly assign (as far as we know from the fragments and testimonies): feeling no pain, feeling no grief, and being bodiless; and (it seems) one property, spatial infinity, that the Master explicitly denied.[32] Thus inferences from Samian doctrines and arguments back to Elea are antecedently of dubious validity; only in desperation would an interpreter rely on Melissus in inferring what Parmenides taught. One is tempted to leave the collimation of Melissus and the Minority position as an exercise for the student.

However, inasmuch as in arguing that Parmenides could not have held the doctrine of the illusoriness of motion and change we have done so partially on the ground that *nobody* could have held such a bizarre view, it is incumbent on us to show that Melissus did not hold it either.

---

31. If so, then Zeno, after all, did maintain, on at least one occasion, that there is such a thing as a motion that is not a delusive appearance.
32. Curd (1993, 15) remarks that "A being that is without body yet unlimited in magnitude seems improbable." Not if the being is Space.

THE NOTORIOUS FRAGMENT 8

The trouble lies in Fragment 8, the relevant portion of which goes as follows:

> (2) For if there were many, they would have to be of the same sort as I at any rate say the one is. For if earth is (*esti*) and water and air and fire and iron and gold, and living and dead, and black and white and the others that men say are genuine (*einai alēthē*), if indeed these are, and we rightly see and hear, each one has to be of the kind that it first seemed to us, and not to alter nor become different, but always be as it is; (3) but it seems to us that the hot becomes cold and the cold hot and the hard soft and the soft hard and the living dies and comes to be from the not living, and all these alter, and what was and what now is are nothing the same, but iron being hard when turned about on the finger is worn down, and gold and stone and everything that seems to be strong, and earth and stone come from water; so that it follows that we neither see nor recognize the beings (*ta onta*). (4) Now these do not agree with each other. For to those who say there are many having their own properties[33] and shapes and strength, all seem to alter and change, as we gather from how they look every time. (5) So it is clear that we did not see rightly nor did those many seem rightly to be; for they would not have altered had they been genuine, but each would have been just as it seemed. (6) But if something alters, being is destroyed, not-being (*to ouk eon*) comes to be (*gegonen*). Consequently if many were, they would have to be just such as the one.

It cannot be denied that this looks like an assault on common sense, on belief in earth and water, iron and gold, and hot food getting cold when people are late for dinner, in favor of a strange teaching that none of these things and processes actually exist—we "do not see rightly." Of course the Majority view is that this is precisely the message of the fragment.

Let us set out Melissus's argument somewhat more formally, supplying (in brackets) suppressed premises:

1. "If something alters, being is destroyed, not-being comes to be."
2. [It is impossible for genuine being to be destroyed or for not-being to come to be.]
3. [Therefore, for all x, if x is genuine, then x does not alter.]
4. [For all x, if x does not alter and x is rightly perceived, then x is not perceived to alter.]
5. Earth, water, etc. are genuine. (Premise for *reductio*.)

---

33. Reading *idia*.

6. Earth, water, etc. are rightly perceived. (Premise for *reductio.*)
7. Therefore, earth, water, etc. are not perceived to alter.
8. But earth, water, etc. *are* perceived to alter.
9. "These do not agree with each other" (i.e., 7 contradicts 8).
10. Therefore, either earth, water, etc. are not genuine, or they are not rightly perceived.
11. [Therefore, if earth, water, etc. are rightly perceived, then they are not genuine.]
12. "Consequently if many (viz. earth, water, etc.) were, they would have to be just such as the one" (i.e., if earth, water, etc. are genuine then they—being unaltered—are not rightly perceived).[34]

WHO WERE MELISSUS'S OPPONENTS?

As we did with Zeno, let us ask who might have been the targets of the polemic. Could they have been ordinary nonphilosophical people—say, the sailors who rowed the Admiral's barge?

No doubt a sailor would accept (1), "if something alters, being is destroyed, not-being comes to be," though the abstract form might be baffling. He might think: "This means, when I eat hardtack, the hardtack is destroyed, and I put on weight. Sure." But then he would be brought up short by (2), seemingly denying this. "What gives?" "Well," Melissus would have to explain to him, "we're talking about *genuine* being." "Hardtack isn't genuine being?" "I'm afraid not . . ." And then he would go on to explain what genuine being is, and why hardtack doesn't qualify. That is to say, Melissus would have to give the sailor a crash course in philosophy before proceeding with the argument, which would otherwise make no sense to him.

Philosophers in and before Melissus's time explicitly asserted (2): Parmenides (DK 28B8, 12-13), Empedocles (31B11), and Anaxagoras (59B17). All of them distinguished between ordinary everyday being and Genuine Being: for Empedocles the latter is the Roots, for Anaxagoras the Seeds. Of course Melissus had no quarrel with Parmenides. Neither did he have any reason to oppose Empedocles or Anaxagoras, on this point at any rate, for each of them *did* assert of his Genuine Beings that they did not alter—they were "just such as the one" of Melissus.

---

34. Melissus, castigated as a sloppy logician by the father of logic (*Soph. El.* 167b12-20), was entitled only to (10), the alternation of the denials of the two *reductio* premises (5) and (6), but he asserted their conjunction: "So it is clear that we did not see rightly *nor* (*oude*) did those many seem rightly to be." However, the conclusion (12) still follows using the weaker premise.

However, many of Melissus's examples of alleged alteration—earth, water, fire, living/dead, cold/hot—echo well-known pronouncements of a philosopher who lived in the same part of the world two or three generations before Melissus. I refer, of course, to Heraclitus:

The cold things warm up, warm cools off, damp gets dry, dry dampens (DK 22B126).

Earth flows through as sea, and is measured in the same proportion as it had before it became earth (DK 22B31).

It is death for souls to become water, but for water it is death to become earth, but from earth water comes, and from water soul. Fire lives the death of earth and air lives the death of fire, water lives the death of air, earth that of water (DK 22B76).

We live their death and they live our death (DK 22B77).

Furthermore, Heraclitus insisted that we *do* perceive rightly:

What there is sight, hearing, learning of, these I prefer (DK 22B55).

Eyes are better witnesses than ears (DK 22B101a).

Although Heraclitus did not (as far as we know) explicitly assert the principle Nothing from Nothing, it is hard to doubt that he accepted it. And as we have seen, in the generation after him it became a philosophical commonplace. I am not suggesting, however, that Heraclitus was Melissus's immediate target. We have the testimony of both Plato and Aristotle for the continued existence of "Heracliteans" in the Ionia of Melissus's time, and that they stressed the dynamism of the Ephesian philosophy, perhaps to the exclusion of Heraclitus's emphasis on the underlying unity of being, which was no less central in his thought than in Parmenides's. If Parmenides and Heraclitus had met, there would have been little occasion[35] for them to quarrel; but it would have been natural for their respective epigones—Melissus, and people like Cratylus—to have at one another. Moreover, if the elaborate account in the *Theaetetus* has any basis in fact, the Heracliteans of the later fifth century had a special interest in sense perception, which to them both revealed and was itself an instance of the unceasing flow of all things. Hence there was a specific motive for their opponents to charge them with "not seeing rightly."

---

35. I do not say no occasion. But pugilistically squaring them off as Thesis and Antithesis distorts their priorities, and is in large part to blame for the belief in Eleatic immobilism.

Because except for what we can glean from the *Theaetetus* and from Aristotle's brief remark about Cratylus's having abandoned speech for finger-wiggling, we know nothing of late Heracliteanism, it is impossible to reconstruct the particulars of Melissus's argumentative strategy. But it seems hardly contestable that Melissus was, like Zeno—and Parmenides himself—carrying on a dialectic with other philosophers and not with the general public; and that therefore he could count on those to whom he addressed his writings to share certain assumptions such as that nothing comes from nothing, and to be aware of certain technical usages, such as Genuine Being (*einai alēthē*)—the Being *sensu stricto* of Parmenides.

Thus we see that Melissus is no obstacle to acceptance of the Minority interpretation of Parmenides.

BEING

A study of Parmenides's poem will show that the participial form, *eon*, is always used in this sense of what fundamentally, objectively, and absolutely exists on its own and is the object of—and in some way identical with—*noein*, which we might render as "the faculty of *a priori* insight." *To eon* does not appear in the Proem or in the meager fragments of the Doxa.[36] *Esti* and other forms of *einai* occur in all three portions, but when they are not merely copulative the context always makes clear whether or not they are intended in the strict sense.

What is it that IS *sensu stricto*? Well, what is ungenerated, indestructible, one, all alike, unchanging, unmoving, indivisible, full, and "like the mass of a well-rounded ball?" De Santillana's answer to this riddle is: the Space of Geometry; certainly all but the last two of these epithets are applicable to that. Tannery said it is Cartesian extension (which is a plenum), and Casertano concluded that it is "the world, reality considered in its unity and totality" (1978, 94). These perhaps fit better with the last two properties listed above. There can be little doubt—at any rate to the Minority—that *to eon* is *at least* geometrical space. The special status of Being assigned to it recognizes it as the domain of pure thought, which to Parmenides as to Aristotle's God is the greatest thing in the world and therefore *must* have a commensurately exalted object—so much so indeed that in the end it must be identical to what thinks it:

to gar auto noein estin te kai einai.

In other words, Space thinks. To which Melissus adds as anticlimactic footnotes that it feels no pain nor grief.

---

36. But neither does *to mê eon*, and there is reason to believe (see Matson 1980, 348f) that that sinister appellation was not to be found in the entirety of the Doxa. The plural *ta eonta* occurs nowhere.

Chapter 6

"Whole-Natured Forms"
in Empedocles's Cosmic Cycle

Joel Wilcox

INTRODUCTION

Empedocles is known to have posited a *cosmos*[1] which oscillates between polar states characterized, respectively, by the hegemony of an attractive force known as Love, and that of a repulsive force known as Strife. During the hegemony of Love all things are drawn together into a more or less *apeiron*-like unity, while during the hegemony of strife all things are separated from one another. Because the fundamental ingredients or "roots" of Empedocles's *cosmos* are the basic materials fire, air, earth and water,[2] the state characterized by the hegemony of love is constituted by a thoroughgoing mixture of the basic materials, while the state characterized by the hegemony of strife is constituted by the separation of each basic material from all the others. *Cosmoi* such as ours occupy some intermediate stage between total Love and total Strife; thus what we are likely to regard as "things" in our *cosmos* are really temporary combinations of the basic materials.

Although this general picture of Empedocles's cosmic cycle is uncontroversial, there has been significant disagreement concerning the symmetry, or lack thereof, of the cycle. The cycle would be symmetrical if (and only if) *cosmoi* such as ours occur both in the period during which Love is increasing to its maximal state, and also in the period during which Strife is increasing to its maximal state. The cycle would be asymmetrical in the event that *cosmoi* such as ours occur in only one of the transitional periods, whether from Love to Strife or vice versa.

---

1. In this chapter the word *cosmos* will be used in an extended sense to refer simply to the totality of existents with which Empedocles's metaphysics is concerned. It need not imply any kind or significant degree of either order or structure, or even unity.

  A tree-dwelling ancestor of this chapter was presented at a meeting of the Society for Ancient Greek Philosophy in October 1995. I am indebted for most of the improvements in the present evolved version to useful criticisms from those who attended, from Dr. Patricia Curd, who chaired the session, and from anonymous referees for the present volume.

2. "Hear first the four roots of all things: bright Zeus and life-bringing Hera and Aidoneus and Nestis, whose tears are the source of mortal streams." For correlations of these "new divinities" with the basic materials fire, air, earth, and water, respectively, see Kingsley (1994); and esp. (1995), 13–68.

Both of these interpretations have been supported by careful philological studies, which have nonetheless arrived at strikingly different conclusions. For example, whereas for Denis O'Brien the symmetrical interpretation honors "the most obvious and distinctive feature of [Empedocles's] philosophy," for Charles Kahn "astonishingly little of the [symmetrical interpretation] is to be found in the fragments."[3] The purpose of this chapter is emphatically not to attempt to supplement the philological expertise of prior studies.[4] It is, rather, to call attention to a single interpretive consideration, which seems to be undervalued, and which supports one interpretation over the other. This consideration is simply a consistent analysis of the natures of Empedoclean Love and Strife which recognizes their fundamental mutual opposition. As it turns out, such an analysis strongly favors the symmetrical interpretation.

The argument will be organized as follows: (1) The two competing interpretations of Empedocles's cycle will be summarized in order to provide a framework for discussion; (2) A univocal interpretation of the natures of Love and Strife, respectively, will be established, employing the key notions of allopathy and homeopathy (the principle of "like-to-like"). Though the content of this section will be based on philological concerns, the idea of univocity *per se* either is, or follows from, the provisional assumption that interpretations should be as internally consistent as possible;[5] (3) At this point the logical criterion of consistency, just introduced *sub specie* univocity, will be applied to the cosmic cycle itself, in that two distinct moments of the cycle will be shown to be incompatible. In particular, the existence of the "whole-natured forms" of B62[6] will be shown to be inconsistent with Empedocles's picturesque story according to which assorted and disconnected body parts come together to form creatures of various sorts, *if* both of these stages of biogenesis are supposed to have developed during the period of time characterized by the ascendancy of Love. Thus, the conclusion will follow, it seems necessary to posit two distinct transitional periods to accommodate the otherwise incompatible features of Empedocles's account.

---

3. O'Brien (1995), 403; Kahn (1969), 442.
4. These studies include, in addition to those mentioned in note 3: Bollack (1965/1969); Graham (1988); Inwood (1992); Raven in Kirk and Raven (1957), 327; Long (1974); O'Brien (1969); Solmsen (1965); and Wright (1981/1995a).
5. In the realm of Presocratic studies, there actually seems to be room for debate regarding this assumption; cf. note 37.
6. Fragments of Empedocles will be referenced by the numbers assigned to them in Diels and Kranz (1961, hereafter DK). However, for ease of reference, footnotes will specify Inwood's numbering (1992) and also that of Wright (1995). For example: B62 = Inwood 67 = Wright 53.

COMPETING INTERPRETATIONS OF EMPEDOCLES'S CYCLE

Since "fr. [B]17 must be the starting point for any analysis of this controversy," a translation of relevant lines of this fragment will be useful:[7]

> I shall tell a double tale. For at one time [they] grew to be one alone from many, and at another, again, [they] grew apart to be many from one.
> And there is a double coming to be of mortals and a double waning, for the coming together [of them] all gives birth to and destroys the one,
> 5 while the other, as [they] again grow apart, was nurtured and flew away.
> And these things never cease from constantly alternating, at one time all coming together by Love into one, and at another time all being borne apart separately by the hostility of Strife. . . .
> 16 I shall tell a double tale. For at one time [they] grew to be one alone from many, and at another, again, [they] grew apart to be many from one—
> fire and water and earth and the boundless height of air; and destructive Strife apart from these, like in every respect,
> 20 and Love among them, equal in length and breadth. . . .
> 34 But these very things are, and running through each other
> 35 they become different at different times and are always, perpetually alike.

One other fragment, B26, will be helpful:[8]

> And in turn they [the four elements] dominate as the cycle goes around,
> and they shrink into each other and grow in the turns assigned by destiny.
> For these very things are, and running through each other they become men and the tribes of other beasts.
> 5 at one time coming together by Love into one cosmos, and at another time again all being borne apart separately by the hostility of Strife,
> until by growing together as one they are totally subordinated.

---

7. Long (1974). All texts and translations (with very minor changes, such as capitalizations of "love" and "strife") are taken from Inwood (1992). B17 = Inwood 25 = Wright 8.
8. B26 = Inwood 28 = Wright 16.

The Symmetrical Interpretation[9]

The fragments just quoted can readily be interpreted so as to support the symmetrical version of Empedocles's cycle: Empedocles announces and repeats the claims that he will "tell a double tale," that "at one time" things come together, and that "at another time" things grow apart. He adds (17, 3) that "there is a double coming to be of mortals and a double waning." The mortals in question would be compounds of the basic materials fire, air, earth, and water, of which Empedocles states (26, 3–4) "these very things are, and running through each other they become men and the tribes of other beasts." Thus, it seems, whatever is happening in the cosmic process of becoming is happening twice, "at one time" under the aegis of Love and "at another time" under that of Strife.

On the basis of such considerations Raven adopted a symmetrical interpretation of the cosmic cycle some time ago, as have (more recently) O'Brien, Wright, Graham, and Inwood.[10] On this view the cycle takes place in four distinct stages: two static, though perhaps momentary, polar states exemplifying the rules of Love and of Strife, respectively, and two process-states constituted by a gradual transition from each of the polar states to the other.[11] This interpretation is represented by figure 6.1.

The polar state of Love, in which "all things are drawn together," is to be found in the *Sphairos* of fragments B27, B28, and B29,[12] of which Empedocles states that:

> There the shining form of the sun is not discerned,
> nor indeed the shaggy might of earth nor the sea. . . .
> Thus it is fixed in the dense cover of harmony,
> a rounded sphere, rejoicing in its joyous solitude.
> For two branches do not dart from its back,
> not feet nor swift knees nor potent genitals. . . .

---

9. A thorough review of previous interpretations, both symmetrical and asymmetrical, can be found in O'Brien (1969). A more recent treatment of competing views, with an argument for the asymmetrical interpretation, can be found in Long (1974).

10. Kirk and Raven (1957), 327; O'Brien (1995); Wright (1995a), 40–41; Graham (1988); Inwood (1992), 40, 42, and n.94.

11. There are of course many interpretive decisions to be made within this general framework, and no claim is implied here that Raven, O'Brien, Wright, and Inwood do or would agree with one another about specific details of the cycle.

12. B27 = Inwood 31, 33 = Wright 19, 21; B28 = Inwood 34 = Wright 22; B29 = Inwood 34 = Wright 22.

Maximum Love   Maximum Strife

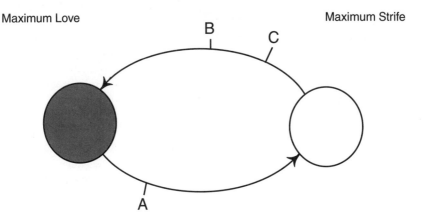

Figure 6.1
The symmetrical interpretation

The polar state of strife is mentioned in B17, 17, wherein things "grew apart to be many from one," and in B21: "in wrath all [the elements are] borne apart separately by the hostility of strife." Glossing B27, Plutarch adds that in this state "earth had no share in warmth, nor water any share in breath [i.e., air]; none of the heavy things was up nor any of the light things down; but the principles of the universe were unblended . . . not desiring combination or communion with one another. . . ."[13]

Thus the polar states are tolerably well evidenced. "Transition-fragments" are very obvious, and show that some sort of developmental sequence or process definitely takes place. Proponents of the symmetrical interpretation take this fact, in connection with Empedocles's references to "double coming to be," "double waning," and so on, to justify their view.

The Asymmetrical Interpretation

According to the asymmetrical interpretation, "In only one half of the cycle is there a world created, in the world of increasing Love; when the *sphairos* dissolves there is no gradual separation permitting temporary stability such as we see in a developed *cosmos*, but a direct return to complete separation under total

---

13. B21 = Inwood 26 = Wright 14; Plutarch's gloss is from *The Face on the Moon* 926d-927a; this text is Inwood CTXT-24; cf. Wright (1981/1995a), 44 n.124, and 186.

strife."[14] This "return" is of "insignificant duration,"[15] and yields a four-stage cycle, consisting of a state of total Love, a transition, however brief, to a state of total strife,[16] a period of total strife, and a period of change during which *cosmoi* such as ours are formed. This interpretation is represented by figure 6.2.

According to this point of view, Empedocles's frequent references to "double tales" and the like do not support the symmetrical interpretation, because there is no evidence in the fragments, or at least there is not sufficient evidence, "of a world created and destroyed by the work of Strife."[17] Such references refer, rather, to the dual operation of Love and Strife in a single linear development, followed by destruction, of a *cosmos*.[18] Thus the difference between interpretations boils down to a difference of opinion concerning the nature of the transition from Love to Strife: "For O'Brien [and the other symmetry theorists] total strife follows the creation and destruction of a world, whereas in Bollack [and the other asymmetry theorists] it is a precosmic condition to be followed by Love's creation of the world."[19] That is, for Bollack (1965–1969) and other asymmetry theorists, total Strife immediately succeeds the homogenous *sphairos*, and does not succeed the creation and destruction of a world.

LOVE AND STRIFE, HOMEOPATHY AND ALLOPATHY

The scholarly disagreement synopsized above suggests that philological considerations do not suffice to determine whether Empedocles's cycle is symmetrical or not. So, at this point it will be useful to invoke a logical expedient—

---

14. Inwood (1992), 42. This quotation characterizes Bollock's (1965–1969) interpretation, which Inwood takes to be the "most influential" of the asymmetric theories. Long (1974, 398), whose interpretation Graham (1998, 297) assesses as "most significant," states that "the evidence of the fragments supports not a pair of oscillating worlds which contain the same events in reverse order [as in the symmetrical interpretation], but a single linear development in which the impulse toward cosmogony is given by Strife, whereas Love acts as the creative power. . . ." Here a very literal reading of the phrase "pair of oscillating worlds which contain the same events in reverse order" might suggest that the symmetrical interpretation requires one world like ours and another that is like a movie run backwards, which of course would be absurd. In this chapter the phrase will be understood to mean that distinct stages of genesis— involving body parts, "whole-natured forms," beings like us, and so on—occur in both periods of transition recognized by the symmetrical interpretation.
15. Long (1974), 399.
16. This transition must be a distinct stage, since the state of total Love is distinct from that of total strife.
17. Long (1974), 412.
18. "In all probability both powers contribute to [genesis], Strife by sorting out the elements, Love by aggregating and mixing them" (Long, 1974, 415).
19. Long (1974), 414.

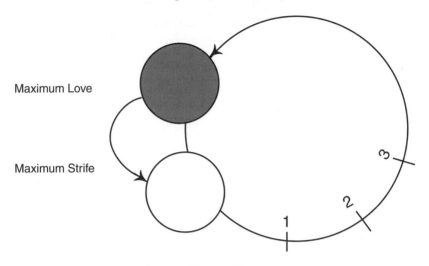

Figure 6.2
The asymmetrical interpretation

viz., interpretive consistency concerning the natures of Love and Strife—which suggests a possible way to resolve the dispute. The idea is simply to provide analyses of the natures of Love and Strife which recognize their fundamental opposition, whereupon it appears that only the symmetrical interpretation coheres with the evidence of certain key fragments.

Prima facie, it is obvious that for Empedocles (as in Greek thought generally, or no doubt in any system of thought for that matter) Love must be a principle of attraction. Assuming that the basic forces Love and Strife are opposites (a widespread "primitive" notion in Greek thought),[20] they must perform opposite functions, so that Strife is a principle of repulsion.

Granted that Love is a principle of attraction, what kinds of things does Love attract to one another? It will not do to simply assume, without qualification, that Love draws "all kinds of things" together. This is so because there are two very different ontological categories in Empedocles's system, whose distinct membership-criteria ensure that Love cannot act as a force of attraction relative to members of both categories. One category includes the elements fire, air, earth, and water, while the other includes all compounds of at least two elements. For Empedocles these must be ontologically distinct categories, because a compound can only be formed by "parceling out" or separating formerly homogeneous aggregates of elements, while homogeneous aggregates of distinct

---

20. Cf. Lloyd (1966).

elements can only be formed by destroying elementally complex compounds. So, any process or force that engenders members of one of Empedocles's onto-logical categories will tend to cause members of the other category to decay.

So, taking Love as a principle of attraction, its function must be either to cause distinct elements to join together, or to cause fragmentary bits of partic-ular elements to form larger, homogeneous, masses, but not both. If the func-tion of Love were to produce homogenous masses of particular elements then, contrary to fact, Love could never affect the uncompounded state of total Strife.[21] Thus the function of Love must be to combine the diverse elements with one another. Empedocles says as much in B21 3–9:[22]

> . . . the sun, bright to look on and hot in every respect,
> and the immortals which are drenched in heat and shining light,
> 5 and rain, in all things dark and cold;
> and there flow from the earth things dense and solid.
> And in wrath all are distinct in form and separate,
> and they come together in love and are desired by each other.
> From these all things that were, that are, and will be in the future
> have sprung: trees and men and women. . .

Assuming that the diverse elements which "come together in love" are drastically "unlike" one another, the function of Love must be to attract dis-similar things.[23] Thus it appears that Love is an allopathic principle in Emped-ocles, in that it draws "unlike to unlike." Allopathy figures much more widely in the early Greek medical tradition than in early Presocratic philosophy (which favors homeopathy[24]), and Empedocles was a physician. It seems reasonable

---

21. Both parties to the dispute agree that Love does act in this way.
22. B21 = Inwood 26 = Wright 14.
23. The possibility remains that Love may combine not only the elements but also com-pounds of the elements. This possibility is innocuous for the present interpretation, and will not be mentioned further. It is worth noting, however, that it does not seem to be possible to argue for the view that Love combines both compounds and ele-ments, since the compounding of elements (of which compounds are constituted) would produce results identical to the alternative. In Aristotelian terms, the opera-tion of Love can be shown to affect the elements essentially, but cannot be shown to affect compounds except accidentally.
24. Homeopathy (the principle of "like-to-like") is far more obvious than allopathy in Presocratics prior to Empedocles, if allopathy is attested at all. For example, the protean quality of both Anaximander's *apeiron* and Anaximenes's *aer* is readily at-tributable to the fact that they are not "opposed" to any definite element. This is ob-vious in Anaximander, and implicit in Anaximenes, in whose system the only true opposition lies between Condensation and Rarefaction which act, not on one an-other, but on *apeiros* air.

to suspect that Empedocles was well-suited to introduce allopathy into the philosophical mainstream in virtue of his medical training.[25] Thus there is additional reason to regard Empedocles as "our best bridge from medicine to philosophy proper."[26]

If Love in Empedocles is a force which causes dissimilar things to come together, and Love and Strife are opposites, the function of Strife must be to cause dissimilar things to disintegrate into their component parts. If Love is allopathic relative to the elements, Strife must be homeopathic relative to the elements,[27] and Empedocles implies as much in the fragment above: "in wrath all [the elements] are distinct in form and separate." That is, under the hegemony of Strife the elements coalesce so as to form four distinct aggregates. Since each element is homogeneous, it can only separate itself from the other elements by a principle which causes like to seek like. Thus Strife is a de facto force of attraction which causes dissimilar things—combinations of distinct elements—to decay so that their elemental components severally segregate from one another and agglomerate into homogeneous masses, while Love is a force of attraction which causes dissimilar things—the various elements—to tend to combine with one another.

The reference to Strife as a "de facto" force of attraction is intended to call attention to the fact that, as suggested above, Strife cannot repel or separate "all things," just as Love cannot combine "all things." Again, as was suggested above, this is so because there are two distinct categories of being in Empedocles's metaphysics—elements and compounds of elements—and neither Love nor Strife can exercise a single kind of effect on both of those kinds of things: Thus, for Love to unite dissimilar elements is ipso facto for it to separate individual elements as it were from themselves, that is, to cause self-contained, segregated homogeneous masses to disperse; and for Strife to cause compounded wholes to disintegrate is ipso facto for it to tend to segregate the several elements into homogeneous masses, each to its own. This is the fundamental interpretive point of the present paper, that the operations of Love and Strife can only be meaningfully (i.e., noncontradictorily) described relative to one of

---

25. Sc. Thivel (1981), 254–255; Vlastos, "Equality and Justice in Early Greek Cosmologies" (1993, 58–61). Both of these sources were found, at the author's suggestion, in Belfiore (1992) 278 and n. 64. I should add here that Professor Belfiore would not necessarily endorse the claims in note 24 above.

26. Vlastos, "Equality and Justice" (1993), 61.

27. Homeopathy is explicitly attested in Empedocles in B109 = Inwood 17 = Wright 77: "By earth we see earth; by water, water; by aither, shining aither; but by fire, blazing fire; love by love and strife by baneful strife." See also Raven in Kirk and Raven (1957), 340. For a discussion of homeopathy throughout Greek philosophy, see Muller (1965).

Empedocles's ontological categories or the other, and not to both (nor of course to neither). Moreover, to suppose that either Love or Strife *could* exercise its influence on both elements and compounds would, contrary to the text, obviate the need for one of these basic forces; for if a given force (whether Love or Strife) were taken to be capable of uniformly affecting both ontological categories, then either Love or Strife could do all the combining or separating Empedocles might wish.[28]

So central is interpretive consistency to this chapter that for present purposes it actually makes no difference how the functions of Love and Strife are interpreted in detail, provided that certain constraints on interpretation are observed. Though an accurate understanding of the precise roles of Love and Strife is obviously desirable in itself—and the discussion above does aim at such understanding—all that is necessary for present purposes is (a) that Love and Strife be regarded as opposite forces, and (b) that they be interpreted as doing whatever it is that they do either to elements or to compounds of elements, but not to both.[29]

---

28. That is, if (say) Strife were to repel both elements and compounds equally, then it would produce not only compounds (in virtue of causing the severally homogeneous elements to separate away from themselves) but also the decay of compounds (in virtue of causing the constituent elements of compounds to separate from one another). The same remarks obviously apply, *pari passu*, to Love, if this force is taken to attract both elements and compounds equally.

29. These constraints license just two consistent interpretations of the functions of Love and Strife, taken together. Letting "dissimilars" denote sets or compounds of at least two distinct elements, and "similars" denote individual, internally homogeneous, elements, there are four possible ways of looking at the functions of Love and Strife, and their corresponding effects:

Function	Effect
(1) Love attracts dissimilars.	Love forms compounds of distinct elements.
(2) Love attracts similars.	Love forms homogeneous aggregates of elements.
(3) Strife repels dissimilars.	Strife destroys compounds of distinct elements.
(4) Strife repels similars.	Strife destroys homogeneous aggregates of elements.

The interpretation offered above accepts (1) and (3); but an interpretation accepting (2) and (4) would equally well support the argument of this chapter. These pairs represent the two consistent ways of characterizing the functions of both Love and Strife. An interpretation holding (1) and (4) would have Love and Strife doing the same thing under different descriptions, thus making the totally segregated polar state of Strife impossible; and an interpretation holding (2) and (3) would also have Love and Strife doing the same thing under different descriptions, but in this case the totally mixed polar state of Love would be impossible.

A CONSISTENT INTERPRETATION OF THE COSMIC CYCLE

For present purposes it will suffice to mention three key biogenetic fragments:[30]

B57 as many heads without necks sprouted up
and arms wandered naked, bereft of shoulders
and eyes roamed alone, impoverished of foreheads

B61 Many with two faces and two chests grew,
oxlike with men's faces, and again there came up
androids with oxheads, mixed in one way from men
and in another way in female form, outfitted with shadowy
limbs

B62 . . . separating fire brought up the nocturnal shoots of men
and women...
First there came up from the earth whole-natured forms

5 having a share of both water and heat;
fire sent them up, wanting to reach its like,
and they did not yet show any lovely frame of limbs,
nor voice nor again the limb specific to men.

Fragment B57 has usually been interpreted to refer to a stage in the cosmic cycle during which bits and pieces of animal (and perhaps also plant) bodies existed, however briefly, independently of the wholes with which they are normally associated. These parts are supposed to have come together in random combinations,[31] of which some of the resulting wholes had survival value and some did not. Thus Empedocles is often credited with a picturesque and bizarre adumbration of the idea of natural selection. B61 and B62 would then refer to more complex compounds.

The strategy at this point is simply to locate the genetic stages described by these three fragments in a sequence within figure 6.2 and then within figure 6.1, in that order, and to note which sequence is more satisfactory. Figure 6.2 represents the asymmetrical interpretation, according to which genesis occurs only during the ascendancy of love, subsequent to the sudden dissolution

---

30. B57, 61, and 62 = Inwood 64, 66, and 67 = Wright 50, 52, and 53, respectively. The translation of B62 substitutes "forms" on line 4 for Inwood's "outlines." Cosmogenesis will not be discussed in this chapter, on the provisional assumption that, if the present argument relying on biogenetic fragments is sound, the cosmo-genetic fragments can be interpreted similarly.

31. B59 = Inwood 65 = Wright 51: "But when daimon mixed more with daimon/and these things came together as each happened to meet/and many others in addition to these constantly emerged [into being]."

of the *sphairos* into its component elements through the agency of Strife. Presumably, B57 must describe a state relatively close to the state of total strife, since so far there are only disconnected pieces of bodies, and Love must form pieces of bodies before it can form entire bodies. Let us suppose that the numeral 2 denotes the stage at which the events described in B57 occur. B61 would then refer to a later development, since it refers to a stage at which additional compounding has taken place. In fact, this stage must still lie in the future relative to beings like us, who have only single faces and a pristinely anthropomorphic aspect. So, let us suppose that the numeral 3 denotes the stage at which the events described in B61 occur.

That leaves B62. Because, according to this fragment, the whole-natured forms came up "first from the earth," the stage denoted by the numeral 1 has been reserved for the events B62 describes. That is, the whole-natured forms are located on the developmental sequence between the polar state of total strife and the disconnected body parts of B57. Now, having constructed the sequence, it is plain that it implies a number of absurd consequences:

1. The asymmetrical view maintains that genesis occurs only during the period of increasing Love; but B62 implies that Strife too, *qua* having "sent them [the whole-natured forms (WNF)] up," plays the role of a generative agent.
2. Because the WNF arise by the agency of strife, the stage of total Strife is followed by a period characterized by greater than total Strife.
3. The body parts of B57 could only come about through the dissolution of the WNF, since they are consequent to the WNF. This process again requires the agency of Strife, which is the force that makes compounds decay. So, Strife must increase beyond its maximal state not just once, as in (2) above, but twice.
4. According to the asymmetrical view, only Love causes genesis.[32] Thus (setting aside (1) above) Love must somehow cause the WNF to arise in the first place, and also cause them to decay into bits. Thus Love has contradictory functions.
5. Fire has no need to "reach its like," since the elements are already segregated in the stage preceding that described by B62. These absurd consequences show that B62 cannot precede B57. On the

---

32. *Pace* Long (1974), n.19: Even supposing that for the asymmetrical interpretation "both powers contribute to genesis," Love must "increasingly predominate" in some sense whose principled specification might well turn out to be another problem for the view. For if Love does not predominate somehow or other, there would be no reason to speak of a climate of "increasing Love" at all.

symmetrical interpretation two possibilities remain, viz., that B62 be sandwiched between the other fragments, or that B62 be placed at the end of the sequence. The former alternative will not do, because (besides being "first") the WNF are not involved with sexual differentiation, as are the complex creatures of B61; thus B61 could only succeed B62 through the agency of Strife, rather than Love.[33] The latter alternative also will not do, because (besides being "first") the WNF "do not *yet*" display limbs, which implies that they occur at a genetic stage prior to the development of limbs, rather than at the end of the sequence. So, in view of the fact that beings with limbs are mentioned in both B57 and B61, the WNF of B62 cannot succeed these fragments.

THE SYMMETRICAL VIEW

Thus there seem to be prima facie contradictions within the asymmetrical view, if Empedocles' genetic stages are construed in terms of a consistent analysis of the functions of Love and Strife. The symmetrical view (represented in figure 6.1), on the other hand, avoids those contradictions. In order to construct a consistent Empedoclean cycle on this view, B57 and B61 can be left in the same sequence as before, within the "cyprogenetic" half of the cosmic cycle. Without the complications introduced by B62, the sequence B57–B61 harmonizes very well with a climate of increasing Love. As for B62, it not only can but must be placed in the "erigenetic" half of the cycle, say at point A. Now there is no inconsistency: Following a state of maximum homogeneity—i.e., at or toward the beginning of the ascendancy of Strife—fire begins to "seek out its like." That is, the dispersed bits of fire in the *Sphairos* begin to draw toward one another. The first results are the whole-natured forms, which combine the

---

33. That is, since the whole-natured forms *are* whole, any other forms—e.g., those of B61, if they are in fact sexually differentiated—must be "partial-natured" to some degree. As the transition from (compound) wholes to (compound) parts requires Strife, then, contrary to the symmetrical interpretation, Strife must be a genetic agent if B62 is to precede B57. Against the objection that the forms of B61 are *themselves* "whole-natured" in some intuitive sense *qua* being constituted of both male and female ingredients, it may be noted that this objection presupposes a prior developmental stage which itself contains forms which are less than whole-natured. This is so because Love would have to compound the putatively whole-natured forms of B61 from prior materials. Thus, even granting the objection, the problem noted in the text would stand, though now with reference to an unknown fragment posited from theoretical necessity (on the part of the asymmetry theorists), rather than with reference to an extant fragment.

traditional Greek opposites water and "heat," that is., fire. This composition is just what one would expect from beings in a state consequent to one in which all the elements, even the paradigmatic opposites fire and water, are commingled. Later stages of eri-genesis would presumably involve the separation of the whole-natured forms into beings like those described in B61, then into beings like us, then into body parts, and finally into aggregates of wholly segregated elements.[34] Such a sequence would, again presumably,[35] have a mirror image in the period characterized by the ascendancy of Love. Thus the symmetrical interpretation readily accommodates textual evidence that seems to generate inconsistency on the asymmetrical view. Thus, if and to the extent that interpretive consistency is regarded as desirable, there is good reason to prefer the symmetrical view of Empedocles's cycle.[36]

---

34. That is, the sequence B62–B61–B57 can be accommodated within the period of increasing strife; thus a revised asymmetrical interpretation might seem possible, according to which genesis occurs only during the ascendancy of strife. However, this view would be contradicted by fragments such as B26 (= Inwood 28 =Wright 16), "these very things [the elements] are, and running through each other [which would require the influence of allopathic Love] they become men and the tribes of other beasts," as well as by the fact that love is manifestly a genetic force in ordinary experience.

35. In this connection the objection raised in note 34 is suggestive. If the forms of B61 are in fact whole-natured forms, then there are WNF in the stages referenced by both B61 and B62. However, as has been seen, these stages cannot both take place during the period of increasing Love. So, if the forms of B61 are WNF, then there is additional reason to view Empedocles's cycle as symmetrical.

36. Whether interpretive consistency is always a genuine *desideratum* where the Presocratics are concerned is a profoundly interesting question, though—perhaps fortunately—it is outside the scope of this chapter. Very probably Heraclitus, for one, thought of fire as both an element among other elements and the set of all elemental interactions; and if he did, then his view cannot be explicated consistently. Cf. Kingsley (1995), esp. 1–10.

Chapter 7

Atomic Independence and Indivisibility*

István M. Bodnár

Aristotle on several occasions voices a two-pronged principle of the atomists, that no plurality may emerge from real unity and no unity from what is real plurality.[1] Understandably, the first injunction has been studied far more extensively than the second. The impossibility of the emergence of a plurality from what is really a unit is a constitutive feature of those indivisible bits of being which, precisely on this account, can be called atomic. In what follows I shall explore the two bans in conjunction. In order to do so, I shall first need some technical vocabulary. Alongside atomic indivisibility—the postulation that atoms cannot be fractured—I shall need to speak about atomic independence. This is the feature of the atoms whereby they do not get absorbed into larger chunks of matter, do not coalesce with one another. What Aristotle stresses in the passages referred to above is that atomic independence *and* indivisibility together account for the permanence of the atoms: both of them are needed so that the atoms can maintain their integrity for time eternal.

The crucial question in a joint exploration of the two requirements is whether the ancient atomists could have a comprehensive account of the permanence of atomic individuality, whether the reasons they provided for

---

* I wrote the first draft of this chapter in March/April 1996, while I was the guest of Fondation Hardt, Vanœuvres, Switzerland. Then I had the opportunity to present my ideas to various audiences at the University of Pécs, the B-Club at Cambridge University, the State University of New York/Buffalo, Cornell University, and the meeting of the Society for Ancient Greek Philosophy at the Central Division Convention of the American Philosophical Association in April 1997 held in Pittsburgh (where my participation was supported by grant 247/6818 of the Soros Foundation, Budapest). Each occasion prompted some significant revision of my account. Here I would like to single out the audiences at the B-Club and at Cornell University, and the written comments of David Sedley, Barry Smith, and Mariam Thalos, who contributed most to the correction and clarification of my views. I also profited from the comments and advice of Christopher Taylor, who kindly let me see chapters of his forthcoming edition of the atomists.

1. *GC* 1.8 325a34ff (=67A7), *De caelo* 3.4 303a5ff (=67A15), and *Metaphysics* 7.13 1039a8ff (=68A42). Moreover, *On Democritus* (fr. 208 Rose =68A37) 166.15-17 also contains the second part of the principle, that two or more things cannot come together and form a single entity.

atomic indivisibility allowed for the independence of atoms. As so often, scholarly opinion is divided on this issue, both about the early atomists and about the Epicureans. Different alternatives have been put forward as to how the account of atomic indivisibility needs to be supplemented in order to provide room for atomic independence, but as I shall argue, none of these could be fully satisfactory, or harmonize with the evidence we have. As a result, at the end of the chapter I shall discuss the implications of the fact that the atomists lacked a credible and comprehensive theory of atomic immutability.

INDIVISIBILITY AND IMMUTABILITY

It is easy to see why the atomists needed to proclaim both principles. Atomic immutability is a cornerstone of the invariability of natural processes.[2] Now indivisibility gives only half of the required immutability. Were atoms indivisible but also liable to put on weight, which from then on forms an integral part of the emerging new unit, and which they cannot lose, atoms would be monotonously on the increase. An infinite past of the world might seem to imply—wrongly—that by this time all atoms should have reached infinite size through this accretion, and because of this impossible consequence it could be claimed that a theory which rules out the divisibility of atomic masses, and at the same time allows for the emergence of new atomic units from formerly independent atomic entities, cannot make sense. But this inference is not mandatory: Atoms may be atomic, and liable to accretion, and nevertheless the laws of nature may be such that not every atomic interaction results in the fusion of the original particles, and that after a while[3] every portion of matter gets integrated into a further immutable unit. Once all the material is allocated in such permanent particles, both constraints of atomic immutability are met.[4]

---

2. See Epicurus *Letter to Herodotus* 38ff, 54, and 56.

3. Or rather, in a counterfactual mode: These couplings should have happened already an infinitely long time ago, hence the universe always had to contain only atoms which cannot combine into indivisible entities. See to this effect the argument in Makin (1993), 88 n.43.

4. Non-atomist philosophers need not be impressed by this argument. On a theory which allows for the divisibility of any chunk of matter the reverse process, the fusion of pieces of matter, needs to be possible also, so that the two can check and balance each other, thereby guaranteeing the stability and invariability of natural processes.

Against such a natural philosophy, where processes of division and coalescence balance each other, the atomists could deploy several arguments. One of these is to ask *what* should effect this alleged balance. The other is what we find in Lucretius: He at 1.551-60 rejects the alleged balance outright, claiming that processes of destruction are always faster than processes of composition, therefore unless there is a barrier to stop these processes of decomposition, the world will always be on a downside.

With atomic indivisiblity and independence in place we can produce a natural philosophy of considerable appeal and simplicity: Eternal and immutable atoms, of the same material, differing only in their shape and size,[5] form different combinations and through this give rise to all sorts of transient phenomena.[6] This line of argument, then, leads to the postulation of the existence of non-splittable pieces of matter, but does not specify yet why any particular piece of matter should be indivisible. Without such an account, however, theories of atomism will inevitably retain an air of arbitrariness.

We should therefore expect some indications of the grounds of the indivisibility of the atoms. Simplicius in his *Physics* and *De caelo* commentaries (67A13 and A14, respectively) mentions several of them. Some, according to Simplicius, were proposed only by the early atomists,[7] and Epicurus did not

---

5. Atomists would not necessarily say that these corpuscles are of the same material. Nevertheless, I think this is a fair characterization of a doctrine in which atoms are ὄντα and full, and considered in themselves they differ only in their ῥυσμός, or in Peripatetic parlance or in σχῆμα. (For this doctrine see 68A38; the other two atomic characteristics—τροπή (i.e., θέσις) and διαθιγή (i.e., τάξις)—are meaningful only for the atoms considered in relationship with their surroundings.) All this suggests that what they are full of is not different for the different atoms.

   Cf. Aristotle's assertion at *De caelo* 1.7 275b29ff (=67A19) and at *Metaphysics* 8.2 1042b11ff that atoms are of the same material, and see also the discussion at *GC* 1.8 326a29-b2, where he considers the difficulties both of a unique atomic material and of the other option, that atoms are made of different stuffs.

   We should notice here that the introduction of different atomic materials is not sufficient for the preservation of the independence of each atom. If atoms cannot merge because of the difference of materials, every pair of atoms which come into interaction through the entire, infinite history of the universe has to contain atoms of different material. As a result of this there needs to be at least an infinite multitude of different atomic materials, and if any two atoms can collide some time or other, every atom will need to have a uniquely distinctive material of its own.

6. In fact a finite number of types of basic variants should have been enough to produce an infinity of surface phenomena, if space is continuous, and these units can take up an infinite number of different collocations (cf. Barnes [1982], 364). On account of this I do not think we should grant Democritus's invalid inference from the infinity of phenomena to an underlying infinite variety of imperceptible atoms, reported by Aristotle in *GC* 1.1 315b6-15 (=67A9).

   Notice, however, that 68A38 (=Simplicius *in Phys.* 28. 15ff) also deploys the *ouden mallon* principle, that there is no reason why atoms should be of this particular shape rather than any other, and so each and every one of the infinitely many atomic shapes has to be present in the cosmos.

7. In this chapter I shall not try to distinguish between Democritus and Leucippus, so I shall use "early atomists" and "Democritus" interchangeably.

accept them. These include atomic partlessness (*amerē*) and smallness. Simplicius mentions alongside these a series of explanations which were entertained by early atomists and Epicurus alike. These are impassibility (*apatheia*), firmness or compactness (*nastas einai*), and the lack of void. Of these we can dispose of impassibility and partlessness rather rapidly. Impassibility is rather an alternative, and more general, formulation of, and not a theoretical underpinning for, atomicity.[8] We have every reason to think that atoms are exempt from any change whatsoever, but on this occasion we are looking for reasons why this is so, and in particular why a certain chunk of matter should be exempt from any further divisions. Simply stating that this is so because these morsels of matter are impassible is not an answer, rather it is a refusal to give an explanation of indivisibility.

Partlessness would be a better answer, and it has had its advocates among historians of early Greek philosophy.[9] Partlessness, however, is an elusive notion, just as the notion of a part is. The claim that atoms lack physical parts, specifically subatomic pieces which could be detached from them by any process whatsoever, may again be nothing more than couching the indivisible nature of these particles in slightly different words, and so no proper explanation of the prerequisites of indivisibility for an entity. Another interpretation would take partlessness to mean a lack of notionally or theoretically distinguishable parts. Although this concept is difficult, we have every reason to believe that Epicurus used it when he distinguished between indivisible atoms and subatomic minimal parts (see *Letter to Herodotus* 56 and 58f). Had the early atomists relied on the notional partlessness of the atoms for their indivisibility, Epicurus's innovation would be most welcome. Although he would still owe us a proper explanation of atomic indivisibility, his distinction between atoms and subatomic minimal parts would at least have signalled that the old account was not tenable, as atoms are surely not without notional parts on the Democritean account either. Democritus's ex-

---

8. In fact Simplicius's *in De caelo* 242.18ff (=67A14) asserts that atomists hold that their elementary particles are impassible *because* they are compact (ἀπαθεῖς καὶ τὸ ναστὰς εἶναι καὶ ἀμοίρους τοῦ κενοῦ), that is, he attributes the same reason for impassibility which is quoted as explaining indivisibility, thereby putting impassibility and indivisibility on a par.

9. See Mau (1954); Furley (1967), study 1, ch. 6; Guthrie (1965), vol. 2, 396 and 503–507; and Stokes (1971), 225ff (although in his case notional indivisibility—and not partlessness—apparently stands for nothing else than continuity). Luria (1932–1933), 106–185, also attributes notional indivisibility to some Democritean entities, but these he claims are the subatomic minimal parts and not the atoms themselves.

planations of atomic interaction mention concave and convex atoms, and even ones which have a hook protruding.[10] Surely in such an entity a notional distinction can be made between the base, the stem, and the curved parts of the particle.

This means that neither the claim that atoms lack physical parts, nor the one that they are devoid of notional parts, can furnish an account of atomic indivisibility. The second claim, as we have seen, cannot be right, whereas the first one, even though in all probability correct, cannot constitute on its own an appropriate explanation. At best we can take physical partlessness as a way of referring to the lack of the sort of internal articulation which would be required for any internal division. That is, we might be tempted to gloss this account with the last one, with firmness or compactness, but then partlessness would cease to be an independent account in its own right.

With the elimination of these options two serious alternatives remain: Atoms might be indivisible on account of their smallness, or they might be indivisible because of their compactness, as they contain no admixture of void.

SMALLNESS

Before turning to the discussion of what an account of atomic indivisibility in terms of the smallness of these particles could mean, two remarks should be made. The first is to notice the rather peculiar historical status of this account. Simplicius explicitly claims that it was only the early atomists who propounded such an account. What is strange about this testimony is that it is precisely these early atomists who are reported to claim that atoms of huge, in fact cosmic, size also exist.[11] These putative atoms surely cannot be indivisible on account of a property they do not even possess. In their case some alternative explanation had to be provided, if there was any explanation at all. This means that if we are to endorse Simplicius's testimony, we should find a way to explain away the embarrassing reports of cosmic atoms.

---

10. For a list of atomic shapes see Aristotle, *On Democritus* (fr. 208 Rose).
11. 68A1 (Diogenes Laertius, ix) 44 may imply this doctrine, when the infinity of atomic sizes and of atomic multitude is mentioned. More unequivocal testimonies are 68A43 (Dionysius *apud* Eusebium) and A47 (Aetius i 12, 6). The doctrine, if it existed, could have been the butt of Epicurus's criticism at *Letter to Herodotus* 55f. (See also 42, where the infinite variety of atomic shapes is rejected. The contrast between Democritus and Epicurus is also a recurrent theme of the doxography: see Aetius i 3, 18 [=fr. 270 Usener, fr. 234 Luria] or Philoponus *in GC* 12.2 [=fr. 141 Luria].)

The other point we need to make concerns the relationship of the two explanations of atomicity, the one by smallness and the other by continuity. Although Simplicius does not stress this, it is clear that an explanation by atomic smallness is a special case of the explanation by continuity.[12] When we claim that an entity cannot be split because it is too small to be cut, we must speak about a small *continuous* entity in the first place. If we could specify a particular size, so that any volume of that size containing noncontinuous chunks of matter would retain its original configuration, this would mean that there could be no rearrangement in the universe. Those who claim that atoms are indivisible on account of their smallness are obliged to maintain that not just any continuous lump of matter is indivisible. Those chunks which exceed some particular atomic threshold size can be fractured, whereas whatever falls below this value will remain intact.

One might wonder in which dimension smallness might be a reason for indivisibility. Is there a specific atomic mass or volume which cannot be further subdivided, or a specific atomic surface area, or a specific atomic linear extension, which makes further fractioning of the particles impracticable? Or should we think of some combination of these? We need not answer these queries. It is sufficient if we suppose that there is *some* measurement of any corporeal entity, and further that there exists a specific atomic measure m along these lines, and lumps of matter of measure m or less are infrangible, whereas bigger ones are liable to split under suitable circumstances. All we have to require from this measurement is that it is additive in a rather weak sense: given two atoms a and b, the size of their sum,[13] *size* $(a + b)$, should exceed both the size of a, *size* (a), and the size of b, *size* (b).

If the sheer size of the particles accounts for the indivisibility of atomic particles, this will mean that atoms can exist only within a rather narrow band of atomic sizes. They have to be below the atomic threshold, the critical extension of splitting. But they cannot be too deeply below this value. To be more precise, for any two atoms which can interact in the course of atomic collisions, the size of the combination of these particles has to be above the critical value,

---

12. Notice, however, that the two criteria of atomicity are conjoined as a matter of fact at Simplicius's *in De caelo* 609.18, where *tas dia* <u>smikrotēta kai nastotēta</u> <u>atomous</u> ("the entities indivisible on account of their smallness and compactness") are mentioned.

13. For the sake of convenience I assume here that the size of the sum of the two particles is the same no matter how they are combined. If we want to drop this assumption, we should reformulate the postulate to the effect that the size of every possible combination of two particles is greater than the size of either of the original particles.

otherwise the emerging combination of the two particles would turn out to be indivisible on account of its smallness.

One striking feature of such an account of atomic immutability is its arbitrariness. It postulates that the course of actual atomic interactions is vastly different from the counterfactual case in which the world would consist of significantly larger, or significantly smaller, units. This arbitrary feature could be objected to by means of an indifference (*ouden mallon*) argument. We could ask why this particular value is the critical extension, what is so different in the properties of slightly larger and slightly smaller lumps of matter. Or even if we admit that the notion of such a critical extension can make sense, and minuscule variations in the initial conditions can lead to tremendously different outcomes, we may ask what it is about the nature of corpuscles that establishes this particular threshold value for atomicity instead of a different one.

Even if we dismiss these objections, and reject these uses of the *ouden mallon* principle as illegitimate, the account of indivisibility referring to atomic smallness alone will have to founder. The crucial consideration is the following: Even if all the atoms are below the critical value of atomic size, and the size of any combination of any pair of atoms is greater than this value, all we can claim is that we do have a reason why this emerging entity is not atomic, why it can be separated into smaller units. What we still lack is an account of why the individuality of the original atoms has to be preserved, why the two atoms after touching will have to separate at exactly the boundary where they came into contact.

In fact an *ouden mallon* argument will rather predict that there should be no specific line of split. Provided there are no preexisting atomic boundaries already present in the superatomic lump of matter, which the procedure of separation is bound to cut along, the principle that particles which are below a certain size are infrangible will not be able to predict where the line of division should run. If atomic indivisibility is founded on atomic smallness, then we shall not know where the masses of the two atoms combined should break. We should bracket the existence of any internal boundaries in this emerging mass of matter, as an appeal to them surely would extend further than claiming that below the threshold size particles are indivisible. Then, however, we have no reason to believe that after atomic interaction we should always and invariably expect the emergence of the very same particles. In fact the *ouden mallon* principle I have appealed to would predict that by default of any further causes the expected outcome of the fracturing of the same superatomic mass should be different on virtually every occasion.

This, then, will mean that the claim that smallness is a reason for atomic indivisibility cannot establish the independence of the atoms without some further, supplementary factors, which together with atomic smallness account for atomic indivisibility.[14]

COMPACTNESS

Last on the list of reasons for atomicity comes the claim that atoms are compact and have no share in the void. This should mean that atoms are continuous chunks of being, uninterrupted by intrusions of the void. Void is then always external to the basic entities, it functions as a separator and not as an ingredient of them. Although it is not an internal component of the atoms, this does not mean that there cannot be concave atomic shapes, where expanses of void separate two distinct parts of the very same particle. Unless this is so, Democritus would not be entitled to explain some of the cohesion between the particles by the suggestion that these atoms have protruding hooks.[15] Without some concavity a hook is not going to be a hook. The assertion that atoms are continuous chunks of matter, however, makes sense in their case, too. We simply would not claim that two portions of matter are the integral parts of the same corporeal entity, unless there is a continuous passage *within* the extension of the entity between these two parts. This much is in accordance with common usage. The atomists' explanation of the indivisibility (and not only the transient individuality) of the atoms by the continuity of their extension adds a further stipulation. This explanation is a direct descendant of the way Parmenides establishes the undividedness/indivisibility of being. Par-

---

14. A single testimony of [Plutarch]'s *Placita* 877D-E (=Aetius i 3, 18, a passage not in the extracts of Stobaeus; fr. 270 Usener) claims that Epicurus did not allow for atoms of every conceivable shape—notably, hook-shaped *(ankistroeidēs)*, three-pronged *(triainoeidēs)*, and annular *(krikoeidēs)* atoms were ruled out, because these would be liable to snap. One might be tempted to regard this testimony as the rudiments of an account in which it is the appropriate shape of a particle which can account for the indivisibility and indestructibility of the atom. Such an account, however, will fail for reasons analogous to those which refute the argument from smallness as a reason for atomicity. The danger of atomic mergers would require that all the possible combinations of any two or more admissible atomic shapes must produce inadmissible shapes, and also that for each emerging inadmissible shape there is a unique division into admissible atomic shapes, for otherwise there will be no reason why the original corpuscles are retrieved at the end of each atomic interaction. As the account we could extrapolate from the passage is hopeless, and more importantly, as [Plutarch]'s testimony is isolated, and contradicted by Galen *De nat. fac.* 137.4 and 13 (Marquardt)—there we are told that the Epicurean account of magnetic attraction did have recourse to *ankistroeidēs* or *ankistrōdēs* atoms—it is best to reject this piece of evidence about Epicurus altogether.
15. For these atoms see Cicero, *De natura deorum* i 24, 66 (=67A11 or fr. 226 Luria); Aristotle, *On Democritus* (fr. 208 Rose); Aetius ii 7, 2 (=67A23); and Lactantius, *De ira dei* 10, 5 (=fr. 235 Luria).

menidean being is not divisible, as it is completely alike—there are no degrees of existence within it which would be necessary for some internal articulation or division; here it is further added that this is why being is continuous (*suneches*), for being holds to being (B8.22-25). The atomists, by transferring this explanation from the all-embracing Parmenidean being to each of the infinite multitude of their corpuscular entities, may have meant to invest all these individually with the analogue of the same metaphysical status that was alloted to Eleatic being.[16]

The explanation of indivisibility on account of the continuity of the atoms, however, no matter how neatly it situates atomistic philosophy in the context of post-Parmenidean puzzles, has a rather serious drawback. If atoms are solid, and so indivisible, precisely because they are continuous chunks of matter, two atoms can stay separate only as long as there is a layer of void actually separating them. Upon impact, when the two particles touch, exactly at the moment when they should rebound from each other there will not be any more distance occupied by the void between the two bodies. That is, at this point the two bodies should form a single, continuous whole, and the reasoning which guaranteed the indivisibility of the two atoms through the time before they would have met will apply just as well to this emerging new unity. The two atoms then should not be able to rebound, rather they will have to be absorbed into this new, indivisible entity.[17] Then, however, instead of a description of the variegated natural phenomena,

---

16. The transference of the same argument, however, will not provide atomic indivisibility with the status of a metaphysical truth. At best atomists have to be content with claiming the status of truths of speculative physics or of applied metaphysics for this account of atomic unity. There has to be something special in the nature of the atoms which allows for the deployment of the Parmenidean argumentation in their case. One can contrast this with the nature of the void: Even though void is a nonentity, it also *exists*, but this existence is not sufficient for the deployment of the Parmenidean argument on that level as well. Otherwise such an argument could either guarantee the permanence of the particular set-up of atoms dislocated in void, or it would not rule out internal rearrangement within a continuous piece of being, and consequently within a continuous piece of full atomic nature, just as it is unable to do so with a continuous combination of void and atomic nature.

17. Stokes (1971, 228f) envisages the meeting of two atoms which dovetail exactly, and claims that "[s]uch a pair, when fitted, ought presumably to present the same solidity as a single atom." As Stokes, however, did not realize that—provided there are not tacit restrictions on atomic shapes, for which see the first half of section 4—almost all pairs of atoms "dovetail" in the relevant sense, that is to say, upon impact the two of them form a continuous whole, he claimed that this problem emerges only in a few atomic interactions, and that consequently "[a]tomist neglect of this by no means obscure point is likely to be a symptom of their concentration on other matters, notably the permanence and indivisibility of the atoms." Once we see that such interactions are pervasive phenomena, and by no means exceptional, we should not be able to dismiss them so easily.

atomism will predict the inevitable conglomeration of all matter. We should be surrounded by black holes—in fact, we ourselves could not be anything else than black holes devouring any material in our ambience upon contact.

In view of this impending atomic conglobulation, short of abandoning an explanation of atomic indivisibility in terms of continuity, proponents of atomism may claim that atomic interaction does not give rise to continuity. This can be maintained in either of two ways: Either there is simply no continuity emerging when two atoms collide, or the continuity which there is is defective compared with the internal one which invests completely continuous chunks of matter with their indivisibility. Before turning to theories of defective touch in the next section, here I shall follow up the first alternative. On this option atoms interact without ever reaching each other directly; what counts as touch between them could be described in more correct terms as a remote touch: A film of void will always remain between the atoms to keep them separate. Accordingly, when atoms are unable to bear the approach of the other particle any longer, just before they would have come into direct contact, they turn their backs upon each other and flee off. If Democritus entertained such a model of atomic interaction, our appreciation of the explanatory models of ancient atomism, and its subsequent history, is bound to change fundamentally. Atomism without remote touch is a mechanistic theory: bits of matter rebound from each other. Atomism with remote touch is completely different, and yet identical. There are no mechanistic interactions; all interactions between atoms happen at a distance.[18] This un-

---

18. Unless the separator is without extension. This is not as impossible as it may sound: If Democritean atoms were open entities, that is, if they were not allowed to contain their boundaries, then when two atoms touch (1) the two atoms do not form a single continuous whole, as some part of the boundaries would be needed in order to connect the two atoms, nevertheless (2) there is no distance between the two atoms, as for any positive distance there can be found parts of the two atoms which are closer than the specified distance. (For a general discussion of the puzzles of touch, and the proposal that one way out of these difficulties is that physical bodies might be open collections of points, see Kline and Matheson [1987].)

Although this would be a feasible answer to our original problem, it cannot be suggested that Democritus could have come up with anything like that. My objections are basically the same as those against the notion of remote touch. Even if the notion of an open entity could have been available for Democritus (and I doubt this), we should expect Aristotle to comment on this basic, or rather constitutive, feature of the Democritean atoms. Moreover, it is not only *e silentio Aristotelis* that we can argue here: If Democritean atoms were intrinsically open entities, we would expect Epicurus to give some new arguments to guarantee atomic independence when he introduces his notion of minimal parts, thereby saddling atoms with their boundaries, and so doing away with the only Democritean buttress of atomic individuality.

derlying field dynamics nevertheless imitates a mechanistic world flawlessly. It would be idle to claim that such a theory is illegitimate. Certainly Democritus is also allowed to join the practices of those post-Parmenidean philosophers who, after the requisite conceptual analysis, where they rejected generation and corruption, could knowingly speak with the vulgar, using the rejected terms.[19] Similarly, after repudiating direct touch Democritus is entitled to speak about the only remaining form of touch in whatever terms he pleases. He should not be taken to task even if, as the testimonies amply indicate, he used *krouesthai* (collide), *haphē* (touch), and the like, and did not bother to repeat and inculcate on each occasion that there is a film of void in between the two touching bodies.

Although it would be idle to deny a Democritean theory of remote touch outright, we should be clear about the philosophical costs incurred by such a theory.[20] Some central atomist tenets will be affected if such a theory is admitted. First, according to the Anaxagorean dictum *opsis adēlōn ta phainomena* ("what appears is the sighting of what is unclear" 59B2la = 68A111), which Democritus also subscribed to as expressing one of his basic criteria, the nature of atomic collisions should be able to be read off from macroscopic collisions. In our everyday experience we are familiar with objects hitting each other and then pursuing a different course after the collision, so the image of atoms directly bouncing against one another readily suggests itself. On the other hand, we never see remote collisions among ordinary objects: Therefore the experience in this case could hardly provide an insight into what is going on at a level not accessible to our senses.[21]

Another consideration that should tell against a doctrine of remote touch is that we could then deploy an *ouden mallon* argument: At whatever particular point the particles would be diverted from their course, we could ask why just there, rather than at any other point before the actual collision, the remote hit should occur. And finally it should be noted that a doctrine of remote touch comes perilously close to rejecting the basic dualism of atomism. On this theory rebounding occurs at some distance from the perimeter of the atom, hence that region of the enveloping void where the particles interact behaves so differently from all other regions of void that it should be regarded as a different, third type of entity alongside the atoms and the void.

Powerful arguments though they are, I do not think either of them could exclude a theory of remote touch altogether. In contrast to the case of Anaxagoras,

---

19. See especially Empedocles B9 and B8, and Anaxagoras B17.
20. I owe the following objections to David Sedley.
21. Note that a similar line of reasoning would rule out the postulation of an atomic threshold discussed in the previous section, below which different laws of physics would apply.

the claim that the experiences we have provide an insight into what is inaccessible cannot establish an uncomplicated correlation between the occurrences of the two domains. After all, we never observe the encounter of infrangible objects in a perfectly yielding medium either. *Ouden mallon* arguments cannot contravene basic regularities of nature: If atomic interactions are at bottom a field physics, atoms have every reason to conform to the regularities of nature and deflect exactly at the crucial point specified by them.[22] And even if atoms experience remote touches, it can be the *atoms* themselves which interact at a distance, without giving rise to a mysterious third basic kind of entity.

Rather, what tells decisively against a theory of remote interactions is the subsequent reception of atomism, both from hostile and from friendly quarters. Had Democritus propounded a theory of remote touch, we surely would expect Aristotle to take cognizance of this in his works on natural philosophy. Let me enumerate a number of contexts in which a reference to such a doctrine might have been expected. Book 6 of the *Physics* analyzes at length the notions of continuity, touch, and succession. Aristotle sets out to establish that physical magnitudes are continuous, that is to say, divisible without a limit. The book begins with Aristotle's recapitulation of his definitions of continuity, touch, and succession: those things touch whose outermost parts are together. Democritean atoms, on a theory of remote touch, would never be touching according to these Aristotelian criteria, and one might claim that this would have deserved at least a brief mention here.

Nevertheless, I do not find this line of thought compelling. Most of the arguments of *Physics* Book 6 are committed to a notion of indivisibility which is more demanding than the mere unsplittability of the Democritean atom. The target there is a doctrine in which not only can further bits not be chipped off from the basic constituents of nature, but these indivisible bits also lack parts. These partless entities lack parts not only in the sense that they cannot be decomposed into these parts, but furthermore they satisfy the restriction that in any of their relationships with external entities the whole chunk of them is involved in the very same way.[23] This means that out of the three major types of

---

22. Similarly an *ouden mallon* argument to the effect that the physics of the atoms has to be isotropic (why should any particular direction be privileged over the other ones, rather than any other direction?) will founder on the fact that the line of fall is a distinguished direction throughout the infinite universe.

23. See, for example, Aristotle's contention at 231a24 that nothing continuous can be made of indivisible entities. When Aristotle gives an argument to this effect at 231b1ff, he expressly claims that the indivisible lacks parts (b2), and so these indivisible entities cannot touch through part or the whole of one touching only part of the other. Therefore the only way for them to touch is if the whole of one of them touches the whole of the other, but then they cannot form a continuous entity.

distinguishing features Democritus deploys, at least one cannot apply to these partless entities, since *tropē*, position, should accordingly be perfectly indifferent. Moreover, the examples for *diathigē*, order, invariably refer to distinctions between different orderings between *two* entities, and with partless entities this could not be possible either. Differences of order can emerge only with three partless entities. And I doubt that there could be any meaningful way of speaking about differences in *rhusmos*, shape, of such partless entities either. Therefore I am inclined to think that Book 6 of the *Physics* is not concerned with the physically unsplittable entities of Democritus, but with theoretically indivisible or non-analyzable beings, propounded in the Academy.[24] And so Aristotle need not be concerned with a peculiar doctrine of Democritus on atomic touch after all at this place.[25]

There are, however, other contexts where Aristotle should have mentioned the doctrine of remote touch. First of all, the treatise *On Democritus* should have stressed this feature of early atomism, and then we would expect to find repeated mention of this in the commentators on Aristotle. Indeed, in the sole fragment of the book, preserved by Simplicius, mention of this special remote touch would have been most welcome, as Aristotle there delineates the fundamental distinction between the permanent unity of an atom and the transient

---

24. By calling these entities theoretically indivisible I do not envisage a process of theoretical cuttings stopping at a point. Such a notion was rightly disparaged by Makin (1989). Nevertheless the distinction between theoretical and physical divisibility can be vested with a perfectly legitimate meaning along other lines. The notion of physical divisibility will refer to possible worlds where things are split up into their constituent bits in all sorts of ways. A philosophy of nature is atomistic if all transitive closures of the possible physical divisions on the same object produce the very same finite set of constituents. The resulting atomic particles may nevertheless be theoretically divisible. This notion of divisibility in thought will refer to possible worlds which contain the very same elementary particles, in the same configuration among themselves, but some of these in a different position (*tropē*). Here we shall have reason to say that these atomic entities may interact with each other differently in the different possible worlds, according to which inseparable parts they touch each other with. Whether theoretical division ends with theoretically indivisible *minima* will depend on what alternative worlds we are allowed to take into account. If an atom has only a finite number of admissible positionings which are causally relevant, this fact can be expressed by the claim that it has only a finite number of theoretically distinguishable minimal parts. Note that Makin (1989, 148) in a similar vein defines minimal parts by possible motions and positions.

25. Even though I do not think Aristotle's argument in *Physics* Book 6 would be applicable against Democritus's atoms, I do not want to contest that later indivisibilists—Diodorus Cronus and Epicurus—could take their cue from these arguments to formulate a revised theory of atomism.

interaction of these bodies, which gives rise to perceptible entities (166.11ff Rose), lines 16–17 expressly claim that it would be "extremely silly to suppose that two or more things could ever become one." If there had been a specific mechanism of atomic touch to safeguard the permanence of the atoms, it would have been appropriate to say so in this context.[26]

It is not only on this occasion that Aristotle's silence is telling against the admission of a doctrine of remote touch. Another, even more striking, case is when Aristotle at *GC* 1.8 326a29ff, in the discussion of whether the nature—as it were, the matter—of the atomic particles is one and the same, asks what should separate them if they are of the same material, or why these entities do not become one upon touch.[27] Had Aristotle known about a doctrine of remote touch, he clearly would not be entitled to formulate his objection this way; instead, he should have proceeded to discuss the inherent improbability of the notion safeguarding the independence of these particles.

After these silent testimonies we turn to John Philoponus, who at two places in his commentary on *GC* attributes a theory of remote touch to Democritus.[28] I would like to argue that we have every reason to believe that these suggestions are guesses of Philoponus, which are solely based on the text of Aristotle, and we should treat them as such.[29] These sentences feature in Philo-

---

26. This also applies to all the other passages referred to in note 1 above.

27. *ei men gar mia physis estin hapantōn, ti to chōrisan; ē dia ti ou ginetai hapsamena hen, hōsper hydōr hydatos hotan thigē;* ("If all of them have a single nature, what is the separating entity? Or why do they not become one upon touch, like water when it touches water?" *GC* 1.8 326a31-3). Note that part of Aristotle's strategy here is to speak about the atomic stuff on the analogy of some liquid. As will be explained in note 52, the individuality of objects made of the same material, when they are in contact, poses notorious difficulties for an Aristotelian account, too.

28. Konstan (1979, 404 n.26) mentions further texts—which had also been included in fragments 236 and 237 in Luria (1970), under the heading *Quid sibi velit ἁφή*—as testifying to a theory of remote touch, but these should not be taken to refer to this doctrine. Simplicius *in De caelo* 609.17ff, as I shall argue in note 37, is noncommittal about the way atomic bodies touch. Konstan's translation of Philoponus *in Phys* 494.20ff might be taken to indicate that atoms are always bounded by void, but this translation is not mandatory. Rather, what Philoponus is arguing against is the identification of limitedness and touch, and he asserts on this account that in the void the limited atoms *may* often be in contact with nothing: this constitutes no basis for a doctrine of remote touch either.

29. Cf. Barnes (1979/1982, 349), in which he attributes a doctrine of remote touch to the early atomists on account of these sentences of Philoponus. Barnes furthermore refers to Alexander *De mixtione* 214.18ff (=68A64), but that passage does not contain any evidence for or against a doctrine of remote touch.

ponus's commentary on *GC* 324b24-325b34, in which, after giving a short overview of the passage on pages 153–155, he proceeds to supply textual notes.[30] The overview stresses how the Eleatic argument for the impossibility of motion and plurality without void was turned into an argument for the existence of void by the atomists. This information comes from Aristotle's text; for this Philoponus did not need to consult any further authorities. Moreover, it is clear that he did not care to check who the Eleatic could have been who argued for the infinity of being from the rejection of void. At 155.19f he attributes this argument to Parmenides, and I take it that his expression at 157.27-158.2 should not be interpreted as a tacit reversal of this: *hoi peri Parmenidēn* need not refer to anyone other than Parmenides, and certainly it cannot refer only to those disciples of Parmenides who, against the authority of the master, held with Melissus that being is infinite.[31]

The first steps toward a theory of remote touch are taken already at 154.2f where Philoponus asserts in a summary fashion that *hoi de peri Dēmokriton kai Leukippon dia tou kenou to poiein kai to paschein ginesthai elegon* ("those around Democritus and Leukippus said that action and passion occur through the void").[32] This sentence is still ambiguous: It may call attention to the role of void as separator, *when* it separates atoms, and to the fact that it gives way to motion by being permeable, and so it is only *through* void that any action can be exerted or suffered; or it can already incorporate the more fundamental claim that it is

---

30. The overview, which could be rather long, was generally called *theōria* or *protheōria*; the technical term for the textual notes is *lexis*. Although this structure in the *GC* commentary is not always strictly observed, we can find Philoponus referring to a *protheōria* at 45.21f, 66.29, 272.11, and 276.14, whereas 29.2, 45.21f, 131.34, and 250.35 mark a transition to the *lexis*.

31. As a further example—in this case about the atomists themselves—the comments on *GC* 325b12-25 may be cited. There Aristotle says that Empedocles analyzed matter only as far as the four elements, whereas the atomists carried the analysis further. Philoponus cannot possibly have any further, corroborative testimony at his disposal when he asserts in his comments at 160.24ff and 161.17f that the atomists also thought that composite bodies are generated from the four elements; they supplemented this theory with an atomistic analysis of the generation of the elements only.

32. Cf. Aristotle *GC* 326a1f *anagkaion apathes te hekaston legein tōn adiairetōn . . . ou gar hoion te paschein all' ē dia tou kenou* ("for each of the indivisible [three dimensional entities] have to be asserted to be impassible . . . for they cannot be acted upon except through the void"), where Aristotle apparently employs his principle that action requires qualitatively different entities (see note 33), and the only qualitative difference present in an atomistic universe is the one between atoms and the void. Philoponus, characteristically, will interpret this argument in 167.4-7 as if it required the presence of an *internal* void.

only *physically* through a film of void that any atomic interactions can take place. Later, by the end of a textual note to 325a25-32 Philoponus reaches the conclusion that division and inclusion of void presuppose each other: Only complexes containing void can be severed into their components; entities containing no void are indivisible. This is when Philoponus turns to interpreting the sentence *Poiein de kai paschein hēi tunchanousin haptomena; tautēi gar ouch hen einai* ("They act and are acted upon in the direction/to the extent/in the way as they happen to be in contact, for in that direction/to that extent/in that way they are not one" 325a32-4). As he has just reached the conclusion that continuous chunks of matter not separated by void cannot split, he understandably takes *hēi tunchanousin haptomena* ("in that they happen to be touching") as a restriction on the mode of atomic touch: There has to be a special sort of touch which, as the next clause of Aristotle specifies, avoids the coalescence of the atomic masses.[33] It is small wonder that Philoponus supplies at this juncture (158.27-159.3) what he perceives to be the missing link, and proposes that the specific atomic touch that preserves the individuality of the meeting parties is through the inclusion of void.

The other occasion in which Philoponus's text refers to a doctrine of remote atomic touch in a straightforward way (160.7-11) is also telling. Aristotle, speaking about Empedocles at 325b9-10, claims *Anankē ara ta men haptomena einai adiaireta, ta de metaxu autōn kena, hous ekeinos legei porous. Houtōs de kai Leukippos legei peri tou poiein kai paschein.*[34] Philoponus here

---

33. This inference, however, is by no means mandatory, as evidenced by the original Oxford translation, which in that instance is superior to the revised one, and by C.J.F. Williams's rendering in the Clarendon Aristotle Series. Moreover, we should keep in mind that Aristotle need not voice any specially atomistic tenets about touch and interaction. The sentence makes perfect sense on his own premises, as he does not allow that anything would induce change in itself. Change requires an active and a passive entity, and these have to be in contact, and to the extent that they are in contact/where they are in contact, they do not form a single, united entity (cf. *Physics* 8.4 255a12f, where a13 *hēi gar hen kai syneches mē haphēi, tautēi apathes* ["To the extent/in the way something is one and continuous not merely by contact, to that extent/in that way it is impassive"]—is almost exactly the contraposition of the *GC* passage). Aristotelian entities, unlike Democritean ones (on which see Aristotle's comments at *GC* 1.7 323b10ff), are qualitatively different—most notably they differ in the characteristic that is passed on by the active entity to the passive one. Therefore the individuality of the two touching parties is not in peril. Nevertheless, the topology of touch will incur the same difficulty as the one stressed by Philoponus: What should it mean that the extremities of the two objects are together, without becoming the same extremity?

34. Cf. the Revised Oxford Translation: "It is necessary, therefore, for his contiguous things to be indivisible, while the intervals between them—which he calls pores—must be void. But this is precisely Leucippus's theory of action and passion."

construes Aristotle as if he were claiming that the things touching are separated by the pores or by the void precisely when they touch. As Empedocles's pores are not empty, touch in his case will be through the contents of the pores, whereas Leucippan touch, as Philoponus hastens to add, is through the void, and not touch properly so called.[35]

There are another two occasions in which Philoponus might have the same claim in mind (159.11-3 and 161.4); but already at the comments on 325b30-3, after reiterating at 163.14-21 the claim that touch occurs through the void, in an astonishing reversal he adds that this is true "no matter whether you speak about touch in the strict sense or touch in the meaning of approximation" (163.21f). Normal, surface-to-surface, touch is no longer ruled out categorically from atomistic physics.

Philoponus has good reasons to drop the claim that with the atomists elementary particles never experience a direct encounter, but interaction is always through the intermediary of a separating layer of void, as Aristotle's text at 326a31ff does not allow this route of escape for the atomists. Were interactions through remote touch admissible, the atomists could easily retort to the question of Aristotle: "For if all of them are uniform in nature, what is it that separated one from the other? Or why, when they come into contact, do they not coalesce into one, as drops of water run together when drop touches drop . . . ?"[36] If, strictly speaking, atomic particles never came into direct contact, there could be no danger of losing their individuality through coalescence with other particles. As this passage of Aristotle tacitly discards this route of escape, Philoponus does not mention it either in his comments on the passage (175.23-176.5). Presumably he takes Aristotle to assault the second line of the atomistic defense. Just as he reached the doctrine of remote touch as something encapsulated in the text of Aristotle, he does not need to entertain it any longer where Aristotle apparently refuses to allow his opponents this refuge.

It was necessary to go into some detail to show that Philoponus's proposal of remote touch does not rest on anything else than an ingenious, if also somewhat feeble, interpretation of the Aristotelian passages he comments on.

---

35. On the first occasion Philoponus spoke about Democritus; here he mentions the circle of Leucippus (*hoi peri Leukippon*). As the second mention unambiguously refers to the earlier passage, it does not provide independent evidence for the same doctrine in Leucippus; rather it reinforces the impression that Philoponus is groping his way through a text of Aristotle, and when that speaks about Leucippus he phrases his comments accordingly: The only change he makes is that he substitutes "the circle of Leucippus" for Aristotle's plain "Leucippus," and thereby indicates that—on the basis of Aristotle's earlier assertion at 325a32ff—he includes Democritus as well in this group.

36. Revised Oxford translation.

Therefore, Philoponus's words cannot constitute an independent witness for this doctrine. If we want to attribute the doctrine to Democritus and Leucippus, we should do so on the authority of Aristotle alone. But we have already seen that Aristotle's presentation of the atomists does not bear out an interpretation on which they could have proposed this very peculiar doctrine.[37]

CONTACT

Another way to salvage atomic independence in a theory where continuity is a sufficient condition of atomic indivisibility is to admit that atoms touch each other surface to surface, and on these occasions they form an uninterrupted, continuous mass, while it can nevertheless be maintained that the continuity is defective where the edges of the corpuscles meet. Continuity can be defective at the seams of the atoms because of different considerations;[38] a general formulation of one of these would be to claim that the major defect of the continuity which emerges upon atomic interactions is that it is unextended in some relevant sense. A proposal of the literature, which would fall in line with this alternative, suggested that atoms touch at single points, or at most along lines only—or in other words these particles are not coupled, because they cannot be in contact across areas.[39] This would mean that these complexes, in which atoms retain their identity, enjoy a continuity which is *spatially* impaired. Only the parts which form the individual atoms are path-connected in the strong sense of the word, whereas the combined mass of these does not have this prop-

---

37. Simplicius *in De caelo* 609.17ff has also been thought to attribute the same doctrine of remote touch to the early atomists. The crucial bit in that testimony is how we take Simplicius's report of the atomists' claim that only the corpuscles are continuous, and all the rest, the seemingly continuous compounds *haphēi prosengizein allēlois*. If *prosengizein* conveyed the restriction that the parties while in contact can only be near to each other, without actually coming to full encounter, Simplicius's text would refer to a doctrine of remote touch. This verb, however, does not exclude the possibility that the particles may be side by side, without anything intervening, and so the passage cannot constitute in itself evidence for a theory of remote touch. (Cf. Parmenides B8.25 ἐὸν γὰρ ἐόντι πελάζει ("for being draws near to being") where there is no ground for supposing on the force of the verb *pelazei* that between the neighboring chunks of being there should be something intervening.)

38. I relegate such an account to the end of the next section. In that account, proposed for Epicurus, the succession and cohesion of internal minimal parts is contrasted with the touch between the minimal parts forming the adjacent boundaries of two atoms.

39. This proposal was first tentatively put forward in Konstan (1979, 407 n.34), for Epicurus—albeit that for a quantized physics such a proposal could not work—and endorsed by Makin (1993, 88 n.43).

erty. Between any two positions in the complex entity there is an uninterrupted path, but when the two positions are not in the same particle, this path cannot be extended into a three-dimensional tube running within the interior of the complex molecule. Those locations of the surfaces of the atoms where they are in contact at single points or single lines do not bond these bodies. After hitting each other and communicating the force of their motion, the particles can then be separated. Or they can even be separated after flying side by side for an extended period of time: If one of these receives a hit, or both of them are struck along lines leading in opposite directions, they can disengage, as there was no bond of atomic cohesion at the places of contact.

Such an account would make a welcome distinction between permanent atomic units and transient molecular combinations, without resorting to the implausible notion of remote touch. But this can be achieved only at rather high price. Somehow it has to be accomplished that atoms encounter each other with positionings in which an area of surface is always hit by an edge. Two atoms which could be fitted on to each other have to be tilted before the portentous encounter. This, however, will be a hard, or even impossible, task indeed. If there are atoms which can be aligned, like a joint and a socket, we cannot simply postulate that these will invariably meet each other the wrong way, and will not be assembled. In fact an *ouden mallon* argument seems to require that between two atoms all sorts of encounters have to happen during the course of time.[40] As we are unable to explain why the particles flying toward each other would always happen to be out of alignment, the best we can do—and this is what was proposed in the literature—is to restrict atomic shapes to those which cannot fit into each other. The serious drawback of this option is that it is in obvious conflict with the atomists' tenet of the equipollence of atomic shapes. According to Simplicius's testimony in 67A7, Leucippus supposed that the multitude of atomic shapes is infinite, as there is no reason why atoms should be such rather than such. Simplicius's wording, the deployment of an indifference argument, is generally acknowledged to go back to the atomists themselves. But even if, in an

---

40. Here we should stress "seem." For reasons which were beyond the ken of theories before the introduction of naive set theory by Cantor, the claim is not correct. In fact, in a universe where the building blocks are unalterable, and where all the points corresponding to real numbers can be traced out in material entities or in space, even the basic atomist claim that all possible atomic forms are instantiated in the universe is itself false. This has to be so, because otherwise the universe would include a non-denumerably infinite multitude of entities of the volume of, say, 1 cubic inch, whereas there is only a denumerably infinite multitude of non-overlapping spatial locations of this size available. Similar considerations will show that out of the non-denumerably infinite number of different encounters between two atoms only a denumerably infinite number of varieties will ever take place.

otherwise unwarranted skeptical mood, we should cast doubt on Simplicius's testimony, and think that he is providing a theoretical framework for Aristotle's repeated comments to the effect that Leucippus thought there was an infinite variety of atoms, as there are an infinite multitude of possible shapes,[41] the idea that some atomic shapes would be ruled out is something which would also undercut this Aristotelian testimony. The infinity of atomic shapes could be asserted only after we had established that any initial set of incongruent atomic shapes can be extended into an infinite set of incongruent shapes, but the Aristotelian testimony does not mention these crucial stipulations.[42]

One might suppose—as I, for one, did in earlier versions of this chapter—that we can provide a significantly different proposal for atomic independence if we maintain that the contact between atoms is unextended *temporally*, and not spatially. This solution would assert that like all other regularities, those which account for the coherence of continuous chunks of matter are operative over stretches of time, and not on points of time. Hence, even if atoms come into surface-to-surface contact and form a single continuous whole in the moment of impact, this continuity will not exist during any stretch of time, and so the encounter will not result in the loss of the identity of the original particles. The solidity of these atoms will see to it that they are separated immediately after the single, unextended moment of the interaction. This way it seems, we do not need to impose restrictions on admissible shapes, and congruent atoms will not run the risk of losing their identity in atomic encounters.

Unfortunately, however, this claim would be unfounded. Even if congruent atoms will not be absorbed into larger units through their mutual collisions, interactions involving several atoms can result in two atoms running on parallel courses touching each other.[43] This is possible once two atoms are not just congruent, but are also able to *slide* on each other. If during the process of sliding on each other one of the atoms runs into some obstacle, and as a result of this reverses direction and acquires a velocity exactly the same as that of the other particle, we have two atoms now forming a non-instantaneous unity. But whether they form a single atom now, or retain their individuality makes a significant difference. There can be atoms along the way of the composite entity

---

41. See especially Aristotle, *De caelo* 3.4 303a10-12 (part of 67A 15).
42. Furthermore, the drift of the indifference argument would suggest a plurality of specimens of each atomic shape, and this is duly reported by Philoponus *in GC* 12.2 (=fr.141 Luria; Epicurus, *Letter to Herodotus*, 42, also reiterates this claim). This, however, will be violated by self-congruous atomic shapes—for example, those with at least one planar surface, as they can be instantiated only once, a second specimen of these will already be in peril of absorption as soon as it comes into contact with the first one.
43. I am grateful to Charles Brittain for bringing this difficulty to my attention.

which deflect only one of the particles, unless it had been incorporated into the emerging joint mass.

The difference between the two accounts of this section, then, will be a difference of degree only. If spatially extended contact is necessary for continuity, and, hence, for atomic indivisibility, congruent atoms will be ruled out, whereas in the other case, if it is temporally extended contact that results in the internal coherence of the particles, we have to eliminate only those congruent atoms that can ethibit lateral translation along each other without interaction, while remaining in contact. As I see no reason to restrict atomic shapes either way, I think that both of the proposals have to be rejected on the strength of the indifference argument of this section.

REMOTE TOUCH

As far as the earlier atomists are concerned, then, remote touch and unextended contact did not prove to be suitable solutions for atomic independence. Turning to Epicurus, it is informative and interesting to see that he did not pursue any of these lines. Informative, because it suggests that these options were not propounded by Epicurus's atomist forebears, and interesting because on balance it shows that Epicurus did not consider the threat of atomic coalescence, and did not provide a theoretical framework which would explain why atoms do not merge.

A major innovation of Epicurus' was that he argued for the granularity of matter (see *Letter to Herodotus*, 56–59). This will certainly inhibit explanations of the permanence of atomic independence that would refer to unextended spatial or temporal encounter between the particles during interaction. First, there is not going to be anything which would be spatially unextended in the strict sense of the word. When atoms touch they do so across the area of a minimal extension. Why such a link would be unsuitable to build an atomic bond between the particles, whereas a finite number of such joints would glue them together forever, is beyond reasonable explanation. Temporally unextended touch will have the same fate. Not because—as I would maintain—time was invariably quantized in the Epicurean theory.[44] That would still allow for a distinction between what is the case in a single, albeit extended, instant, and what holds in

---

44. It is a moot point *when* Epicurus might have introduced minimal spatial and temporal extensions, as the *Letter to Herodotus* refers to minimal bodily parts only. Long and Sedley (1987, vol. 1, 41–44, and vol. 2, 34), suggest that minimal bodily parts were postulated by Epicurus independently from the other three *minima* and accordingly in vol. 1, 51, they propose that Epicurus took over temporal, spatial, and kinetic *minima* only later from Diodorus Cronus. This claim compels

(*continued on page 144*)

44. (*continued from page 143*)

Long and Sedley to attribute a roundabout explanation for the Epicurean postulate, announced at *Letter to Herodotus*, 61 (and cf. 46), that all the atoms possess a uniform, though unimaginably great, atomic speed. This would be a trivial consequence in quantized space and time: atoms cannot stay put, and they are allowed to take one step at a time. Long and Sedley, however, need something else, and argue (Long and Sedley [1987] vol. 1, 50) that Epicurus took his cue from Aristotle's premise about the proportionalities of speed and resistance, which had the absurd consequence at *Physics* 4.8 215a24-216a21, that motion of all bodies in void should happen at the same, infinite speed, and accommodated the resulting difficulties in his system by postulating a uniform, unimaginably great atomic speed. I find this proposal unlikely: In order not to have an infinite, but only an excessively great, finite speed, Epicurus had to *reject* the Aristotelian proportionalities altogether.

Moreover, it is significant that *Letter to Herodotus*, 61, is at pains to stress that the speed of atomic motions is uniform in all directions. In justification of this Epicurus stresses that void does not impede motion in any way. This, however, is only a necessary condition, and is not sufficient in itself to establish uniform atomic velocity in a non-isotropic universe, where atoms fall in a perpendicular line, that is, up and down, are built into the basic regularities of nature. The need for further support for Epicurus's thesis can be well illustrated with the following exposition of the last clause of the passage (proposed by Furley [1967], 122f): Every atom travels in any direction at the same speed "until it is hit against, either from outside, or from its own weight against the force of what had hit it." The second option apparently envisages situations where an atom, ascending because of a previous hit is overcome by its own weight without anything obstructing in its way, and starts to descend. That on both limbs of the trajectory it has to travel constantly at the same speed, and its own weight, which forced it to turn in the end, could not exert some drag on the upward motion and slow it down, is an unlikely presupposition, and warranted only if some other physical constraints—like the granular structure of space and time—impose a uniform atomic speed. (It should be noted here that the passage is interpreted differently in Konstan [1979], 413f and in Long and Sedley [1987], vol. 1, 48, the crucial difference being whether one takes the force of the aorist participle πλήξαντος as indicating temporal precedence, as Furley and I do, or as indicating the instantaneous character of the hit, which is, however, simultaneous with the change of direction.)

On balance we have either of two options: We can rephrase Long and Sedley's claim, and propose that Epicurus's doctrine in *Letter to Herodotus* contained some hidden tensions, which Epicurus could eliminate only later; or, as I would suggest, we should suppose that in a work containing only the rudiments of his creed Epicurus may avoid mentioning some intricate but indispensable details of his position. In this second case the easiest way to account for Epicurus's stance is to suppose that he already had his doctrine of spatial and temporal *minima*, and these required the postulation of uniform atomic velocities.

a series of them, which corresponds to a stretch of time here.[45] This proposal will founder rather because, as we have seen, it rules out atomic shapes which can slide along each other. On a quantized theory of matter, however, this is almost impossible to ensure. Atoms which have protrusions of at least two minimal extensions can already slide on each other for the length of this part of their boundary. This would mean that only atoms which have the shape of a ziggurat everywhere on their periphery are admissible, and again this restriction on atomic shapes seems to be unwarranted and unacceptable.

Remote touch would fare better in an Epicurean setting than these unextended contacts. The first thing we should notice is that remote touch would fit in excellently with the way Epicurean atoms interact. When two atoms are flying toward each other this happens in jerks. For each minimal extension of time they occupy a given location, and then by the next one they will have moved exactly one spatial extension's worth. Consequently, atomic speed is a constant of nature: Atoms cannot stand still; every atom has to be located at a neighboring position in the following instant. This is presumably also true about the moment of impact: When two atoms have reached each other they do not try to push forward and do not come to a halt, rather what they do is detect that there is an obstacle ahead and change direction without waste of time.[46] That atoms "sense" each other only when they have reached adjacent locations, and not when they are one or two spatial units ahead of collision, does not seem to make a crucial difference in the description of natural processes.

Moreover, not only would action at a distance be able to safeguard atomic independence, it would answer another puzzle which emerges on quantized theories of space and time. The puzzle is best posed in Sextus's *Adv. Math.* x, 142ff. There Sextus ridicules the notion of minimal extensions and minimal jerks as the constituents of motions along these extensions with the following example. Imagine two atoms at a distance of nine units and moving toward each other. The query is when and how they will interact; as there would always be an odd number of spatial *minima between* them, they can never reach adjacent locations.

It is clear that an optimal solution Epicurus could have proffered would have been to claim that atoms interact whenever they enter the perimeter of each other in, say, two atomic units or less.[47] But although this would be a satisfactory answer to several queries, we hear nothing of it in works of the Epicureans, or

---

45. To this extent I hold that space and time are not analogous. In space, isolated links can occur between two particles simultaneously, and then we can ask what the adjacency of these links contributes to the permanence of the attachment. In time, only a single instant is simultaneous with itself.
46. So Konstan (1979), 395f.
47. One might want to add further clauses to allow for near misses within the restricted perimeter, that would not result in the atoms coming into direct contact.

doxographical reports of their doctrines. So we have no reason to suppose that Epicurus might have approved of such a theory of action at a distance between atoms.

Finally, after these options we have to explore whether Epicurus had some account as a derivative of his novel, granular account of matter with which he could distinguish between the transient juxtaposition of particles and the cohesive and permanent continuity of the atoms.

Introducing minimal parts may be—and in fact has been—viewed as just the right sort of move with which we can establish this distinction. With that additional layer of analysis Epicurus should be able to formulate a "deep structure of matter," and through this there is at least some hope of solving the problem of simultaneous contiguity and discreteness.[48] The description of a special deep structure (or in more Peripatetic parlance, the formal aspect of the atom: cf. note 52), however, is missing from our Epicurean texts. In the absence of such a theory, as Long and Sedley stress ([1987]), vol. 2, 33f), interrelationships between atoms will have to be described in terms of interrelationships between the respective minimal parts which serve as their extremities. Then, however, the suggestion that internal *minima* are in succession, and so cannot touch in the Aristotelian sense,[49] cannot answer our puzzle, as Long and Sedley would have it. Even if two atoms on this account were not allowed to touch (or rather, we were not allowed to speak about them as touching), whatever relationship there is between the minimal parts inside an atom will also apply to the adjacent minimal parts which formed the extremities of the two particles before the encounter. Therefore, contrary to Long and Sedley's contention, unless some considerations preempt talk of the non-overlapping but exhaustive parts of the atoms,[50] the two exact halves of, for example, an atomic cube with sides of eight units would not share an extremity in any stricter sense of the word than two adjacent particles of $4 \times 8 \times 8$ units do when these two particles make up a transient cube upon touch. And so I submit that we can expect no solution to our puzzle from the mere introduction of new, subatomic entities.[51]

---

48. The phrases are borrowed from the programmatic propositions in Konstan (1979, 407).
49. Proposed in Sorabji (1983, 372–375).
50. It is very unlikely, though, that there could be such considerations: Even if the minimal parts themselves were strictly speaking not parts of the atoms, the fact that Epicurus at *Letter to Herodotus*, 58f can specify the relationship between individual adjacent *minima*, that they are in succession, suggests strongly that there should be no intrinsic impossibility in referring to any uninterrupted array or group of these entities.
51. What would be needed, for example, would be a theory according to which "a packing of matter inside the atom is of a qualitatively different order of density than that achieved when corpuscles are placed adjacent to one another, and that accordingly there is a sense in which void continues to intervene between contiguous atoms," as Konstan (1979, 405 n.28) aptly formulates.

INDIVIDUATION

As I have argued, none of the proffered explanations for atomic indivisibility guarantees the permanent individuality of all the possible atoms. As we have seen in and around note 5, atoms are made of the same, single atomic stuff. Hence, whatever individuates these entities has to be some sort of formal aspect of these entities in the Peripatetic terminology. This certainly would be the case even if one of the explanations for atomic indivisibility could guarantee atomic integrity. In that case the atomists could have claimed that they could reduce the notion of the formal aspect of the atomic particles to some initial (or in fact to any intermediate) state of the allocation of matter across the universe *and* to the laws or regularities of natural processes, which bring with themselves the conservation of the form of the particles. Then the account of atomic independence and indivisibility would be a fundamental part of the general reductionist enterprise. The completion of the enterprise requires that qualities of composite objects be reduced to the interaction of the atoms making up this object and that we also have an account of the permanence of the characteristics of the atoms. If my contention in the preceding sections is correct, this complete reduction has never been achieved, in fact the atomists have not even endeavored to provide such a comprehensive account. This suggests that they were tacitly operating with a notion of further irreducible, formal principles of the atoms, and these were not, and as a matter of fact could not be, eliminated by the official atomist explanations for indivisibility.

This might appear a crucial defect at the very foundations of atomistic reductionism, and so it may seem surprising that proponents of atomism apparently never seriously discussed, and critics of atomism never paid more than cursory attention to, these issues. But we have to keep in mind that even if the issue of atomic independence and indivisibility is settled—and we have seen above that it can be settled in a number of different ways—the derivation of the features of macroscopic objects still remains an issue of contention. As the crucial alternatives of teleological versus reductionist explanation concern the status of these higher-level features, the disputing parties rightly passed over the issue of atomic forms as being of lesser importance only.[52]

---

52. Notice also that these problems of the status of atomic forms can be paralleled with the problems surrounding the form of a particular elemental mass in Aristotle's philosophy. This form will have an irreducible causal role in the explanation of the behavior of this elemental mass: it will at least specify the direction of natural motion for this object. But it is not clear whether the speed of this motion will also be determined by this form. If so, we should like to know how the forms of two clods of earth give rise to the new form of the aggregate object when these are joined. Otherwise we shall be anxious to know how the form specifying the direction, and the mass of matter, determining the speed of the motion, interact.

Chapter 8

Why Democritus Was Not a Skeptic

Patricia Curd

THE PROBLEM

Was Democritus a skeptic?[1] Jonathan Barnes presents a skeptical Democritus in *The Presocratic Philosophers*, and skepticism is attributed to Democritus by Kirk, Raven, and Schofield, and by others.[2] In this chapter I try to show that Democritus did not embrace skepticism, arguing that Democritus's distinction between what is by convention and what is by reality does not entail a skeptical view of knowledge. By understanding what Democritus means by this distinction, we shall see that both his famous claim (B117) that "In truth we know nothing; for

---

1. References to Presocratic philosophers are made through the standard numbering system of Diels and Kranz, (hereafter: DK) *Die Fragmente der Vorsokratiker.* With the exception of Antiphon B44, translations are my own.
2. See Barnes (1979), Chapter X, part (e); Kirk, Raven, and Schofield (1983), 409–413; O'Keefe (1996) (although O'Keefe modifies his position in [1997]; see O'Keefe [1997], 120–121). O'Keefe, following Hankinson, makes a useful distinction among various versions of skepticism. He argues that Democritus's views on sense perception appear to commit him to a moderate version of global epistemological skepticism (120). Asmis argues that Democritus embraced a skepticism similar to that of Sextus; see Asmis (1986), 337–348. Makin (1993, Ch. 3, 65–84) discusses the role of indifference (*ou mallon*) arguments in Democritus's epistemology and argues for a moderately skeptical interpretation of Democritus's views. DeLacy (1958) argues that Democritus's use of *ou mallon* arguments "carries no suggestion of scepticism" (59). C.C.W. Taylor (1967) argues for a moderate interpretation of Democritus's epistemology, but believes that the theory is finally contradictory, both relying on and rejecting the evidence of the senses. See Weiss (1938) for a statement of a non-skeptical interpretation of Democritus. Sedley (1992) rejects the strongly skeptical interpretation, but Sedley himself doubts that there is "an overall position" to be found in Democritus (24, n.7). McKirahan (1993) adopts a position similar to that of Weiss. McKim (1984) rejects a skeptical account of Democritus, but thinks that Democritus must begin by adopting as an "axiom" the claim that all perceptions are true (I shall suggest that this is a conclusion that Democritus reaches, rather than a starting point). See also Baldes (1981) who argues that for Democritus "empirical statements are true, not absolutely, but relative to man;" they can be the basis for reliable ontological claims. Farrar (1988) also argues for a non-skeptical Democritus, although I have doubts about the overall interpretation that Farrar offers, especially in the way she connects the physics and the ethics.

truth is in the depths" (ἐτεῇ δὲ οὐδὲν ἴδμεν· ἐν βυθῷ γὰρ ἡ ἀλήθεια), and other fragments that have traditionally been used to support a skeptical interpretation do not require Democritus to deny that knowledge is possible.[3] My discussion will not begin with the epistemological fragments, or with Democritus's account of perception, for it is these aspects of his thought that are in contention. Rather, I shall first explore the consequences for ethics of the Democritean claim that the world reported by the senses is not genuine, but is rather "by convention." I will then discuss Democritus's own ethical views and then finally turn to the issue of Democritus's supposed skepticism about knowledge and his worries about the re- liability of sense perception. Having argued that Democritus's views leave no room for skepticism in ethics, I suggest that in epistemology, too, a skeptical in- terpretation is not forced on us by the evidence.

The second half of the fifth century (BCE) was marked by the activity of the Sophists, who, through challenging traditional moral and social judgments and inquiring whether morality is a matter of convention (*nomos*) or of nature (*phy-sis*), brought into question both the proper relation between the individual and the state, and the very nature of ethical claims.[4] Part of this debate is recorded in the fragments of Antiphon, who argues that *nomos* and *physis* are opposed to one another, and that following the dictates of *nomos*, conflicting as they do with those of *physis*, can be harmful to an individual (although the requirements of *nomos* may benefit the many).[5] Here are a few of Antiphon's claims about the contrast between *nomos* and *physis* (in McKirahan's translation):

---

3. Nor does it entail that Democritus should claim that we ought to withhold judg- ment about the possibility of knowledge. Metrodorus of Chios adopts the view that no justified claim about knowledge can be made; in 70B1 he says that "none of us knows anything, not even this, whether we know or we do not know; nor do we know what to not know and to know are, nor on the whole, whether anything is or is not" (text as in DK). Clement says that Metrodorus was a student of Democritus, but Diogenes Laertius (in his discussion of Anaxarchus—IX.58 = 72A1) asserts that Metrodorus was a student of Nessas of Chios, "although some say he heard [i.e., was a student of] Democritus" (οἱ δὲ Δημοκρίτου φασὶν ἀκοῦσαι). Although Metrodorus follows Democritus in adopting atomism, this need not imply that his skepticism was also inherited from Democritus.

4. On the opposition between *nomos* and *physis*, see Reinhardt (1959) and Heinemann (1945). See note 32.

5. I take it that the Sophist known as Antiphon is identical with Antiphon of Rham- nous. See the section on Antiphon by J.S. Morrison in Sprague (1972). For discus- sions of the issues in the identification of the two Antiphons, see Guthrie (1971, 285–294, esp. 292–294); see also Kerferd (1981), 49–51. Guthrie suggests that the two are different; Kerferd seems to opt for their identity. Barnes, on the other hand, takes no interest in the question: "There is no decisive evidence telling for or against the identification of any two, of any three, or of all four of these [An- tiphons]; nor is the question of great moment" (1979, vol. II, 207).

Justice is a matter of not transgressing what the laws (*nomima*) prescribe in whatever city you are a citizen of. A person would make most advantage of justice for himself if he treated the laws (*nomoi*) as important in the presence of witnesses, and treated the decrees of nature (*ta tēs physeōs*) as important when alone and with no witnesses present. For the decrees of the laws are extra additions, those of nature are necessary; those of the laws are products of agreement, not of natural growth, whereas those of nature are the products of natural growth, not of agreement. If those who made the agreement do not notice a person transgressing the prescriptions of laws, he is free from both disgrace and penalty, but not so if they do notice him. But if, contrary to possibility, anyone violates any of the things that are innate by nature, the evil is no less if no one notices him and no greater if all observe. For he does not suffer harm as a result of opinion, but as a result of truth (*ou gar dia doxan blaptetai, alla di' alētheian*). This is the entire purpose of considering these matters—that most of the things that are just according to law are established in a way which is hostile to nature (*hoti ta polla tōn kata nomon dikaiōn polemiōs tēi physei keitai*). (87b44 = Oxyrh. Pap. XI n.1364 ed. Hunt, col. 1, lines 6–33; col. 2, lines 34–66)

The extant fragments of Antiphon do not contain a systematic treatment of ethical or social issues.[6] Nevertheless, there is a kind of social and ethical skepticism to be found in them. This skepticism severs moral judgments from judgments about truth, and suggests that moral claims are merely conventions (*nomima*) that are not subject to rational inquiry. If we paid attention to nature, according to Antiphon, we would act to acquire pleasure and avoid pain, in ways that would prolong our lives. We would avoid the dictates of conventional justice and morality when we can because such dictates are contrary to nature (*physis*) in not furthering our own self-interest. Antiphon seems to be claiming that ethical rules and judgments, as mere human conventions, are as a matter of

---

6. Commentators on Antiphon routinely point out that he has not worked out these claims in a fully coherent manner, that there is, in the extant fragments at least, no proper account of what is meant by nature (*physis*), and that it is left unclear just what a life devoted to "following nature" would be like. See Kerferd (1981) and McKirahan (1993). For a dismissive view of Antiphon, see Barnes (1979). Commentators often—and justifiably—point to Callicles in the *Gorgias* and Thrasymachus in *Republic* I for fuller treatments of these issues, although it must be kept in mind that Callicles and Thrasymachus are characters in dialogues written by Plato, who had a strong bias against the Sophists. So, we cannot be sure that Antiphon would agree that his claims about *nomos* and *physis* should be understood as endorsing the Calliclean or Thrasymachean positions.

fact false, but are adopted by a society as a matter of convenience; at any rate, one should (if possible) ignore or avoid them in favor of "following nature."

What is intriguing in these claims (and others like them, such as Protagoras's pronouncement that "of all things, *anthrōpos* is the measure, of things that are, that they are, of things that are not, that they are not"[7] [80B1]) is the question of the philosophical support that might be marshaled in favor of them. What metaphysical and epistemological theories might be appealed to in order to support the view that morality is a matter of convention (*nomos*) and so that one who wants to follow nature would do best to avoid when he can the dictates of the *polis* if these are inimical to his own pleasure or welfare?[8] We have no fragments that suggest a "Sophistic metaphysics"[9]; and indeed anyone who propounded a genuine metaphysical theory might not be classified as a sophist in the first place.[10] But the history of Presocratic philosophy suggests a source for just such a skepticism: the atomism of Democritus.[11] This link between Democritus and sophistic social thought is made by Kerferd when he claims that

---

7. The translation of this fragment is controversial. Does Protagoras mean that *a* human being is the measure, or does he use *anthrōpos* collectively? Should *hōs* be translated "that" or "how"?

8. Consider this from Barnes: "Democritus's practical philosophy has no metaphysical or physical basis. Nor should we really expect it to have one. For what, after all, would a physical basis for ethics look like? Ethics and physics, so far as I can see, have no systematic interconnexion at all. . . . The long scholarly discussion of the possible 'materialistic foundation' of Democritus's ethics is empty: it follows a will-o'-the-wisp" (1979, II, 232). Barnes might agree that this is anachronistic; both the *Republic* and the *Nicomachean Ethics* offer examples of what "a physical basis for ethics" would look like, particularly if we keep in mind that "physics" for the classical Greeks means the study of nature, or what there is, and so included metaphysics.

9. One exception to this claim might be Gorgias. His arguments in *On Nature* clearly take on metaphysical assumptions adopted by Presocratic philosophers (Eleatics and others). But Gorgias's arguments seem primarily negative: No account of what it is to be can be given such that we can claim with certainty that anything is. See Kerferd (1955–1956) and (1981), 93–100; Mansfeld (1985); and de Romilly (1992), 95–97.

10. This is not to claim that the Sophists were not interested in scientific or mathematical issues; see Kerferd (1981), 39–44.

11. On Democritus and Antiphon, see Moulton (1974), who suggests both parallels and differences between the two, noting that although we probably cannot know which of these influenced the other (if indeed there was influence), the work of both suggests "probable doctrines 'in the air' in the late fifth century" (132). Plutarch's *Reply to Colotes* indicates that Colotes took the doctrines of Democritus and Protagoras to be related.

Hippias's comment in Plato's *Protagoras*, that "law . . . constrains us contrary to nature in many things" (*Protag.* 337d2-3) begins from a "starting point" that is "not different from that of Democritus" when he himself contrasted *nomos* and *physis* in his atomic theory.[12]

Democritus famously declared that sensory properties of physical objects are what they are by convention (*nomos*):

> By convention (*nomōi*) sweet and by convention (*nomōi*) bitter, by convention (*nomōi*) hot, by convention (*nomōi*) cold, by convention (*nomōi*) color; in reality atoms and void (ἐτεῇ δὲ ἄτομα καὶ κενόν). (68B9; cf. B125)

Moreover, in the passage in Sextus Empiricus in which the fragment appears, the claim is made that Democritus "sometimes did away with things appearing to the senses," presumably by denying that such things are real and declaring that they are merely "by convention."[13] Diogenes Laertius, who also quotes the fragment, adds that, according to Democritus, "in reality we know nothing; for truth is in the depths" (B117: ἐτεῇ δὲ οὐδὲν ἴδμεν· ἐν βυθῷ γὰρ ἡ ἀλήθεια). These pronouncements seemingly give us a skeptical Democritus, one whose skepticism is firmly grounded in his metaphysics. For if the only things that are in reality are atoms and void, then we cannot have genuine knowledge of physical objects because they are merely temporary combinations of atoms and void and known through sense experience.[14] This view of the skeptical Democritus is supported by one variant of the "by convention" fragment that has come down to us. Plutarch includes combination itself as one of the things that are "by convention": his version says, "for color is by convention and by convention sweet and by convention combination (*nomōi sunkrisin*)."[15] Thus

---

12. Kerferd (1981), 114.
13. See Sedley (1992), who argues that the discussion of Democritus is actually taken from Posidonius by Sextus.
14. See O'Keefe (1997) for a recent discussion that stresses Democritus's claims that "sensible qualities are, in some sense, unreal" (121). Their unreality lies, according to O'Keefe (and I think he is correct in this) in their not being intrinsic properties of atoms. But whether the unreality (in this sense) of sensible properties entails a strong skepticism (as Barnes seems to claim) remains to be seen. I return to the issue of Democritus on perception later in this chapter.
15. Plutarch, *Adv. Colot.* 1110F. For an extended discussion of the implications of this version of the fragment, see Wardy (1988). Furley (1993) accepts that Plutarch most likely wrote *sunkrisin*, but argues that it is nevertheless unlikely to be what Democritus himself actually wrote: "The word σύγκρισις seems to me likely to be anachronistic. It occurs in the *Timaeus*, but not in the B-fragments of the Presocratics nor in the Hippocratics (except in a spurious work), nor in Herodotus, Thucydides, or tragedy" (1993, 76–77, n.7).

Democritus could seem to be both in sympathy with and supplying a metaphysical basis for the skeptical views of certain of the Sophists. Protagoras, for instance, offers a claim that is in agreement with a skeptical interpretation of Democritus's assertion that truth is in the depths, when he says:

> Concerning the gods I am not able to know, either that they are or that they are not, nor how they appear. For the things preventing knowing are many: the unclarity of the matter and the shortness of a person's life. (80B4)

Note that neither Protagoras nor Democritus assert that there is no truth of the matter about such things; but both seem to deny that such truth can be grasped by human beings.[16]

One immediate objection to interpreting Democritus's claims about convention and his metaphysics as support for skeptical views like those of Antiphon and Protagoras is that Democritus himself provided an ethical theory. But it may be that Democritus's own views are grounded in an ethical skepticism, and that he himself thinks of ethical principles as no more than human *nomoi* to be adopted only if no other alternative is possible.

DEMOCRITUS'S ETHICAL CLAIMS

The majority of the fragments that have come down to us from Democritus deal with ethical issues, but it is difficult to cull from them a systematic theory.[17] The fundamental principle of Democritus's ethics is to be found in a

---

16. Compare this claim with Xenophanes B34. For a non-skeptical interpretation of Xenophanes, see Lesher (1978) and (1992, 159–166).

17. Any discussion of Democritus's ethics must deal with the vexed issue of the authenticity of the ethical fragments. This issue is complicated by the "Democrates" fragments and here I follow Kahn's account; see Kahn (1985), 2–4. As Kahn points out, the "Democrates" fragments (B35–115) should probably be used with care, as their authenticity is particularly open to question (this difficulty may be found in C.C.W. Taylor's [1967] interpretation of Democritus, which relies heavily on those fragments). Procopé (1989) discusses the origin and nature of such collections as the "Democrates" fragments. But see West (1969) for a more sanguine view of these fragments, and a suggestion of how they came to be collected. Stewart (1958) provides a good discussion of the possible role of the Cynics in preserving the ethical fragments, and points out that if the ethical fragments formed part of a Cynic collection, "they will not represent in many cases the style and organization of their author" (188). Stewart does not intend to offer an attack on the authenticity of the fragments, rather he offers "a rather more detailed and better defined warning for the exercise of a caution which others have already felt on other grounds" (187).

short summary provided by Stobaeus. After quoting B170 and B171, he says this about Democritus:

> He calls *eudaimonia* cheerfulness (*euthymia*) and well-being and harmony, due proportion and tranquillity. It arises by distinguishing and judging among pleasures (*ek tou diorismou kai tēs diakriseōs tōn hēdonōn*), and it is the finest and most beneficial thing (*kalliston te kai symphorōtatōn*) for humans. (68A167 = *Ped.* II.vii.3i)

Like other Greek moralists, Democritus finds happiness to be the ordered, contented, and cheerful life, and most of his ethical maxims are directions toward achieving this life as an end. Here is Clement quoting Democritus:

> The Abderites also taught that there is a goal of existence. Democritus, in his *Peri Telous* ("On Goals"), says that it is cheerfulness (*euthymia*), which he also called well-being (*euestō*); and he often adds, "For delight (*terpsis*) and joylessness (*aterpiē*) [are] the boundary-mark <of advantage and disadvantage>." (Clement, *Strom.* II. xxi.130.4 = 68B4; cf. B188)

All the Democritean ethical fragments seem to reach this conclusion, that the best and happiest life for a human being is a well-ordered one in which pleasures are moderate, and in which one seeks modest enjoyment.[18]

But Democritus also has things to say about *nomos*, occasionally seeming to contrast it with *physis*. In fragments 258, 259, and 260 he discusses the killing of dangerous persons or enemies:

> It is right (*chrē*) to kill anything contrary to justice (*para dikēn*) no matter the cost; . . . (68B258). Just as I have written about cunning beasts and animals, so it also seems to me right to act with respect to humans: one should kill an enemy according to the inherited laws in every society (*kata nomous tous patrious kteinein polemion en panti kosmōi*), in which law (*nomos*) does not prevent it; but the holy customs (*hiera . . . epichōria*) in each different country, treaties, and oaths are prohibitions. (68B259)

---

18. Barnes dismisses Democritus's ethical system on two grounds. First, he does not think it constitutes an ethical *theory* ("it does not pretend to tell us what, morally speaking, we ought to do, or how to live the moral life. It is a recipe for happiness or contentment, not a prescription for goodness"). Second, Barnes "do[es] not care for it"; he says he finds it "peculiarly unappetizing. Calm and placidity are tedious virtues; moderation in all things leads to a confoundedly dull life" (1979, vol. II, 231). For a more sympathetic account of Democritus's ethical views, see Farrar (1988).

The claim in B259 that one should kill enemies in accordance with the customs of the city where one happens to be would seem to echo Antiphon's claims about *nomos*: Democritus says that one should kill that which offends against justice, but the justifications for killing (and, hence, justice itself) may differ depending on the customs that certainly differ in different *poleis*. This accords with Antiphon's assertion in 87B4. But we should not be too hasty in thinking of Democritus as sympathetic to Antiphon's claim. For B260 goes on to say: "Anyone killing a highway robber or a pirate ought to go unpunished, whether doing it by his own hand, by exhortation, or by a vote." Here, there is no reference to justification being tied to the *nomoi* of different cities; Democritus seems to be issuing a universal claim about the justified execution of highwaymen and pirates. If this is correct, then the reference to justice in B258 ("It is right to kill anything contrary to justice no matter the cost"), must be to an objective justice, not to justice conceived of as the *nomos* of a particular *polis*.[19] A similar appeal to that which is objectively the case occurs in B264:

> Feel no more shame before men than before yourself; nor perform
> evil any more if no one is to know than if all men are: but feel shame
> most of all before yourself and establish this as a law (*nomos*) in your
> soul so as to do nothing unfitting. (B264)

Here Democritus clearly rejects the possibility that those things about which one ought to feel shame are simply a matter of social convention, to be avoided if no one knows what one has done (as Antiphon prescribes). Democritus, then, must assume that there is a way to avoid moral skepticism of the sort that grows out of conventionalism as adopted by Antiphon and Hippias. I think that this is indeed the case, and that seeing how Democritus avoids moral skepticism can help us see how he avoids more general skepticism as well, despite the claim that sensory qualities are "by convention" and are thus, strictly speaking, unreal.

Democritus relies on pleasure and pain (or joy and lack of enjoyment) as the mark of what one ought or ought not to do. We have already seen how B188 and B4 claim that joy and its absence are the boundary (*horos, ouros*) of advantage; Democritus is committed to the view that what is genuinely right will be good for oneself. Thus, one must have a correct account of what sorts of actions are likely

---

19. There is a possible reference to the distinction between nature and custom (though not quite in terms of *nomos* and *physis*) in B278. There Democritus contrasts nature (and necessity) with convention in the raising of children. While men and animals deem the raising of offspring to be ordained by nature and thus necessary rather than for some end, "for human beings it has been made a convention, so that something enjoyable actually comes from children" (there is a problem in the text here; I follow Natorp who reads τῷ δὲ ἀνθρώπῳ νόμιμον).

to be accompanied by pains or pleasures.[20] This account is not to be derived by examining the *nomima* of one's particular polis, but by the correct use of right thinking or reason (as *logos* is often translated[21]). Stobaeus makes this clear in A167 (quoted above) when he claims that for Democritus *euthymia* comes about "by distinguishing and judging among pleasures," and the crucial role of right reasoning in Democritus' ethics comes out particularly strongly in fragment 181:

> Making use of urgings and the persuasions of reasoning (*logou peithoi*) will appear stronger encouragement to virtue than law (*nomoi*) and necessity (*anagkē*). For someone who is impeded from injustice by law (*hypo nomou*) is likely to do wrong in secret, but one who has been guided to that which is right by persuasion is not likely to do anything discordant either in secret or openly. For this reason the man who acts rightly from both wisdom and knowledge (*synesei te kai epistēmē*) is at the same time courageous and straightforward (*andreios hama kai euthygnōmos*).

At first glance, one might be tempted to take *logos* here in the Sophistic manner, thinking of it as a means of persuasion that is separated from what is actually the case (as in Gorgias, for instance). But the claim at the end of the fragment, that one who is persuaded by *logos* acts well "from wisdom and knowledge," shows that Democritus must mean by *logos* reasoning or rational argument. In using both *sunesis* and *epistēmē* in this fragment, Democritus is aligning his views with traditional Presocratic accounts of knowledge and truth, rather than with Sophistic practices of rhetorical persuasion.[22] Clement tells us that, according to Democritus, "Medicine heals the diseases of the body, and wisdom (*sophiē*) clears the soul from passions" (B31—it is unclear whether this is paraphrase or quotation). Wisdom, the right use of reasoning, allows the soul to have the proper passions in the proper amount, so that one is not led

---

20. I am not claiming here that pleasure and the avoidance of pain are the end of the good life for Democritus; rather, my claim is that things one ought to pursue will be pleasurable and those one ought to avoid will be painful; pain and pleasure are marks through which one can determine whether or not an activity should be pursued. See Kahn (1985), 26–28; Vlastos (1995), 335–340.

21. I am not convinced that "reason" is the best translation of *logos* when dealing with Presocratic thinkers. Perhaps "reasoning" or "rational argument" might be better. The suggestion of a separate faculty here is tricky, particularly when dealing with Democritus. On the issue of the separation of the functions of soul into different faculties in Presocratic thought, see Kahn (1985).

22. See, for instance, Heraclitus's uses of *sunesis*. On Heraclitus's epistemological claims, and their connections with traditional Presocratic views about knowledge, see Lesher (1983) and Curd (1991).

astray by them. Democritus's contempt for people who are governed by passion is evident in his claim that:

> The courageous person is the one overcoming not only his enemies, but also pleasures. Some master cities, but are slaves to women. (68B214)

Failures of judgment result in needless pains:

> Of the things required by the body (*to skēnos*), all are easily available to everyone without difficulty and suffering: the things which require difficulty and suffering and make life distressing are not yearned for by the body but by misapplication [or: aimlessness] of judgment (*all' hē tēs gnōmēs kakothigiē*. (68B223; following the text as in DK)

Thus, it is proper reasoning and judgment that will prevent one from pursuing inappropriate desires, and that will guarantee that the pleasures one pursues will indeed be part of a life of enjoyment or *euthymia*. It is not enough just to choose the proper pleasures; Democritus seems to assert that one must choose them in a knowing manner. The correct relation between soul (knowledge) and body is set out in 68B187:

> It is appropriate for men to take more account of[23] their souls than of their bodies; for perfection of soul corrects the bad state of body, but strength of body without reasoning (*aneu logismou*) in no way makes the soul better. (68B187 = B36)

The "taking more account of the soul" of the first part of the fragment is explained in the second part: To do so is to gain and to maintain the power of reasoning (*logismos*); I assume that Democritus here has in mind correct reasoning.[24] Such reasoning will prevent the pursuit of useless or even harmful pleasures. As B74 (a "Democrates" fragment) puts it, "It is pleasant to receive nothing that does not confer advantage"; and knowledge of how to avoid the useless and pursue the useful is consonant with knowledge of which pleasures to pursue.[25] The life that

---

23. On this as the proper translation of λόγον ποιεῖσθαι, see C.C.W. Taylor (1967, 14).
24. Vlastos reads B187 as arguing that the correct way to do ethics is to have a correct physical account (i.e., an understanding of atoms and void). But see Taylor's criticisms of Vlastos's view in (1967), 14. Taylor's other criticisms of Vlastos also seem correct.
25. C.C.W. Taylor (1967) thinks that B74 and B188 are inconsistent: "the former . . . says that some things may be pleasant but not useful, which is a direct contradiction of our interpretation of fr. 188" (16–17). According to Taylor, B188 says that "something is useful if and only if it is pleasant" (16). I do not see that B74 says what Taylor says it does; it seems rather to suggest that to receive that which is not useful is not pleasant, which is perfectly consistent with his interpretation of B188. Taylor resolves the perceived contradiction by seeing B74 as concerned with individual pleasure while B188 is concerned with the pleasantness or unpleasantness of one's life as a whole. As I see no contradiction, I see no reason to assume that B74 and B188 differ in scope.

is devoted to the rational pursuit of these pleasures will be full of useful things and will be both composed and content, which is, I take it, Democritus's account of the life of *euthymia*.[26]

How does reasoning determine which desires are proper, or which pleasures should be pursued? And how is Democritus's account of proper reasoning in ethics connected with his view of the role of reasoning in epistemology? Was Democritus the kind of skeptic who could join with Sophists such as Antiphon and Hippias in backing the *physis*-based claims of the individual against the *nomos*-based claims of the *polis*? It is to these issues that I now turn.

DEMOCRITUS'S EPISTEMOLOGY

The basic claims (and problems) in Democritus's epistemology are laid out in a long passage in Sextus Empiricus:

> Democritus sometimes does away with the things appearing to the senses and says of them that none appears in accordance with truth but only in accordance with opinion, truth among the things that are being that there are atoms and the void. For he says, "By convention sweet and by convention bitter, by convention hot, by convention cold, by convention color: in reality atoms and void" [68B125 = B9]. That is to say, the perceptibles are thought and believed to be, but these things do not exist in truth, but only atoms and void do. In the *Confirmations*, even though undertaking to attribute trustworthy power to the senses, he is nevertheless found condemning them. For he says, "In reality we grasp nothing precisely, but only what shifts around in accordance with the disposition both of the body and of the things entering it and the things resisting it" [68B9]. And again he says, "Now, that in reality we do not understand how each thing is or is not has been shown in many ways" [68B10]. And in *On Ideas* he says, "it is necessary that a person know by this rule that he is separated from reality" [68B6], and again, "And it is clear from this argument too that in reality we know nothing about anything, but that belief is in each case a remolding (*all' epirusmiē hekastoisin hē doxis*)" [68B7]; and again, "it will indeed be clear that to know how each thing is in reality is bewildering" [68B8]. And in these passages he nearly (*schedon*) does away with apprehension, even if it is only the senses that he expressly attacks. But in the *Rules* he says that there are two kinds of knowing, one through the senses and the other through the understanding. The one through the understanding he

---

26. See Procopé (1989) for a comprehensive account of Democritus's views on the vital connection between politics and the best life for a human being.

calls genuine, witnessing to its trustworthiness in deciding truth; the one through the senses he names "bastard," denying it steadfastness in the discernment of what is true. He says in these words, "There are two forms of knowing, one genuine and the other bastard. To the bastard belong all these: sight, hearing, smell, taste, touch. The other, the genuine, has been separated from this" [68B11]. Then preferring the genuine to the bastard, he continues, saying, "Whenever the bastard is no longer able to see more finely nor hear nor smell nor taste nor perceive by touch, but something finer . . ." [68B11].[27] (Sextus Empiricus, *Adv. math.* vii. 135–139[28])

In this passage Sextus (or his source) claims that Democritus distinguishes between atoms and void, which are genuine or real, and what is reported by the senses and only apparent.[29] What is reported by sense perception is "by con-

---

27. Sedley suggests that in order to understand B11, we should remove the gloss between the two parts of the fragment, joining the two by a comma. He then suggests that we should "delete the comma after αἰσθάνεσθαι and accentuate the next word ἄλλ', 'other things' " (1992, 42; the argument about the passage extends from 39 to 42). The last words then read αἰσθάνεσθαι ἄλλ' ἐπὶ λεπτότερον. Sedley translates: "Of knowing there are two forms, the one genuine, the other bastard. And of the bastard kind this is the complete list: sight, hearing, smell, taste, touch. The one which is genuine, but separate from this one, is when the bastard one is no longer able either to see in the direction of greater smallness, nor to hear or smell or taste or sense by touch other things in the direction of greater fineness" (42; see also 42, note 59).

28. This treatment of Democritus is followed (in VII.140) by a shorter account of Democritus on the criteria from a certain Diotimus. This Diotimus says that for Democritus there are three criteria: appearance for what is non-evident, the concept for inquiry, and feelings for choice and avoidance. Sedley (1992, 43–44) argues that the Diotimus referred to is not the Democritean Diotimus of Tyre but the Stoic Diotimus who was a critic of Epicurus. Sedley suggests that Diotimus attributes the three criteria to Democritus in order to bolster the claim that Epicurus plagiarized from Democritus (among others). If Posidonius (another critic of Epicurus) is indeed the source of the passage in Sextus (see next note), then we should treat this second account of "Democritus" with caution; as Sedley puts it, "It looks like an attempt, on the flimsiest evidence, to show that Epicurus's three criteria of truth— αἰσθήσεις, προλήψεις, and πάθη—were not original to him but anticipated by Democritus" (44).

29. As always with the Presocratics, one should keep in mind the context of the fragments and the question of the philosophical aims of the person quoting the fragment. McKim (1984, 288) concludes that Sextus overemphasizes Democritus's skeptical tendencies in order to find support for his own views. This view is challenged by

(*continued on page 161*)

vention" *because* it is only apparent (or sensed) and not real.[30] A distinction between what is genuinely the case and what the senses report is a common Presocratic theme. It is found in Anaximenes' assertions that the first principle of everything is air (13B1, B2) and that the reality of everything reported by the senses is air that has been altered through condensation and rarefaction, in Parmenides' distinction between truth and the opinions of mortals, and in Empedocles' claim that the roots earth, water, air, and fire are genuine realities that "become" other things by running through each other, a process that humans class as "coming-to-be" (see 31B8, B9, B11, B12). Democritus is quite clear that atoms and void constitute reality (*eteē*) while all other "things" are the result of the mixture of atoms. Phenomena, having no nature as such to be known, are unknowable in the strict sense. Phenomena have no nature because they are merely temporary arrangements of atoms and void, and natures are genuinely real things that are not subject to coming-to-be and passing-away.[31] Because we do not have direct access to atoms and void, we are

---

29. (*continued from page 160*)
   Sedley (1992). Sedley carefully analyzes the text in Sextus, concluding that Sextus is actually quoting from Posidonius, and Sedley shows that in these passages Posidonius is demonstrating that in Democritus reason is the criterion, although, Sedley points out, Posidonius is also "quite happy to leave intact the 'no criterion' interpretation of Democritus" (39). Sedley suggests and argues for a coherent reading of the troublesome last line of B11. Although Sedley is not convinced that there was an overall Democritean view on the possibility of knowledge (see note 2, above), I shall suggest later in the chapter that Sedley's view supports a non-skeptical interpretation of Democritus. For a series of discussions of these issues with respect to Sextus Empiricus, see *Elenchos* 13 (fasc. 1–2), 1992: "Sesto Empirico e il Pensiero Antico." On Sextus Empiricus as a source for Democritus, see also Spinelli (1996) who claims that Sextus tends to use the Democritean material he deals with to show that Democritus was a dogmatist and that he cannot be a genuine forerunner of Pyrrhonian skepticism (Spinelli disagrees in part with Sedley on the source of *Adv. Math.* vii. 136–139).

30. The question of Democritus's exact views on the reliability of sense perception is a vexed one. Aristotle counts Democritus among those who say that "truth is in the appearance." But Democritus also seems to deny that the evidence of the senses is reliable, given the variability of sensory experience and the phenomenon of disagreement between persons about similar experiences. KRS (1983) conclude that "Democritus did indeed commit himself to a far-reaching skepticism about the reliability of the senses—if not, indeed, about the possibility of knowledge of any kind whatsoever" (411). Furley (1993) offers an account of Democritus on perception that does not require that we attribute skepticism to him.

31. I have discussed this notion of a nature in *The Legacy of Parmenides* (Curd, 1998), arguing that it is a fundamental part of Presocratic philosophical thought.

removed from reality (68B6). What is reported to us by the senses is suspect because the objects of perception are not literally real but rather conventional; that is, they are phenomenal.[32] Although we may believe we have knowledge gained on the basis of sense experience, we must realize that belief based on sense experience is not an instance of genuine knowledge, but rather of the bastard sort, because it is not connected in the proper way with what is real. Thus, by itself, it is not trustworthy.[33] In contrast, understanding (*dianoia* is the term in Sextus; but I suspect that it is Democritus's as well; he uses it in B155 and B191) connects with what is real (atoms and void). Because atoms and void are what is real, they have a nature, and are something in their own right (see B156). Knowledge of them is thus genuine and legitimate. Understanding allows us to claim correctly that there are atoms and void. The senses can tell us of the phenomenal characteristics of sensible objects—those characteristics that are "by convention."

There is, I think, in Democritus no questioning of the character of sensible objects. We are entitled to believe the evidence of the senses about the phenomena. The senses cannot tell us how things are by nature, for neither atoms nor void are proper objects of sense experience. But this does not mean that we can have no knowledge of the real nature of what there is. When the senses can no longer function, because of the smallness and fineness of what is to be perceived (atoms), a correspondingly finer, that is, more discriminating mode of cognition (understanding or reason) takes control.[34] Similar roles for the understanding are posited by other Presocratics. Heraclitus, for instance, claims that grasping the *logos* is a requirement for genuine understanding, and judging by *logos* is a fundamental requirement in Parmenides. For Democritus, sense perception is the starting point, but perception must be accounted for and explained by an understanding of the

---

32. The fact that such things are not genuine, but are only by convention does not mean that what is reported by the senses is necessarily false or that it is arbitrary or capricious. Reinhardt (1959, 82–88) argues that in Greek thought *nomos* should be understood in exactly this way, and he traces the use to Parmenides. Things are conventional because they are phenomenal, not because they are arbitrary or merely agreed upon by a society. Thus, the distinction between *nomos* and *physis* is primarily epistemological (and has this force in the atomists). It is only later that the sense "merely conventional" becomes attached to *nomos*. He is followed in this by Heinemann (1945).

33. The connection between what is known and what is real gives genuine knowledge its legitimacy. It is precisely this lack of connection with the genuine that makes the other form of *gnōmē* "bastard."

34. This claim is made explicit in Sedley's version of B11 (see note 26, above), but it can also be made even on the basis of the text as it stands.

nature of the genuinely real things. These metaphysically basic entities are atoms and the void, and it is they that account for the world reported to us by the senses because the character and arrangement of the particular atoms that make up a thing and the quantity of void included are the sources of the qualities of objects reported by the senses.[35] These qualities are the result of the temporary arrangements of atoms, and are not, in the technical sense of being metaphysically basic, real things; rather they are dependent and so are "by convention."

Democritus's denial that things that are "by convention" are real does not entail that what they are is a subjective matter, or that there is no truth about them.[36] There may be disagreements between perceivers about some properties of objects, but Democritus insists that perception is a function not only of the characteristics of the objects being perceived (determined in some sense by atoms and void) but also of the state of the perceiver, for perception involves a reshaping of the atoms that constitute the perceiver. When different perceivers have different atomic configurations of their sense organs (because of illness, or some other difference), the interactions will be different, and different sensations in different perceivers will be the result. But these

---

35. I provide a fuller account of the reality of atoms and void in Chapter V of *Legacy*, arguing that both atoms and void have natures and thus can be the objects of knowledge. See B156, together with Plutarch's explanation that "when [Democritus] declares that the thing is no more than the nothing, he is calling thing body and nothing void, and declaring that this too [void] has some nature and existence of its own" (Plutarch, *Adv. Colot.* 4.1109A = 68B156). See Theophrastus's account of the role of atoms and void in accounting for the sensed characters of physical objects: "he [Democritus] makes sweet that which is round and quite large, astringent that which large, rough, polygonal and not rounded" (*de Caus. Plant.* 6.1.6 = 68A129); Theophrastus also reports that the heaviness of lead is to be attributed to the number of atoms it has, while its softness depends on their even spacing with void. In contrast, iron has more void (and fewer atoms) and so is lighter than lead, but those atoms are spaced in such a way that it cannot be easily cut, because there are no long passages of void along which one could cut as in lead (*de Sensu* 62 = part of 68A135). Simplicius says that objects made up of sharp and very fine atoms in similar positions come to be hot and fiery; those made of atoms with the opposite character come to be cold and watery (*in Phys.* 36.3-6 = 67A14).

36. This point is made in Baldes (1978b, 1981) and also in Furley (1993). The claim that sweet and bitter are "by convention" should not be seen as incompatible with the view that there are properties of atoms that account for such characteristics. Thus, I disagree with Theophrastus's interpretation of the "by convention" passage and would reject his criticism of Democritus in 68A135.

differences in perceptual states do not entail that there are not, as a matter of fact, atoms of a certain size and shape in the object being perceived.[37] The characters "sweet" and "bitter" may not be real—they are simply the result of the effect of atoms in the sensed object on atoms in the perceiver, and so they are "by convention." There is, nevertheless, something that is real by nature—the atom itself.

The fundamental distinction here is between, on the one hand, what is genuinely real by being metaphysically basic, having a nature, deserving of the name "what is," and known by understanding, and, on the other hand, that which is in a dependent manner, real only "by convention," and the object of sense perception. Democritus is quite clear that the name "the real" actually applies only to atoms and void, for only they meet the criteria for genuine entities that were set out by Parmenides in the *Alētheia* section of his poem.[38] But other things—those things that we perceive—are constituted by atoms and void and thus have a derivative claim to reality. They are not genuine, for they are subject to change and to coming-to-be and passing-away through the shifting movements of the atoms. But they are nonetheless things that are grounded in atoms; their character is determined by the arrangements of the atoms that compose them and by the characters of the particular atoms themselves. Theophrastus, for instance, attributes the heaviness of lead to the fact that it contains little void; yet because the atoms in lead are evenly arranged, it is soft to the touch (*de Sensu* 62 = 68A135), and he reports that sweet and bitter are determined by the shapes of atoms (*de Sensu* 65-67 = 68A135). Thus, the properties of physical objects are ultimately traceable to atoms and void, though atoms and void themselves do not have these properties.[39] For instance,

---

37. See Furley (1993), 78. The exact details of Democritus's account of perception remain vague and are beyond the scope of this chapter; I do not discuss here the mechanics of perception for Democritus. He apparently follows Leucippus in claiming that objects give off effluences or *eidōla* that impinge on and interact with atoms in the perceiver. On Democritus's account of perception, see English (1915), Burkert (1977, who questions whether the *eidōla* are actually part of Democritus's theory of perception rather than part of his account of parapsychological phenomena), and Baldes (1978a, 1975). Baldes rejects the view that Democritus's theory of sight requires emanations from the eye of the perceiver as well as emanations from the sensed object.

38. For a discussion of this, see Chapter II of *Legacy*.

39. The question of whether Democritus attributed weight to the atoms them-selves still awaits a definitive answer. For discussions, see for instance, Chalmers (1997), Furley (1983), and O'Brien (1981). Even if atoms have weight, they certainly do not have softness, sweetness, or bitterness. On this aspect of Democritus's account, see also McDiarmid (1959).

a large round atom is not itself sweet-tasting, but, in interaction with the normal arrangement of atoms in the tongue and mouth of a perceiver, it can produce the sensation of sweetness.[40] These properties are thus not real, but "conventional." But to call them "conventional" does not imply that these properties are arbitrary or that it is merely a matter of agreement that things are soft or sweet, but rather the term is used to contrast their status with the genuine reality of atoms and void. When the senses have told us all they can about these things, reasoning or understanding takes over and theorizes how atoms and void could account for these characters, and so gives us insight into the objects reported by the senses. Thus, because each report of the senses can be explained by referring to atoms and void, Democritus can say, as Aristotle reports (*de An.* 1.2 404a28-29; *Met.* 4.5 1009b12-15) that all sense perceptions are true. This simply means that an account of each that explains its content can be given. The extant fragments and testimonia contain no precise explanation of how this process is supposed to work in the case of reports by the senses, but Democritus seems confident that it will.

Democritus claims that reasonings about pleasures (based perhaps on past experiences and on right judgments about the nature of persons, and the effects of certain atomic configurations on them) can tell us which pleasures are to be pursued and which avoided, so as to escape from those large swings between states (of pleasure and pain, I think) that Democritus so deplores.[41] B191 claims that "enjoyment comes to humans through moderation in joy and through due proportion in life: Deficiencies and excesses are apt to change the soul and to bring about large movements in it. Those souls which move across large intervals are neither steady nor cheerful."[42] As feeling beings we are attracted by pleasures and repelled by pains. But, it is only though the use of reasoning, the "something finer" than sensation, that we can understand that not all pleasures are to be pursued indiscriminately and all pains avoided. It is reasoning that

---

40. For a clear discussion of this issue, see Furley (1993).
41. This account is similar to C.C.W. Taylor's (1967), but differs from it in that I claim that the same process of reasoning or thinking is at work in both the ethical and the metaphysical cases. Democritus has a single epistemological process: Working out what is true in any case is done in the same way, whether one is searching for ethical or metaphysical truths. See also Couloubaritsis (1980) on *Nous* in Democritus. (By referring to atomic structures and to large fluctuations, I do not mean to endorse Vlastos's view of the connection between atomic physics and Democritean ethics. Rather, certain feelings of pleasure and pain produced by certain objects are to be traced to certain atomic structures and, thus, can be explained and understood. With this knowledge, one can either pursue or avoid similar objects in the future.)
42. For the proper interpretation, see C.C.W. Taylor, against Vlastos.

works out what pleasures we should seek out, and which pains we should shun. This is the process that is recommended in B187:

> It is appropriate for men to take more account of their souls than of their bodies; for perfection of soul corrects the bad state of body, but strength of body without reasoning (*aneu logismou*) in no way makes the soul better. (68B187 =B36)

This is the same mode of reasoning (*logismos*) that Democritus appeals to when he discusses our apprehension and knowledge of the world. In the epistemological fragments quoted by Sextus, Democritus uses such terms as *gnōmē*, *dianoia*, and *dianoesthai*. *Dianoesthai* also appears in B155 (the discussion of the cone cut by a plane parallel to its base). In B129 *noesthai* appears, and as Kahn remarks, "apparently refers to nonsensory cognition."[43] In fragments that are primarily ethical, Democritus uses *nous* (B175 and B282), *logismos* (B187 and B290), and *dianoia* (B191). *Logos* appears in B181, while B187 and B290 refer to *logismos*. The fact that most of these terms are found in both ethical and what we might call "purely epistemological" contexts indicates that the *same* process of thinking and working out the truth of the matter is operating in both sorts of cases.[44] In B187 (=B36), for instance, the knowledge and reasoning required is not limited to prudential claims or to the working out of what we might (anachronistically) call a practical syllogism. Indeed such reasoning *could not* be limited to prudential cases. Knowledge about atoms and void is essential here; we must know the true nature of a thing (in terms of atoms and void) in order to know what sorts of pleasures or pains it will cause. This epistemological side of Democritus's ethics appears clearly in B181, is implicit in Stobaeus's summary of Democritus's views in A167, and is surely part of B223. Genuine knowledge of sensory objects is presupposed by Democritus's non-skeptical ethics.

Although we may all take pleasure in different things to different extents, it is no less true that there is a truth to be known about what is and is not worthwhile (or useful) to pursue. A "Democrates" fragment appears to undermine this claim, but this appearance is deceptive:

> For all men the good and the true are the same; but pleasure differs one to another. (B69)[45]

---

43. Kahn (1985), 20.
44. Kahn remarks that "the fact that *logismos* is attested only in a practical sense is probably an accident of our documentation" (1985, 21, n.47).
45. As one of the fragments from the "Democrates" collection, and one for which there is no parallel in other, better-attested fragments, this fragment should perhaps be used with caution.

While, at first glance, this suggests a subjective account of pleasure, and, given pleasure's role in the good life, a subjective view of such a life, this is not, I think, what Democritus is claiming here (if indeed the fragment is genuine). There may be variations in perceptions and appreciations of pleasure, but without a genuine account of the range of pleasures and pains likely to be produced by certain things or actions, one cannot know what a good life is. If the good is the same for all, then pleasures and pains will have to be objective in a sense that depends on tracing their sources to atoms and void. This is inconsistent with any Sophistic appeal to a subjectivist or relativist distinction between *nomos* and *physis* in Democritus's ethics. Rather, Democritus's account of the good life requires that the good *polis* pursue the truth about what is best for its citizens, and undermines Antiphon's claim that the requirements of the individual can justify a rejection of the laws of the *polis*, because such laws are mere *nomoi*, to be avoided if one can. Other fragments support this view: B252 claims that the state that is well-conducted is the best means to success and B255 requires that the *polis* conduce to "companionship, mutual defense, and concord among the citizens."

In the same way, Democritus can insist that there is a truth of the matter to be found in epistemological contexts. Truth may be in the depths (B117) but this is not a denial that there is a truth to be known. According to Galen (in the context of his quotation of B125), Democritus composed a dialogue between the senses and the mind. Galen writes:

> when he [Democritus] brought charge against the senses, saying "by convention color, by convention sweet, by convention bitter, in reality atoms and void," he made the senses (*aisthēseis*) respond to the understanding (*dianoia*) this way, "Wretched *phrēn*, taking evidence from us do you throw us over? Our overthrow is your fall." (B125)

Galen quotes the convention claim as evidence that Democritus brought charges against the senses, and the overthrow response as evidence of counter-charges by the senses against the *phrēn*. The fragments that Sextus Empiricus quotes, including B7 which repeats the claim of B117 that in reality we know nothing about anything (*eteēi ouden ismen peri oudenos*), could be part of that dialogue. It is worth noting that B7 does not claim that our lack of knowledge is because "truth is in the depths" as the B117 version does, but rather adds that "belief is in each case a remolding—*epirhusmiē*." If the reference is to a change in atomic movements, here is an explanation for the "in the depths" claim of B117. Democritus's conversation between senses and understanding, referred to by Galen, suggests that Democritus was aware that neither reasoning nor the senses alone can be sufficient for knowledge: both must cooperate in any act of understanding. We cannot be certain of Democritus's intentions in these passages, but together they may imply that genuine knowledge must be composed of both sensory matter and intellectual activity.

Barnes considers and rejects a non-skeptical interpretation of Democritus's epistemology:

> we may find a positive epistemology for Democritus: "All knowledge rests on perception: and perception will not, directly, yield knowledge of what exists *eteēi*. But by perception we may come to know about what is *nomōi*, and intellectual attention to those sensual pronouncements will enable us to procure an inferential knowledge of genuine reality." Alas, that happy picture is mistaken. The *doxis epirhusmiē* [in B7] argument is resolutely skeptical; and B6, B7, B8, and B117 leave no room for any knowledge at all.[46]

If Barnes is right, my account of Democritus must be wrong. Barnes's strongest evidence is his interpretation of B7, for, as I have argued, the other fragments do not commit Democritus to skepticism. Barnes interprets the B7 assertion that "belief is in each case a remolding" as committing Democritus to the view that "belief is never anything more than atomic rearrangement." "But," according to Barnes, "if every belief is simply a cerebral alteration . . . then no belief can be rational. To put it crudely, causally determined cerebral mutations cannot be identical with rationally accepted beliefs."[47] But we need not accept this interpretation of B7. We have already seen how sense perception involves a "remolding" of the perceiver through the interactions of the atoms of the perceived object with those in the perceiver. That such remoldings follow regular patterns (in normal perceivers) seems to be a part of Democritus's account, and these regular patterns are the basis of rational belief. We are justified in accepting them, and when the pattern is broken, we look for reasons (such as an illness of

---

46. Barnes (1979), vol. II, 261. (I have omitted the paragraph break before the penultimate sentence.)

47. Barnes (1979), vol. II, 258–259. Barnes would reject any materialist account of mind apparently on the grounds that if beliefs are physical states that are caused, then they cannot satisfy the justification condition for knowledge. Barnes (seemingly approvingly) cites Bertrand Russell's argument (in Barnes's words) "that naive realism leads us to accept the assertions of modern science; and that modern science then proves realism false. Realism is false if it is true; hence it is false. And if science rests on realism, then it is built on sand" (261). Barnes then says "the parallel with Democritus is plain." But Russell's argument is not valid (because "leads to," in the first premise, does not mean "entails") and so cannot support his (or Barnes's) conclusion. Barnes implies that, for Democritus, "atomism rests upon the senses." But this is false. Atomism (like all Presocratic cosmologies) may begin with the world reported by the senses, but there is a role for reasoning acting independently of perception to play here (as there is in Heraclitus, Parmenides, Anaxagoras, and Empedocles).

the perceiver) to explain that break. The causal connection (arrived at through reasoning) gives one the best possible reason for accepting that a remolding of this sort is a justified belief. We don't *know* that honey is sweet on the basis of this remolding, because, in truth (or, in reality), the honey is not sweet, and honey is not the sort of thing of which we can have genuine knowledge. But the sweetness is phenomenal, or "by convention," and we can explain it by reference to the character of the atoms that constitute the honey, and are thus justified in believing that the honey is sweet. We are separated from reality (B6 and B117) and it is difficult (and even bewildering) to know about honey (B8) because it is difficult to know about atoms. Knowledge about atoms is inferential, but Democritus claims (in B11) that such inference is possible. That inference, the result of the use of the "finer," genuine knowing, itself would result in a remolding which constitutes the basis of a knowledge claim. We will, perhaps, never know the relations that hold among the works that Sextus Empiricus refers to as the *Confirmations*, the *On Ideas*, and the *Rules*. But the evidence from Sextus, and from Galen, indicates that Democritus realized that any coherent atomistic account of knowledge would have to accord equal importance to both the senses and reason or understanding. This will involve a delicate balancing act (as B125 shows), but taking the evidence of the epistemological and the ethical fragments, we are, I think, justified in believing that Democritus thought it could be done.

I have argued that Democritus was not a skeptic. When properly understood, it is clear that Democritus's ethical theory requires genuine knowledge, and that Democritus was not an ethical skeptic in the Sophistic mold. Moreover, none of the epistemological fragments unequivocally commits Democritus to epistemological skepticism and most can be plausibly understood as implying that genuine knowledge is possible. Even the claims that sensible characters are not real but are only by convention and that "truth is in the depths" can be understood in ways that do not entail skepticism. Democritus had an atomist metaphysics and an atomist epistemology. In his epistemology both sense and reason play crucial roles, and the result of their proper use is genuine knowledge.

Chapter 9

The Truth of Antiphon's *Truth*

Michael Gagarin

My starting point for this chapter is the title the fifth-century thinker Antiphon gave to his main theoretical work, *Alētheia* or *Truth*. What did Antiphon mean by *Alētheia*? Can this title help us interpret any of the surviving fragments, especially the papyrus fragments? These questions form part of a larger set of issues concerning truth and language in the works of many pre-Platonic thinkers, especially the sophists, and the strong reaction to their views we find in Plato. Plato had a very strict idea of the nature of truth, which for him included such features as the law of non-contradiction and the requirement that one be able to give a rational account of truth, and he was highly critical of the less rigorous views of earlier thinkers. "Protagoras's *Truth*," he maintains, "is true to nobody" (*Theaetetus* 171C), rhetoric deals in falsehood (*Gorgias* 458e-59c, etc.), and his predecessors honored probabilities more highly than truth (*Phaedrus* 267A, 272D-273C).

These well-known criticisms are not my concern here. Rather, I want to examine the pre-Platonic sense of truth in the context of a tradition of thinkers going back to Hesiod who understood truth quite differently from Plato. To this end we must put aside Platonic notions and examine the sophists in their own terms and in terms of this tradition. I will therefore begin by looking briefly at Hesiod, Parmenides, and the sophists, especially Protagoras, and then consider the works of Antiphon. I will argue that Antiphon is promoting a view of truth as multiple and ambivalent that goes back to Hesiod, who first proposed a pattern of language in which a single *logos* (word or concept) is analyzed into opposing meanings which then are seen to merge in a problematic and unstable synthesis. For Hesiod, the multiplicity of language—and therefore of truth—corresponds to the multiplicity of the real world[1]; for the sophists and orators this ambiguity inheres both in *logoi* (language, argument, rhetoric) and in *erga* (things or events).

For the Greeks up through the fifth century, at least, truth was always a property of *logoi* (statements or propositions), and the truth of a *logos* was determined by its correspondence to some external reality, whether this was

---

1. I leave aside here the many complex and interesting issues surrounding the notion of "reality." In my view, even if reality is, say, a social construction, the term usefully conveys a meaningful notion. See further, Searle (1995), 149–197.

the observable, material world or some deeper, unobservable reality.[2] When Hesiod, for example, has the Muses assert that they know how to tell lies that are like the truth but also how to sing the truth when they wish (*Th.* 27-28), he apparently is distinguishing between stories that are made up and stories that correspond to actual events, including those that we would label "myths." Even passages such as his description of Hades (*Th.* 720-28) presumably correspond to reality as he conceives it. The Presocratics continued this task of describing a deeper, unobservable reality with such claims (apparently) as Thales's that everything is water; and the trend culminates in Parmenides's "Way of Truth (*Alētheia*)" describing a reality (*esti*) that "must be."

The sophists quite consciously directed their intellectual activity away from these rather abstract speculations of the Presocratics and toward areas we would call ethics, political and social theory, religion, myth, and education. Parmenides was the obvious target of works like Gorgias's *On Not Being* which, whatever its true purpose, must have been intended in part as a parody of Parmenides's reasoning. Moreover, Protagoras certainly aimed his work entitled *Truth* (*Alētheia*)[3] at least in part at Parmenides's Way of Truth, and the first sentence of Protagoras's work, the famous *homomensura* assertion, clearly points to a rejection of the entire thrust of Parmenides's thinking, and in particular his view of truth. And it seems almost certain that Antiphon's *Truth* (*Alētheia*) should be understood within the same traditions as Protagoras's.[4] In the third papyrus fragment

---

2. For other views of truth and a survey of modern views, see Haack (1978, 86–134). For truth as correspondence see Searle (1995, esp. 199–226).

3. The title *Alētheia* is given only by Plato (*Tht.* 161C, etc.). Since it clearly serves Plato's purpose in the context of the *Theaetetus*, it has been argued that the title is Plato's own invention (see Untersteiner [1961–1962], 1.72). But Plato's persistent mocking of the title *Alētheia* can also be taken as evidence for its authenticity; otherwise (as Heitsch [1969/1976] argues), Plato's use of it would be perverse. The alternate title for Protagoras's work is *Kataballontes*, for which see later in this chapter. Protagoras may have given his book both titles.

4. We have no good evidence for dates of Protagoras's and Antiphon's treatises, but it is very likely that Protagoras's work is the earlier. In a recent plausible interpretation of Antiphon's views on morality and self-interest, Nill (1985) takes them to be a response to Protagoras. The fourth-century sophist and cynic philosopher Antisthenes is also reported to have written a work entitled *Alētheia*, of which Diogenes says that it especially was written in a rhetorical style learned from Gorgias: "He [Antisthenes] first studied with the orator Gorgias, from whom he took the rhetorical style (τὸ ῥητορικὸν εἶδος) found in his dialogues, especially in *Truth* and in *Protreptics*," D.L. 6.1; cf. 6.16). Socrates's pupil Simmias is also reported to have written an *Alētheia* (D.L. 2.124).

of this work (44C),[5] Antiphon speaks of "testifying the truth" μαρτυρεῖν τἀληθῆ 44C I.3-4, I.17-18, I.38-II.2), which must imply a fairly straightforward correspondence between the witness's *logos* and reality, or what really happened. In choosing the title *Truth*, however, I think Antiphon intended more than this, and I shall suggest later in this chapter that the work as a whole conveyed the view that the reality to which a true *logos* corresponds is complex and ambivalent, and, consequently, the *logos* itself is similarly complex and ambivalent. Thus, I shall argue, although Antiphon assumes a correspondence theory of truth, his title *Truth* incorporates an intentional ambiguity: The truth of Antiphon's *Truth* is that there is more than one reality, and thus more than one truth. A true *logos* must comprehend more than one truth and more than one true *logos*.

The first suggestion that a *logos* may be ambivalent because the reality to which it corresponds is ambivalent can be found in Hesiod's discussion of *eris* at the beginning of the *Works and Days*.[6] After a short prologue (1–10) ending with the assertion, "I would speak the truth" (ἐτήτυμα μυθησαίμην, Hesiod declares (11–13) that there is not, after all,[7] one *eris* ("strife") but two *erides*, one good, the other evil. The first descriptions of these two *erides* maintain this opposition, but in the second part of the passage (20–26) the distinction between the two begins to break down, and it becomes evident that the two poles, good and evil, are collapsing into one another. Thus, *eris* first becomes two *erides* and then these turn out to be so similar that in the end we have a single *eris* (which is also two). Moreover, the verbal ambivalence of the word *eris* corresponds to a similar ambivalence in the real world, where the division between strife and striving, constructive and destructive competition, and harmful and beneficial activities in general, ultimately collapses into a nexus of sameness and difference. Word and reality do in fact correspond, because the ambivalence of the one corresponds to the ambivalence of the other.

This passage of Hesiod sets a pattern of analysis that recurs in later thinkers: A unity divides into opposites which then recombine into a new unity, resulting in a complex tension among the unity and its parts. The few surviving fragments of Protagoras contain no clear statement of the pattern, but there are

---

5. 44 is the traditional Diels-Kranz numbering, but the standard text is now Decleva Caizzi's (1989), which includes the most recent papyrus fragment (*POxy* 3647). There are English translations in Ostwald (1990, 293–296), and Gagarin and Woodruff (1995, 244–247). The new fragment has necessitated a reordering of the three main fragments. Following Decleva Caizzi, I shall use the numeration 44A, 44B, and 44C; in Diels-Kranz and other editions before 1989, these fragments were numbered 44B, 44A, and 44 (or 44C), respectively.

6. For a fuller treatment of this passage, see Gagarin (1990).

7. With most scholars (e.g., Verdenius [1985], *ad loc.*) I take οὐκ ἄρα as an indication that Hesiod is correcting *Th.* 225–226, where *eris* is portrayed as an unambiguous evil.

hints that it may have guided his understanding of the *homomensura* statement.[8] One example Protagoras himself apparently used in explicating this sentence is that of a wind that appears hot to some and cold to others (*Tht.* 152b-c). Protagoras may have explained that each perception, and thus each *logos*, is true because the wind is somehow both hot and cold. In terms of Hesiod's pattern, a single wind is simultaneously both a hot wind and a cold wind, and these two apparent opposites are thus one and the same wind. We cannot know whether Protagoras gave this explanation himself, but a Hesiodic view of ambivalent truth would also be consistent with such reported Protagorean views as "contradiction does not exist," or "it is impossible to tell a lie."

Also revealing is the fact that the work Plato calls *Alētheia* was otherwise known as *Kataballontes* (sc. *Logoi*) or *Overthrowing Arguments*. This title employs a metaphor from wrestling and implies a struggle, an *agōn* between *logoi*.[9] The present tense implies that the struggle is not completed, so that no single *logos* necessarily emerges the final victor. This notion may have provoked the complaint of a Hippocratic author (*On the Nature of Man* 1):

> Someone would best understand this [that others are wrong], if he were present when they were debating (*antilegein*). For when the same speakers debate in front of the same audience, the same man never wins the debate three times in a row, but sometimes one wins, sometimes another, and sometimes whoever happens to have the most fluent tongue in addressing a crowd. And yet someone who says he has correct knowledge of the facts should, in all justice, always make his own argument (*logos*) prevail, if indeed he knows what is the case and demonstrates it correctly. But I think that out of ignorance such people overthrow (*kataballein*) themselves by the wording of their arguments.[10]

---

8. Scholars have advanced widely diverse interpretations of this fragment; for a good survey, see Kerferd (1981, 83–110).

9. The sophists and their contemporaries often used wrestling imagery to describe intellectual conflict. Heitsch (1969/1976, 299 n.4) gives examples of καταβάλλω applied to arguments in other authors; for other wrestling imagery during this period, see Stanford's (1958) note on *Frogs* 775 and O'Sullivan (1992, 65) with notes. None of these scholars notes the Hippocratic discussion quoted here although it seems most relevant to Protagoras.

10. γνοίη δ ' ἂν τις τόδε μάλιστα παραγενόμενος αὐτέοισιν ἀντιλέγουσιν· πρὸς γὰρ ἀλλήλους ἀντιλέγοντες οἱ αὐτοὶ ἄνδρες τῶν αὐτέων ἐναντίον ἀκροατέω οὐδέποτε τρὶς ἐφεξῆς ὁ αὐτὸς περιγίνεται ἐν τῷ λόγῳ ἀλλὰ ποτὲ μὲν οὗτος ἐπικρατέει, ποτὲ δὲ οὗτος, ποτὲ δὲ ᾧ ἂν τύχῃ μάλιστα ἡ γλῶσσα ἐπιρρυεῖσα πρὸς τὸν ὄχλον. καίτοι δίκαιόν ἐστι τὸν φάντα ὀρθῶς γινώσκειν ἀμφὶ τῶν πρηγμάτων παρέχειν αἰεὶ ἐπικρατέοντα τὸν λόγον τὸ ἑωυτοῦ, εἴπερ ἐόντα

(*continued on page 175*)

Protagoras's title seems to imply that *logoi* are continually struggling against each other and any final truth must incorporate this struggle. Each *logos* may nonetheless correspond to (an aspect of) reality, as in the example of the hot and cold wind: because the wind is both, then each *logos* (the wind is hot; the wind is cold) corresponds to a reality. Both *logoi* are true, as is the overall *logos* (the wind is hot and cold) because all these *logoi* correspond to reality.

These speculations about Protagoras are intended only as background for Antiphon's view of truth,[11] for which we need to examine not just the fragments of his *Truth*, but also his other works, especially the Tetralogies.[12] These are intellectual exercises modeled on a courtroom contest (*agōn*); in two speeches by each litigant Antiphon explores arguments about issues that are relevant not only to legal cases but also to other intellectual debates of the period. The *Second Tetralogy*, in particular, raises interesting questions about the ability of a *logos* to express the truth of reality; the *First Tetralogy*, focuses specifically on the relationship of truth to likelihood or probability (*eikos*).[13]

The issue in the *First Tetralogy* is one of fact: Did the defendant murder the victim, or did someone else do it? Both sides acknowledge that direct evidence of the facts would be best, but in the absence of good direct evidence,[14] probability arguments are necessary. It is clear that both parties conceive of truth in this case as the account that corresponds to the facts; they only disagree about what these facts are. The reader has no sure guide to the truth, since no good external evidence is introduced and no verdict is delivered in any of the

---

10. (*continued from page 174*)

γινώσκει καὶ ὀρθῶς ἀποφαίνεται. ἀλλ'ἐμοί γε δοκέουσιν οἱ τοιοῦτοι ἄνθρωποι αὐτοὶ ἑωυτοὺς καταβάλλειν ἐν τοῖσιν ὀνόμασι τῶν λόγων αὐτέων ὑπὸ ἀσυνεσίης. Cf. the astronomers mentioned by Gorgias (*Helen* 13), "who replace opinion with opinion: displacing one but implanting another, they make incredible, invisible matters apparent to the eyes of opinion."

11. Thucydides, who was said in antiquity to have been Antiphon's pupil, has even more complex views about the relationship of *logos* and reality (see Parry's fine study [1957/1981]); Gorgias, on the other hand, seems more interested (in *Helen*) in a *logos's* power to move or persuade others than in its truth.

12. My use of the Tetralogies to illuminate the sophistic work *Truth* rests on two assumptions: that the orator and the sophist are, in fact, the same Antiphon, and that he is the author of the Tetralogies. The arguments for unity on both these points are sketched in Gagarin (1997, 5–6, 8–9). I will present these more fully in a future work. We have no certain date for the Tetralogies or *Truth*. Antiphon's three courtroom speeches were probably composed in 420–411. Many would date the Tetralogies to the 430s or even 440s and would put *Truth* a bit later, perhaps in the 420s.

13. For *eikos* in the *First Tetralogy*, see Gagarin (1994).

14. There is secondhand and perhaps biased testimony that the victim's attendant before dying identified the defendant as the killer.

Tetralogies.[15] We must therefore be guided by the litigants' speeches alone; and as in a dramatic *agōn*, we must be skeptical of both litigants' claims to speak the truth. Thus, Antiphon explores statements of fact and probability arguments and the interaction between these without reaching a conclusion about these claims of truth. Any reader may assess the conflicting *logoi*, but the overall truth of the work cannot rest with only one side.

The *Second Tetralogy* begins (3.1.1) with an apparent nod to the *First Tetralogy*, as the plaintiff distinguishes between cases where the facts (*pragmata*) are agreed on and cases where they are in dispute, adding that in this case he expects no dispute.[16] Antiphon then gives a simple statement[17] of these facts: "my boy, struck in the side by a javelin thrown by this young man on the playing field, died on the spot. Therefore I charge him not with intentional but with unintentional homicide."[18] As expected, the defendant accepts the *pragmata* as stated, but to the plaintiff's surprise and chagrin, he disputes their interpretation, arguing that the boy caused his own death by running out to pick up the javelins at the wrong time; thus, it was not the thrower who erred but the boy.[19] This makes the boy in essence his own killer, and as a result the killer has in fact already been punished! Thus, the question in the *Second Tetralogy* is not factual (what happened?) but interpretative: given certain facts, is the defendant guilty?[20]

---

15. Unless we take the defendant's departure during the *Third Tetralogy* as a tacit admission that his case will lose; cf. Gagarin (1997) ad 4.4.1. An alleged alibi is introduced too late in the case (2.4.8) to be conclusive.
16. This is essentially the position of the *First Tetralogy*, that if the facts were known and agreed to, there would be only one corresponding *logos*.
17. For the style of this sentence in comparison with the more elaborate style of the rest of the argument, see Zuntz (1939).
18. In Athenian law unintentional homicide was punishable by exile for one year.
19. The possibility is raised that a supervisor may have erred in sending the boy out (3.3.6, cf. 3.4.4), but Antiphon makes little of this and apparently wants to exclude it from our consideration (while making us aware of the possibility).
20. Perelman (1963) makes a distinction (esp. 101) between "judicial proof," which is "concerned only with fact," and "juridical proof," which is concerned with interpretation of the law. The same difference can be seen in the different approaches to the defense of Helen: Gorgias does not argue, as others like Stesichorus had, for a different set of facts (i.e., that Helen never went to Troy); instead he accepts the traditional story that Helen did sail to Troy but proposes a different interpretation of these facts. Gorgias's *Palamedes*, where the issue is factual (did Palamedes betray the Greeks?) forms a pair with *Helen* much like Antiphon's first two Tetralogies. This dichotomy of fact and interpretation is the basis for later *stasis* theory, though it is unclear whether the sophists exerted any direct influence on the later rhetoricians who developed this theory.

The defendant states his position at the beginning of his argument (3.2.3): his son "threw [his javelin] but did not kill anyone, according to the truth of what he did" (κατά γε τὴν ἀλήθειαν ὧν ἔπραξεν). This is essentially the same expression the defendant in the *First Tetralogy* used in asserting that he trusts in "the truth of the things that were done by me" (τῇ ἀληθείᾳ τῶν ἐξ ἐμοῦ πραχθέντων). There the expression implies the existence of an unambiguous "factual truth," a single truth corresponding directly to the facts, but in the *Second Tetralogy*, where the expression is more common,[21] each of the two opposed *logoi* (the youth killed the boy; the boy killed himself) corresponds directly with the same *pragmata*.[22]

We have clearly moved beyond the plaintiff's assumption that an accepted set of facts will lead to a single interpretation or the view that a direct correspondence with the facts will be sufficient to determine truth. But correspondence is not insignificant, as the defendant immediately makes clear with his next argument (3.2.4): "If the javelin had hit and wounded the boy because it carried outside the boundaries of its proper course, then we would have no argument (*logos*) against the charge of homicide." In other words, if the *pragmata* were a little different, the defendant's *logos* corresponding to those facts would necessarily be different. This implies that each speaker's *logos* is to some extent constrained by the facts, and that the number of *logoi* corresponding to the facts, though perhaps more than one, is limited.

Must we then consider both *logoi* true? Is one more true than the other? Or, as these are court cases, must we become jurors and vote for one of them? And if so, on what grounds should we decide? Perhaps with such questions in mind, Antiphon has the defendant tell the jurors at the beginning of his second speech (3.4.1–2): "your task is to recognize that we litigants judge a matter from our own point of view,[23] and we each naturally assume our own case is just. You, however, must examine the facts impartially, for the truth of these facts is only discernible from what each side says."[24] In other words, the jurors

---

21. 3.2.3, 3.2.10, 3.3.3, 3.4.1-2; cf. Ant. 5.3.
22. One could, of course, distinguish the two cases by further precision of the *prag-mata*—e.g., by adding "at the wrong time" to either "the young man threw" or "the boy ran out"—but Antiphon seems to want to retain a single statement of the facts for both sides.
23. For *eunoia* as a natural bias, cf. Thucydides's complaint that eyewitnesses may differ because of *eunoia* or *mneme* (1.23.3).
24. ὑμᾶς δὲ χρή, γιγνώσκοντας ὅτι ἡμεῖς μὲν οἱ ἀντίδικοι κατ' εὔνοιαν κρίνοντες τὸ πρᾶγμα εἰκότως δίκαια ἑκάτεροι αὐτοὺς οἰόμεθα λέγειν, ὑμᾶς δὲ ἴσως ὁρᾶν προσήκει τὰ πραχθέντα· ἐκ τῶν λεγομένων γὰρ ἡ ἀλήθεια σκεπτέα αὐτῶν [sc. τῶν πραχθέντων] ἐστίν.

must decide the truth of this case from the two *logoi* alone, and in view of the fact that each *logos* corresponds to the same *pragmata*, the jurors will have to determine this truth by the relative coherence of the two *logoi*. There is no other basis for their decision. On the other hand, a verdict is only necessary in a real case, and though we readers may be tempted to try to decide the case ourselves, in fact no final truth is ever determined.

In the end, therefore, the truth of the *Second Tetralogy* lies not in the *logos* of either litigant alone, nor in some choice between them, but rather in a dialectical tension between the two arguments. This is the same pattern we saw in Hesiod: An initial unity consisting of a single *logos* or statement of facts and a single interpretation of them (the defendant threw his javelin and killed my son) divides into opposed interpretations, both corresponding to these facts (the young man killed the boy, the boy killed himself). But in the Tetralogy as a whole these two *logoi* collapse into the larger truth that both the thrower and the victim (and perhaps others as well) are in some sense responsible for the death, and the defendant is both guilty and innocent. The truth of the *Second Tetralogy* is thus a *logos* about the complexity of shared responsibility, and (we should further understand) the ambivalent truth of this *logos* corresponds to an ambivalent truth about the real world, that events have complex causes and responsibility often belongs to more than one agent.

Against this background it is now time to turn to Antiphon's *Truth*. This work began, "Someone who says one thing does not in fact have one mental concept, nor is there for him one thing, neither any of those things the one who sees best sees with his sight nor any of those things the one who knows best knows with his mind" (fr. 1).[25] Morrison follows Galen in understanding the importance of this statement to lie in the opposition between cognition and sense perception implied in the neither/nor expression at the end. He also understands that the sentence makes a claim about language: A single *logos* does not correspond to either a single thought or a single perception. Antiphon thus appears to be saying that someone who speaks a single *logos* has more than one mental concept, and that more than one thing in reality corresponds to that *logos*.

If in fact Antiphon here associates the complexity of things, of mental concepts, and of *logoi*, this suggests that the work entitled *Truth*, which this statement introduces, is not intended to present a single unequivocal statement

---

25. ἕν τῷ λέγοντι οὐδέ γε νοῦς εἷς, ἕν τε οὐδὲν αὐτῷ οὔτε ὧν ὄψει ὁρᾷ <ὁ ὁρῶ>ν μακρότατα οὔτε ὧν γνώμη γιγνώσκει ὁ μακρότατα γιγνώσκων. The text of this fragment from Galen is uncertain. I follow Morrison (1963/1976), whose text and interpretation are vast improvements over Diels and Kranz and are accepted by, for example, Guthrie (1971, 202–203). Even with Morrison's text, however, the sense is not easy to extract from the Greek.

of a truth, such as that *physis* (nature) is more real than *nomos* (law, custom), as scholars have often thought,[26] but rather presents a complex *logos* about a multiple truth. I shall examine three possible examples of ambivalent truth in the papyrus fragments: the relationship between Greek and Barbarian, the relationship between *physis* and *nomos*, and the idea of justice.

> **44A.** <The laws (?)[27] of nearby communities> we know and respect, but those of communities far away we neither know nor respect. We have thereby become barbarians[28] toward each other, when by nature (*physis*) we are all at birth in all respects equally capable of being both barbarians and Greeks.
>
> We can examine those attributes of nature that are necessarily in all men and are provided to all to the same degree, and in these respects none of us is distinguished as foreign or Greek. For we all breathe the air through our mouth and through our nostrils, and we laugh when we are pleased (col. 3) in our mind or we weep when we are pained, and we take in sounds with our hearing, and we see by the light with our sight, and we work with our hands and we walk with our feet.

Clearly, one aim of these remarks is to challenge the opposition that by Antiphon's day was entrenched in Athenian thought between Greek and barbarian—two mutually exclusive and exhaustive categories that are positively and negatively charged respectively. When we consider "the attributes of nature," according to Antiphon, the opposition disappears; no one is Greek or barbarian. The fragment seems to have continued (col. 4) with an account of the historical differentiation of the two groups by means of *nomoi* (laws and customs), but even if it did not, the opposition Greek/barbarian is clearly a matter of *nomos* and does not exist in *physis*.

The majority of scholars[29] understand the thrust of these remarks to be that the natural similarity of all people is more real than the difference in law and custom, though Ostwald (1990) has argued that Antiphon intends to give equal weight to both perspectives. But there is another perspective here too, for

---

26. For good summaries of earlier views, see Ostwald (1990) and especially Narcy (1989).
27. The intelligible papyrus text begins in mid-sentence; an alternative suggestion for "laws" is "gods." My translations are slightly modified from Gagarin and Woodruff (1995, 244–247).
28. "Barbarian" (*barbaros*) originally designated anyone who did not speak Greek, in other words, a foreigner. In the fifth century it gradually acquired its negative connotations.
29. A recent example is Furley (1981, 90).

Antiphon also asserts that "we" (Greeks) "have become barbarians" (*bebar-barōmetha*). In other words, an original identity, based on *physis*, became an opposition by means of *nomos*, but is now once more an identity, as we Greeks are also barbarians—the familiar pattern of unity divided into opposites re-combining into a more complex unity: (we) Greek-barbarians. And the pattern may be even more complex if Antiphon is evoking the ambivalence of current Greek views of barbarians as both better and worse than Greeks.[30]

> **44B.** Justice (*dikaiosynē*), therefore, is not violating the rules (*nomima*) of the city in which one is a citizen. Thus a person would best use justice to his own advantage if he considered the laws (*nomos*) important when witnesses are present, but the conse-quences of nature (*physis*) important in the absence of witnesses. For the requirements of the laws are supplemental but the require-ments of nature are necessary; and the requirements of the laws are by agreement and not natural, whereas the requirements of nature are natural and not by agreement. (col. 2) Thus someone who vio-lates the laws avoids shame and punishment if those who have joined in agreement do not notice him, but not if they do. But if someone tries to violate one of the inherent requirements of nature, which is impossible, the harm he suffers is no less if he is seen by no one, and no greater if all see him; for he is harmed not in reputation (*doxa*) but in truth (*alētheia*).
>
> I inquire into these things for the following reason, that most things that are just according to law are inimical to nature. For rules have been made for the eyes what they should (col. 3) and should not see, and for the ears what they should and should not hear, and for the tongue what it should and should not say, and for the hands what they should and should not do, and for the feet where they should and should not go, and for the mind what it should and should not desire. Thus the things from which the laws dissuade us are in no way less congenial or akin to nature than the things toward which they urge us. For living and dying both belong to nature, and for humans living is the result of advantageous things whereas dying is the result of disadvantageous things. (col. 4) The advan-

---

30. Cf. Euripides, *Orestes* 485–486, where the same verb is used with some irony as the resumed difference between the two categories is called into question (Tyndareus accuses Menelaus of having become "barbarized" because he continues to support his nephew Orestes, whereas Menelaus replies that it is Greek to honor one's fam-ily). Cassin (1992) has a very interesting discussion of the complexity of conflict-ing attitudes toward barbarians in *Orestes* and in Antiphon's fragment.

tages laid down by the laws are bonds on nature, but those laid down by nature are free. Thus things that bring pain do not, according to a correct account (*orthos logos*), help nature more than things that bring joy. Nor would things that bring pain be more advantageous than things that bring pleasure; for things that are in truth advantageous ought not to harm but to benefit. Thus things that are advantageous to nature. . . .

. . . and those who (col. 5) defend themselves when attacked and do not themselves begin the action, and those who treat their parents well even when they have been badly treated by them, and those who let their opponent swear an oath when they have not sworn one themselves. One would find many of the things I have mentioned inimical to nature; and they involve more pain when less is possible and less pleasure when more is possible, and ill treatment which could be avoided. Thus, if the laws provided some assistance for those who engaged in such behavior, and some penalty for those who did not but did the opposite, (col. 6) then the towrope of the laws would not be without benefit. But in fact it is apparent that the justice (*to dikaion*) derived from law is not sufficient to assist those who engage in such behavior. First, it permits the victim to suffer and the agent to act, and at the time it did not try to prevent either the victim from suffering or the agent from acting; and when it is applied to the punishment, it does not favor either the victim or the agent; for he must persuade the punishers that he suffered, or else be able to obtain justice by deception. But these means are also available to the agent, [if he wishes] to deny . . . (col. 7) . . . the defendant has as long for his defense as the plaintiff for his accusation, and there is an equivalent opportunity for persuasion for the victim and for the agent.

The second fragment further explores issues relating to *physis* and *nomos*, though its initial focus (col. 1) is on justice—here defined as following the city's laws—and advantage. The question is, How can justice be most advantageous? There is a two-part rule: It is advantageous with witnesses present to follow the laws but without witnesses to follow nature. The direct opposition of *nomos* and *physis* is clear: the former is "by agreement and not natural," the latter "natural and not by agreement." This opposition is then linked (col. 2) to a parallel opposition between opinion or reputation (*doxa*) and truth (*alētheia*).

The opposition of law and nature runs throughout this fragment, but several remarks suggest that it is not so strong or clear-cut as one might think. "Most things" (not "all things"), says Antiphon, "that are just according to law are inimical to nature," implying perhaps that some things are consistent with both. Later (col. 3) Antiphon remarks that unlawful things are equally congenial or akin to nature as lawful things,[31] implying an open relationship between the two rather than an opposition. Then nature is said to include both living and dying, associated respectively with advantage and disadvantage, so that now nature, like justice, includes advantage and disadvantage. And then (col. 4) pain and pleasure are seen (apparently) as equally helpful to nature. The overall flow of Antiphon's argument is not entirely clear in this fragment, but these remarks, interspersed among other indications of an opposition between law and nature, suggest several respects in which the two opposites are more similar than initially indicated. In general the demands of the law impose a restraint on nature, but whether this is advantageous or not remains problematic.

Thus we can see the same pattern here, though less clearly. *Nomos* and *physis* at first form a strong opposition, but as the work progresses more similarities become apparent, so that by the end the opposition is both present and absent. The only unequivocally positive value assumed in this section is advantage; sometimes it is more advantageous to follow *nomos*, sometimes *physis*. But each of these turns out to be complex and ambivalent. It is not clear where this argument will lead Antiphon,[32] but if he wishes to reunite law and nature later in this work, he has prepared the ground for it here.

After a short gap, 44B returns (col. 5) to issues of law and justice, citing specific cases where adhering to the laws is "inimical to nature" in that it brings more pain and less pleasure. Three specific examples of this are: waiting until one is attacked before defending oneself, treating one's parents well despite being mistreated by them, and allowing one's opponent to swear an oath (presumably false) without doing the same oneself. However, although these examples could easily be used to support a continued attack on justice per se and a corresponding defense of nature, Antiphon (col. 6) ties the harm done to those who follow the law to the ineffectiveness, not the unnaturalness, of the law. He seems to envision the possibility that the law could be benefi-

---

31. Two expressions I treat here as equalities are in fact negative comparisons, but it seems legitimate to interpret these as in effect statements of equality: "the things from which the laws dissuade us are in no way less congenial or akin to nature than the things toward which they urge us" (col. 3), and "things that bring pain do not . . . help nature more than things that bring joy (col. 4)."

32. I am sympathetic to Ostwald's conclusion: "It rather looks as if Antiphon's theme was to delineate the advantages that accrue to a human being from following, respectively, the dictates of society and those of nature. Partial truth is to be found in both" (1990, 303). Cassin (1992), too, finds positive value on both sides and rejects the primacy of nature.

cial, even if it currently is not; once again a value seems more problematic than it initially appeared.

44C. To testify truthfully for one another is customarily thought (*no-mizetai*) to be just (*dikaios*) and to no lesser degree useful in human affairs. And yet one who does this will not be just if indeed it is just not to injure (*adikein*)[33] anyone, if one is not injured oneself; for even if he tells the truth, someone who testifies must necessarily injure another somehow, and will then be injured himself, since he will be hated when the testimony he gives leads to the conviction of the person against whom he testifies, who then loses his property or his life because of this man whom he has not injured at all. In this way he wrongs the person against whom he testifies, because he injures someone who is not injuring him; and he in turn is injured by the one against whom he testified, in that he is hated by him (col. 2) despite having told the truth. And it is not only that he is hated but also that for his whole life he must be on guard against the man against whom he testified. As a result he has an enemy who will do him whatever harm he can in word or deed.

Now, these are clearly no small wrongs (*adikēmata*), neither those he suffers nor those he inflicts. For it is impossible that these things are just and that the rule not to injure anyone nor to be injured oneself is also just; on the contrary, it is necessary either that only one of these be just or that they both be unjust. Further, it is clear that, whatever the result, the judicial process, verdicts, and arbitration proceedings are not just, since helping some people hurts others. In the process those who are helped are not injured, while those who are hurt are injured.

The third and last fragment leaves the issue of *nomos* and *physis* and returns to the question of justice. In 44B Antiphon examined justice in the sense of obeying the laws (justice$_a$) and showed that it could be a disadvantage but could also bring benefits, if witnesses were present. Now he introduces a different way of understanding justice (justice$_b$): "not to injure anyone, if one is not injured oneself."[34] Since this sense of justice is apparently being tested ("if indeed it is just . . ."), we may speculate that justice$_a$ was also being tested (and that Antiphon may perhaps have tested other senses of justice in this work). In any

---

33. There is an untranslatable ambiguity in *a-dikein* in this passage between its literal meaning, "not be just," and its normal meaning with a direct object, "wrong" or "injure."

34. This sense echoes the very traditional Greek sentiment that one should help one's friends and hurt one's enemies.

case, the direct confrontation of these two senses leads to a conflict, because behavior that is just on one understanding is unjust on the other. Thus, the fragment concludes that both understandings cannot be just.

We have no way of knowing how Antiphon's argument continued. The preserved text presents a more positive picture of justice$_a$,[35] but lost portions may have modified this impression. Beyond this, we cannot say if Antiphon will ultimately reject justice in every sense or is seeking (like Socrates) to find some more general understanding of justice that would avoid the problems apparent in these traditional views. But we can say that in this fragment Antiphon points to ambiguities and contradictions in our thinking about justice in a way that echoes the pattern we have been tracing elsewhere. An initial unity—justice—is split into justice$_a$ and justice$_b$, which at first, at least, appear strongly opposed; obey one and you violate the other. Only the beginning of the pattern is evident here, but it is not impossible that Antiphon went on to bring these opposites closer together into a new complex unity, as we have seen in other cases.[36] This is speculation, but the text we have is enough to say, paraphrasing the sense of fragment 1 of *Truth* (see above), that anyone who uses the word "justice" has more than one mental concept of justice and there is more than one justice for him. The ambivalence in justice that exists in human society is thus mirrored by the ambivalence in Antiphon's *logos* about justice.

In sum, I propose that in his work entitled *Truth* Antiphon espoused the view that words or concepts (*logoi*) that may appear at first to consist of polar oppositions can also be seen as more complex or ambivalent notions in which the oppositions break down as each pole takes on characteristics of the other. Truth may at times appear unequivocally associated with one pole—nature in col. 2 of 44B—but in other places it will be allied with the other pole—law in 44C (testifying truly). As in the Tetralogies, where each side may claim an exclusive truth but the truth of the whole work is a larger synthesis, the truth of Antiphon's *Truth* lies in a discourse of opposites. *Truth* presents a complex and ambivalent discourse about a complex and ambivalent world, in which we can see Antiphon manipulating different arguments and seeking suggestive contradictions to illuminate some of this complexity. His particular concern is to explore different views of justice and its effect on human conduct, and despite his fondness for intellectual paradoxes, he seems to be trying at the same time to assess practical issues in the Athenian legal system. But his

---

35. Indeed, if justice is not injuring anyone unless injured by him (justice$_b$), then almost every human act will be unjust toward someone.

36. He could, for instance, argue that justice$_b$ is a form of *nomos* that like justice$_a$ violates *physis*.

method is apparently not to propose a clear solution or to develop a comprehensive or consistent theory, for clarity and consistency would be inadequate tools for expressing the complexity of reality. As Hesiod understood, only a complex and ambivalent *logos* can adequately express the complex ambivalence of reality.[37]

---

37. This chapter was originally written for presentation at the meeting of the Society for Ancient Greek Philosophy in Chicago in 1991. It was also presented at the Center for Hellenic Studies in Washington and the Frei Universität in Berlin, and I thank the audiences on all these occasions for their comments. I also thank an anonymous reader for helpful comments. I am particularly grateful to Anthony Preus for the initial invitation to address the Society and for encouraging me to prepare this version.

Chapter 10

The *Dissoi Logoi* and Early Greek Skepticism

Thomas M. Robinson

Dissoi Logoi ("Contrasting Arguments") is the name of a little-known anonymous document that is found appended to the works of Sextus Empiricus in the manuscripts containing his writings. It was first published in Paris in 1570, and since that date there has been dispute, among its handful of readers, concerning its date, authorship, purpose, and overall philosophical commitments.[1]

That it was perceived by some, at any rate, of its earliest readers as generally "skeptical" in tone seems clear enough from the fact that it is invariably found in conjunction with the works of Sextus Empiricus, but the precise nature of its skepticism is less clear. From various pieces of internal evidence it seems to have been written long before the time of Sextus, in fact in the first or second decade after the end of the Peloponnesian War (404 BCE),[2] and most people now believe it is the work of a Sophist teacher of the day.[3] For purposes of this chapter I shall assume the general correctness of both of these beliefs and confine my discussion to the nature and purpose of the work's contents.

I begin with a brief outline. The 4000-word treatise, which ends abruptly, and looks unfinished, consists of nine short chapters. The structure of the first four is strictly antilogical. Chapter 1, for example, entitled "On Good and Bad," begins:

> On the matter of what is good and bad contrasting arguments are put forward in Greece by educated people: some say that what is good and what is bad are two different things, others that they are the same thing, and that the same thing is good for some but bad for others, or at one time good and at another time bad for the same person.

---

1. In Stephanus, *Diogenes Laertius Opera* 1 (Paris 1570, 470–482). For the most recent edition of the work see T.M. Robinson (1979), from which the various translations in this chapter are taken.
2. See especially I.8, "And in the matter of war (I shall speak first of the most recent events) the Spartan victory over the Athenians and their allies was good for the Spartans, but bad for the Athenians and their allies . . ."
3. For the various views on authorship that have been put forward over the years, see T.M. Robinson (1979, 41–54). A notable recent exception to the currently accepted view is that of Conley (1985), which upholds the possibility of anonymous Byzantine authorship.

The author then goes on to offer a series of reasons why good and bad might reasonably be thought to be one and the same, and then immediately afterward a series of reasons why they might reasonably be thought to be different. An example of the first runs: "Illness is bad for the sick but good for the doctors. And death is bad for those who die, but good for the undertakers and gravediggers." Examples of the second have a uniformly hypothetical cast to them, each one amounting to an assertion of the (presumably self-evident) contradiction it would entail if the identity thesis in question were true; for example, "Being sick is bad for the sick and also good for them if what is good and what is bad are the same thing."

Chapter 2, "Seemly and Shameful," follows a similar pattern to chapter 1, as does chapter 3, on "Just and unjust." As in chapter 1, the author has an easy time making out a case for the identity thesis, but in maintaining the difference thesis once again does little more than simply assert the (self-evident) contradiction it would entail were the identity thesis in question true. Chapter 4, likewise, "Truth and Falsehood," offers a list of uncontroversial examples in support of the identity thesis, though this time, in his defense of the difference thesis, he bolsters the familiar charge of self-contradiction on the part of those maintaining the identity thesis by the interesting deployment of what looks like an early version of the Liar Paradox (4.6).

> It is also said that the false statement is different from the true statement; as the name differs, so likewise does the reality. For if anyone were to ask those who say that the same statement is false and true which of the two their own statement is, if the reply were "false," it is clear that a true statement and a false statement are two different things, but if he were to reply "true," then this statement is also false.

Chapter 5 is untitled, and the familiar phrase *dissoi logoi* is missing from it, but the basic structure of the treatise as seen so far is maintained: a conglomerate identity-thesis is propounded, and then a refutation of it offered. The thesis in question consists of two parts:

1. People possessed of contrary properties may in fact act and speak identically (various common speech acts and activities of the sane and the demented, the wise and the ignorant are offered as examples; e.g., "The demented, the sane, the wise and the ignorant both say and do the same things. First of all they call things by the same name: "earth," "man," "horse," "fire," and everything else. And they do the same things: they sit, eat, drink, lie down, and so on, in the same way").

2. The same person/thing is himself/itself possessed of contrary properties "The talent," he says, for example, "is heavier than the mina and lighter than two talents; the same thing then is both lighter and heavier." And "what ex-

ists (is the case) here [sc. in Greece] does not exist (is not the case) in Libya; nor does what exists (is what is the case) in Libya exist (turn out to be the case) in Cyprus . . . Consequently, things both exist (are the case) and do not exist (are not the case)."

As far as the difference thesis is concerned, this is for the first time in the treatise defended with a set of arguments far surpassing the simple assertion of apparent self-contradiction on the part of identity-theorists, the first of them interestingly distinguishing identical speech acts by the varying appropriateness of the occasion of utterance (5.9-10), the final one (5.15) drawing a careful distinction, two generations before Aristotle, between existence simpliciter and existence secundum quid. In the author's own words:

As for the affirmation that the same man exists and does not exist I ask, "Does he exist in some particular respect or in every respect?" Thus, if anyone denies that the man in question exists, he is making the mistake of asserting "in every respect." The conclusion is that all these things exist in some way.

Chapter 6, "On Whether Wisdom and Moral Excellence are Teachable," preserves the structure of the first five, setting out first the one case (in this instance the case that wisdom and moral excellence are in fact unteachable) and then the counter-case with arguments remarkably similar to a number of those found in Plato's *Protagoras* (328c, 324dff) and *Meno* (93b-94e). At 6.3-4, for example, we read:

Another (proof that wisdom and moral excellence are unteachable) is that, had wisdom and moral excellence been able to be taught, there would have existed recognized teachers of them—the way there have been recognized teachers of the arts. A (further) proof is that those men in Greece who became wise would have taught this wisdom to their children and their friends.

Chapters 7, 8, and 9 are untitled, and the structure of case and counter-case has now apparently started to break down. The first of the three chapters propounds the single logos that it is absurd that offices should be—as many were in Athens—assigned by lot; the essence of the counter-case consists of a single statement at the end asseverating the value of electing qualified people for such offices. The second chapter consists of a little essay on the characteristics of the paradigmatic sophist/orator/politician, and defends among other things the remarkable view that such individuals are by definition both omniscient and omnicompetent. The treatise ends with a short discussion of the value of memorization and with what looks like the beginning of a list of a few specific mnemonic techniques.

Opinions on the author's own stance in the treatise have varied. For Diels and Kranz[4] he is simply "talentlos," and his views—if he has any—unworthy of further investigation. For others,[5] he is simply a paradigmatic Protagorean, and as such a common-or-garden relativist, convinced that on any topic contrary arguments can be proffered, and offering examples of such arguments in his treatise. For others he is Protagorean in a further, tougher sense, not only proffering contrary arguments on various topics but attempting while so doing to make the weaker of each pair the stronger. And the matter is further complicated by items here and there in the treatise that look to be possibly Gorgian or Hippian or even in a couple of places possibly Socratic[6] in influence, suggesting to some that the author is more of an eclectic than a proponent of any specific philosophical Weltanschauung.

That the author is, in general terms, Protagorean in the weaker sense seems undeniable. He clearly does believe that on various topics contrary arguments can be proffered, as he spends the greater part of his time offering examples illustrating the proposition's truth. Whether relativism on his part can be inferred from this is however debatable, both in his own case and in that of Protagoras. As is well known, Plato argued in the *Theaetetus* that relativism was the logical conclusion of Protagoras's "man the measure" doctrine. As is less well known, and as Levi has pointed out,[7] there was no suggestion on Plato's part that Protagoras himself ever drew any such conclusion. What we do know is that, according to Diogenes Laertius,[8] Protagoras was the first to say that there were contrary arguments on every topic, and also "the first to institute contests between arguments" (*protos . . . logon agonas epoiesato*). One natural inference from this is that the "contest" Protagoras saw as basic to philosophical disputes was one between arguments, not people; any further inference is hazardous.

Not long after Protagoras's floruit, however, we find Aristophanes—followed later by Aristotle—attributing to him the view that he set out to "make the weaker argument the stronger."[9] But there is no independent evidence to support such a claim, which has all the appearances of popular prejudice based on (legitimate) irritation at the verbal game-playing—apparently for its own sake—practiced by sophists, such as Plato's Dionysodorus and Euthydemus, claiming Protagoras as their inspiration. Protagoras himself, by contrast, when

---

4. Diels and Kranz (1951) ad loc.
5. For details, see Robinson (1979), 55ff.
6. Robinson (1979), 59ff.
7. Levi (1940), 292–306.
8. 9.50ff. = Protagoras A1, B6a DK6.
9. Aristophanes, *Clouds* 882–884; Aristotle, *Rhet.* 1402a 23 = Protagoras B6b DK6.

placed on the stage by Plato, comes across, not as a relativist, but as a man adhering to the straightforward and uncomplicated beliefs of his day.

If this picture of Protagoras is the correct one, all that the author of the *Dissoi Logoi*, if he saw himself as in general terms a follower of Protagoras, should be credited with is the view that on a large number of topics contrasting arguments can be and, in terms of sound philosophy, should be proffered; the quality of the individual arguments however remains open for discussion and assessment.

Before looking at those arguments, we should first examine briefly two general claims about them that have been thought to offer evidence of the author's own philosophical stance.

1. The author makes it clear that, in the opening chapters at least, he backs the difference thesis.[10] In addition to his own statements on the matter, we have the facts that:
   a) the identity thesis is invariably placed first in sequence, and
   b) the difference thesis is in chapters 1–4 the one spelled out at greater length.
2. The difference thesis invariably attacks a version of the identity thesis wholly different from the one that has just been defended.[11]

Let us look at these claims and their supposed implications.

1. (The author invariably backs the difference thesis.) In fact, however, the author on a number of occasions expresses clear support for the identity thesis (1.2, 2.20, 3.7, 4.2), and this evidence must be weighed in the balance along with the evidence (1.11, 2.26, 5.6, 6.7, 6.13) that suggests a commitment to the identity thesis. One possible conclusion from this is that the author has little idea of what he is doing, and is indeed as Diels suggested "talentlos." There are, however, other possible conclusions, which I shall discuss later.
   a) (The identity thesis is invariably placed first in sequence.) It has been argued from this that it is consequently the difference thesis and its supporting arguments that are invariably left ticking over in the reader's mind, and that this is a suasion in support of the view that the author himself supports such a difference thesis. There may be something in this, but against it one should point out that the identity thesis invariably propounds views, the factual accuracy of which is open to relatively simple testing and observation. This being the case, and something readily ascertainable by even the most unsophisticated reader, the author may well, it seems to me, have intended the reader to notice that the difference thesis

---

10. For proponents of the view, see Robinson (1979), 73.
11. Robinson (1979), 76.

possesses whatever strength it does thanks to a witting or unwitting mis-
representation of the identity thesis, and the point will be made with particular clarity if the identity thesis is placed first in sequence.

b) (The difference thesis is in all four of the first four chapters spelled out
at greater length.) This is as it happens simply false; it is in fact the identity thesis that in those chapters is the longer, as a glance at the text
makes clear. Even if it were true, however, nothing of any clarity concerning the author's commitments, *pace* Untersteiner (1961–1962), can
be inferred, except by those who find a causal connection between an argument's length and its plausibility.

Of much greater substance (and possible implication) is the point ([2] above)—
glossed over or not noticed by commentators—that the difference thesis invariably attacks a version of the identity thesis different from the one that has just
been defended. I say "defended," rather than "proffered and defended," because
typically the identity thesis will be proffered as an (extreme) identity statement
but actually defended as a (very moderate) predicative statement. Among many
examples, one might take chapter one of the treatise. The opening lines, as we
have seen, read as follows:

> On the matter of what is good and bad contrasting arguments are
> put forward in Greece by educated people: some say that what is
> good and what is bad are two different things, others that they are
> the same thing, and that the same thing is good for some but bad
> for others, or at one time good and at another time bad for the
> same person.

What is interesting here is the fact that the identity thesis is first expressed as
an identity statement ("[what is good and what is bad] are the same thing")
and then immediately afterward as a predicative statement ("the same thing is
good for some but bad for others," etc.). The thesis is then defended (1.2-10),
but only in its predicative version ("death is bad for those who die, but good
for the undertakers and the grave-diggers," etc.). When it comes to the difference thesis however (1.11ff), the author defends it by reference to the extreme
version of the identity thesis—i.e., as an identity statement—that had been
mentioned but in no way defended. He has as a result a very easy time pointing out that such a thesis is self-contradictory. It is indeed, and would no doubt
have been admitted to be such by the proponents of the predicative version of
the thesis who had just had their arguments aired. But he has of course
knocked down a straw man, and we are no further forward as to his views on
the value of the arguments that uphold a moderate—and perfectly defensible—version of the identity thesis, as against the value of arguments in defense of the extreme version.

What we have instead is a constant reiteration that he favors the difference thesis (i.e., that *x* and *y* are, as he puts it, as different in reality as they are in name [1.11]) but with no hard arguments in defense of that thesis other than the claim that its opposite leads to self-contradiction, and—as we have seen—with the occasional asseveration that he does in fact support various identity-theses. Two major interpretations of all this seem possible.

The first is that of Diels, to wit, that our author is simply devoid of talent. Though Diels does not spell the matter out, presumably he means either that the author has failed to notice that the version of the identity thesis he attacks is never the version of it the arguments for which he has just propounded; or, more seriously, that he could not in fact recognize the difference between identity statements and predicative statements in the first place. The result in either case is a lamentable failure to realize that the supposed difference thesis he supports is wholly compatible with if not in fact the very same as the moderate identity thesis he has just in fact outlined.

The second interpretation leaves open the possibility that the author is fully aware of the difference between an identity statement and a predicative statement, but for propaedeutic reasons not unsimilar, perhaps, to those underlying Plato's aporetic dialogues, constructs arguments predicated upon their supposed sameness. If this is the case, the treatise will consist of more than rote-lists of arguments and counterarguments for the use of sophists. It will in fact be a genuine teaching manual for sophists, with arguments displayed in such a way as to challenge readers (or hearers) to hone their rhetorical skills by working out for themselves the relative worth of such arguments.

I am inclined to accept this latter interpretation, on the grounds that it fits the facts as well as the first and has at the same time the merit of crediting our author with a modicum of philosophical intelligence. It does not, however, tell us anything specific about the author's own stance on particular issues, and more generally whether those who, in appending the treatise to the works of Sextus Empiricus, clearly thought he was reasonably classifiable as a skeptic, even if only in some fairly moderate sense of the term.

As far as content is concerned, if the interpretation outlined immediately above is correct, it might be thought that we may be forever precluded from knowing the author's own philosophical stance, for that stance was irrelevant to his objective in writing the treatise. There is, however, a case for saying that his position emerges regardless.

As we saw earlier, while for the most part strongly backing the difference thesis he also on occasion makes affirmative noises concerning the identity thesis. This would on the face of it constitute evidence that he is putting up the best case he can for both sides, and thereby blocking any rash attempt on the reader's part to waste time attempting to unmask his (the author's) own private opinions. But this could be mistaken. The affirmative noises are all, as it turns out, in favor of the straightforward, easily verifiable predicative version of the identity thesis in question. And in view of the fact that this version is, on the face of, comfortably compatible with the difference thesis that is its supposed contrary, it seems eminently possible that the author's "own" stance will in fact coincide with this thesis.

If this is true, our Sophist-author will turn out to be—not surprisingly— an empiricist, and one firmly convinced of the worth and importance of the wealth of empirical evidence he uses in support of the predicative statements of various identity theses throughout the treatise. And the type of skepticism appropriately thereby attributed to him will consist of the skepticism of all those who, before and since, have demanded evidence before drawing general conclusions.

Whether such empiricism and skepticism was an all-embracing feature of his thinking is a conclusion less easy to draw. At 1.17, for example, the author disclaims any intention of telling us "what the good is" (*ti esti to agathon*), a phrase that would not have been surprising on the lips of Socrates. And at 4.5 he writes: "It is clear, then, that the same statement is false when the false is present to it, and true when the true is present to it." The doctrine of "presence" of universal to particular is, as is well known, thought by many to be character-istic of the Platonic/Socratic Theory of Forms and indeed a specifically Pla-tonic/Socratic contribution to philosophical speculation. This may well be the case and our author—given the presumptive date of publication of the trea-tise—may be one of possibly many influenced by Socratic argumentation. On the other hand, it seems equally possible that such an argument was "in the air" in sophistic circles at this time, and actually drawn by Socrates from such cir-cles. In view of the lack of evidence either way, the matter must be left in tan-talizing doubt.

However that may be, it seems beyond question that the author is strongly affirming in this instance at any rate a position more appropriately character-ized as essentialist than empiricist. In combination with the empiricism that ap-pears to characterize so much else of the treatise it constitutes a view of the real and of language used to describe the real that Socrates (if not Plato) would al-most certainly have found respectable, and for that matter Aristotle too.

Two further pieces of evidence, already noticed in passing, to support such a view should be mentioned.

1. In the chapter on truth and falsehood we read the following statement, as a defense of the difference thesis begins (4.6):

> It is also said that the false statement is different from the true state-ment; as the name differs, so does the reality. For if anyone were to ask those who say that the same statement is false and true which of the two their own statement is, if the reply were "false," it is clear that

> a true statement and a false statement are two different things, but if
> he were to reply "true" then this statement is also false.

The argument is a shrewd one, and incorporates elements of the so-called Liar Paradox. In its fully articulated form this was first set out a generation later by Eubulides, a disciple of Euclides of Megara (who was himself a contemporary of the author of the *Dissoi Logoi*). Perhaps for present purposes more significantly, an analogous argument is, with some effect, set out by Socrates in Plato's *Theaetetus* (170eff), as part of his criticism of Protagoras's "man the measure" doctrine.

2. At the end of chapter 5 the author concludes:

> As for the affirmation that the same man exists and does not exist I
> ask: "Does he exist in some particular respect or in every respect?"
> Thus, if anyone denies that the man in question exists, he is making
> the mistake of asserting "in every respect." The conclusion is that all
> these things exist in some way.

The simpliciter/secundum quid distinction employed in this argument is remarkable to come across two generations before the appearance of Aristotle's *Sophistical Refutations*, and suggests an expertise on the author's part far greater than is usually attributed to him. We also know, from Aristotle himself, that little manuals of sophistic arguments were in circulation in Athens and elsewhere in his day. That opens up the intriguing possibility 1) that one such manual was the *Dissoi Logoi*, 2) that it was actually read by Socrates/Plato and Aristotle, and 3) either that its use of features of the Liar Paradox influenced Socrates/Plato or that its use of the simpliciter/secundum quid distinction influenced Aristotle, or both. As in the earlier case of the origin of the doctrine of "presence," no evidence is unfortunately available either way, and the matter must once again be left in tantalizing doubt.

To return to the question at hand: Can the author of the *Dissoi Logoi* be meaningfully described as a skeptic? The answer it seems to me must be Yes, on two counts, though hardly in the technical sense of the term that Sextus would himself have recognized.

1. As far as the content of his beliefs is concerned, he is committed to the adducing of empirical evidence in areas where such evidence is either actually or potentially available. In the area of true and false propositions, by contrast, he seems more essentialist in his analysis. The total package might reasonably be described as one of moderate empiricism and moderate skepticism, in that empirical evidence, when adduced, will serve to dispel the septicism that fueled the investigation, but not all problems it seems are deemed to be amenable to the adducing of such empirical evidence.

2. His methodology, by contrast—and here he draws directly on Protagoras—
is uncompromisingly empirical, in that no investigation is deemed to have
been properly conducted unless both sides of the question—and there always are two, at any rate in the matter of the particular questions he raises—
have been aired.

Whether the above arguments alone would account for the work's invariably being found in Sextus Empiricus manuscripts is certainly open to question,
given the broader and more searching range of Sextus's own brand of skepticism. But three further features of its style and contents may have served as
suasions in favor of such a collocation.

1. If the author was understood (wrongly, as I have argued, but not surprisingly,
given what we know of the way in which Protagoras's views on logos/
counterlogos came to be interpreted in antiquity) as himself adhering to the
view that in his various chapters logos and counter-logos were equipollent, a
compiler could be forgiven for seeing an affinity between this view and the
doctrine of equipollence that so characterizes the writings of Sextus.

2. A more specific suasion is found at 5.13-14, where, after mentioning instances of changes in meaning brought about, not by the subtraction of
anything but by a mere change of accent, he goes on:

> Since, therefore, there is such a difference when nothing is taken
> away, what if in that case somebody does either add something or
> take something away? I shall give an example of the sort of thing I
> mean. If someone were to take away one from ten <or to add one to
> ten, Diels>, there would no longer be ten or even one, and so on in
> the same way in all other instances.

As I have put it elsewhere (*Commentary*, ad loc.):

> The argument turns on a particular use of the word "ten." The form
> can be used collectively (*ta deka*—cf. words like "score," "dozen,"
> etc., in English) or distributively (*deka*), leaving open the possibility
> for the author to argue (as he apparently does here) that to (suppos-
> edly) take away from "the ten" (*ta deka*) that I have is to leave me
> without my ten, and so apparently without even one of them! (In the
> same way, one might argue, one cannot take one away from a "rugby
> fifteen" and get a "rugby one" plus a "rugby fourteen;" one either
> has a rugby fifteen or one has not.)

Similar addition-subtraction puzzles crop up in Plato (*Crat.* 432a-b) and
Aristotle (*SE* 22.178a29-37),[12] but are as it happens a particular feature of the

---

12. For discussion of the passage, see Sprague (1990), 20.

writings of Sextus; see *Pyrr. Hyp.* 3. 85, *Adv. Math.* iv. 23-24, *Adv. Phys.* 1. 303-330, 2. 308-309.

3. A final possible specific suasion is to be found at 2. 20, where the author is arguing that the difference between seemly and shameful actions is that the former are performed "at the right moment" (*kairoi*), the latter "at the wrong moment" (*en akairiai*). An analogous—though far from identical—argument is expounded by Sextus at *Adv. Eth.* 64-67 and credited to the Stoic Ariston of Chios; and, possibly tellingly, an analogy is drawn from the different placing of letters in the spelling of names (cf. *Dissoi Logoi* 5.12 for the same point), which is said to depend upon the force of *hoi kairoi* (cf. ibid. 2.20, *kairoi*).

Such suasions, small though they may be as individual items, could well, it seems to me, have been deemed to have sufficient collective force to persuade a hesitating compiler to place the *Dissoi Logoi* alongside the works of Sextus. Whether we were meant to infer from such a collocation that the work should be attributed to Sextus himself or simply to his philosophical entourage we cannot tell, and in any case the compiler was wrong. Where he was less obviously wrong was in his appreciation of the fact that there are features of its style and content which, as I hope I have shown, the master might well have interpreted as significant gropings towards the light.

Chapter 11

Moral Dilemmas and Integrity
in Sophocles's *Philoctetes*

Carol Steinberg Gould

"Tragic drama," D.D. Raphael remarks, "was the moral philosophy of fifth-century Athens."[1] Few philosophers currently working in Greek philosophy would disagree; indeed many scholars have brought out studies of various dramas as enactments of efforts to resolve moral dilemmas and to face the difficulties of the human ethical situation. Sophocles has long attracted attention from philosophers, starting with Plato, who tacitly allies himself with Sophocles early in the *Republic* (329b-c) when he refers to Sophocles' rumored relief at the impotence that accompanies old age and the deliverance it brings from an unrelenting slave master. Given Plato's concern in the *Republic* to show the trouble wrought by misdirected passion, he seems to take Sophocles' cast of thought quite seriously.[2] Moreover, Sophocles's now deeply-mined *Antigone* shows not only a pre-Platonic commitment to unwritten laws, but also a familiarity with the intellectual debates of his contemporaries, especially the sophists, as to whether justice is natural or conventional (another concern in the *Republic*). Philosophers have, however, lavished less attention on Sophocles' *Philoctetes* than on many other Greek dramas, such as *Oedipus, Medea, Agamemnon*, and *Antigone*—to name a few. In this chapter, I show that the *Philoctetes* deserves as central a place in the philosophical canon as the more thoroughly probed plays. More specifically, I argue that Sophocles anticipates a model of virtue drawn by Plato in his *Republic*,[3] another work dealing from the start with coercion, moral

---

1. Raphael (1983), 4. Nussbaum reflects on this at the start of her article on the *Philoctetes* (1976). I am grateful to the Schmidt College of Florida Atlantic University for a summer research grant that enabled me to work on this chapter. For helpful comments on an earlier version, I extend thanks to Berel Lang, Anthony Preus, Josiah Gould, Gary Meltzer, and an anonymous referee for this volume.

2. As Anthony Preus has pointed out to me, Aristotle, too, considers Sophocles a serious thinker. See, for example, *Metaphysics* 1015a 30; *Eudemian Ethics* 1242a 37; and *Rhetoric* 1373b 9, 1375a 33, 1417a 28–33.

3. Interpretations linking *Philoctetes* with the *Republic* are rare. One substantially different from mine appears in the now classic Edmund Wilson essay, "The Wound and the Bow" (1947). Wilson views the wound as symbolic of the diseases in each

(*continued on page 200*)

reasoning, and the uneasiness at the heart of political *philia*, another work attacking the then entrenched sophistic ethic of expediency.

Sophocles produced *Philoctetes* in 409, during some of Athens's darkest moments, when fear so routinely unseated judgment that shifting loyalties and betrayal of principle must have become a condition of life. Socrates himself, as he reports in the *Apology* (32b-e) felt caught up in this maelstrom. Today, we can only speculate on how some Athenians must have winced to see Sophocles's image of the lonely Philoctetes, a brave soldier who had lived for ten years with only the beasts of Lemnos, abandoned there by those for whose cause he had left his home to fight. We can imagine, too, how others must have squirmed to see Odysseus return in search of this man, now necessary, though no less abhorred, or as they saw Neoptolemus vacillate between compassion and ruthlessness. Sophocles must have found this myth a promising one for exploring integrity, moral reasoning, and the dialectic between self-sufficiency and regard for others.[4]

Sophocles, I argue in this chapter, expresses in the *Philoctetes* a version of moral realism, one which allows for the resolution of moral dilemmas. He gives us a proto-Platonic account of the moral self, embodied in the eponymous Philoctetes. Let us recall that in his *Republic*, Plato draws with a fine brush the beautiful interior of the just person, who may appear mad, unjust, or repulsive to others. He contrasts this person with the unjust one who may have a fine, successful appearance, but a morally deformed interior, like that of the democratic or tyrannical soul. We find a similar juxtaposition in the *Symposium*, in which Socrates, a Silenus, ugly to behold, but beautiful within, contrasts with the alluring, but corrupt Alcibiades. Sophocles, as we shall see, uses the same sort of opposing portraiture in his *Philoctetes*: He draws an excellent man with a noxious, repulsive exterior in the character of Philoctetes, while portraying a dazzling exterior in the character of Neoptolemus, a man who appears just and morally authentic, but who in reality, I submit, is ignominious. In tacitly contrasting the two characters in this way, Sophocles prefigures the Platonic as-

---

3. (*continued from page 199*)
   of us for which Plato prescribes a life of disciplined rationality as a treatment (293–294). More recently, Rose (1992) connects the works more obliquely in terms of their political concerns. In chapter 5, he analyzes the play as a response to sophistic anthropology and political theory. His analysis, Marxist in orientation, complements mine, but deals more with the structure of Athenian society. For an intriguing discussion relating the play to Plato's *Meno*, see Kieffer (1942).

4. The Athenian condition of 409 stands silently in the background of the play. Some scholars have speculated on its connection to the Athenian political scene and on the real identities of the characters. Though many of their conclusions are fanciful, to put it charitably, some of these discussions cast much light on the play. See Wilson (1947), Rose (1992), Calder (1971), Jameson (1956).

sault on the sophistic instrumentalist view of value and correlative denial of the appearance/reality distinction in the moral realm.

My interpretation of *Philoctetes* is at odds with two other philosophical approaches to the play. First it conflicts with the widely accepted reading of MacIntyre,[5] who contrasts Sophocles with Plato on the possibility of moral knowledge and the nature of moral dilemmas. Tragedy depicts the human being in crisis, facing an ethical conflict. Plato clearly takes moral dilemmas to admit clean, logical resolution, at least when adjudicated by an agent primed by nature and rigorous education. The Platonic moral agent grasps moral facts and the logical relations among them, having made a precise study of value as well as the world of the polis. In this, Plato, like Socrates, responds to both the philosophical relativism of the sophists and the pre-reflective prudential ethic of the Athenians who were their patrons or aspiring patrons.

Focusing chiefly on the controversial epiphany of Heracles at the end of the play, MacIntyre views Sophocles as accepting Plato's belief in moral facts but rejecting his optimism about the human capacity to ascertain such facts. On MacIntyre's reading, then, Sophocles needs a divinity to "end" the conflict "rather than resolve" it.[6] If human beings must rely on the gods or their signs as the final court of appeals, then we can never rationally settle matters of conflicting moral claims.

This line of interpretation, however, leads to a paradox: Sophocles seems to value integrity, as even a cursory reading of his extant plays reveals.[7] But on MacIntyre's reading, integrity can have no role in a Sophoclean ethical life. Integrity involves fidelity to one's ethical judgments, whatever the practical consequences. But if human moral knowledge is so limited, then holding fast to one's ethical commitments would seem indefensible. For Plato, integrity is essential to the moral life,[8] whereas for the sophistic relativist, it would have at

---

5. MacIntyre, *After Virtue* (1981), 133–136.
6. MacIntyre (1981), 134.
7. One notable exception would be the *Trachiniae*.
8. One might contrast Plato and Socrates on this matter. The Socrates of the early dialogues purports to have no absolutely justified beliefs that cannot be scrutinized further. But when Socrates claims to have no knowledge, in some cases, he is speaking ironically, and in both the *Apology* and *Crito*, in which he professes a willingness to die for his beliefs, he asserts many moral claims with confidence: that a person should not leave his post, that he should not stop investigating the foundations on which his fellow citizens base their beliefs, and that even a wrong sentence must be respected. He clearly thinks that a responsible agent must not stop reflecting on and refining his beliefs. But this does not entail skepticism. Plato, most notably in his *Republic* and *Symposium*, strikes a more confident stance with regard to moral knowledge. One ascends from one insight to a higher order one. Though space does not permit me to expand on this further, the contrast is worth exploring. If Socrates is closer to Plato than he often appears, then integrity does not burden him logically.

best prudential value in certain kinds of situations. If Sophocles considers moral knowledge so inadequate, then his skepticism would compel him to follow the sophistic route, even if halfheartedly. But this interpretative line would do great violence to Sophocles' ethical convictions that emerge so clearly in the plays, and the interpretation I offer in this chapter will demonstrate that, at any rate, with regard to his *Philoctetes*.

The second philosophical approach to the play in conflict with mine is that focusing on Neoptolemus. Many interpreters of the play[9] take it to depict the moral awakening of Neoptolemus as he struggles successfully with a moral dilemma and completes a rite of passage to adulthood. In the course of this chapter, I argue against this line. I shall first discuss the nature of a moral dilemma, which many contemporary scholars rightly discern as the conceptual *agon* at the heart of most tragedies. I shall argue that Neoptolemus is incapable of facing, let alone resolving, a moral dilemma. For in order to confront a moral dilemma, one needs to be committed to some principles, to have a moral worldview. Appearances to the contrary, Neoptolemus has no such commitments, as I explain below, page 212. Philoctetes, I argue, stands firmly at the moral center of the drama; it is his moral nature that unfolds. In placing Philoctetes in the context of a more primal Greek archetype, I then propose an interpretation of the notoriously problematic Heracles scene that supports my assessment of Sophocles as anticipating Plato and opposing the sophists. Exploring the ethical terrain of the play will illuminate both the philosophical issues and some artistic problems.

MORAL DILEMMAS

The nature of moral dilemmas is itself a vexing philosophical issue, but one especially felicitous for exploring the philosophical scaffolding of a Greek tragedy. First of all, simply characterizing a moral dilemma takes one to the heart of ethical philosophy: Whether a dilemma can be resolved rests on whether two principles or sets of values can genuinely have competing claims on an agent, and one's stance on this reflects more fundamental views on the nature of a moral reasoning and the reality of moral facts. The tragedians depict characters struggling with dilemmas, and they reveal such struggles as part of the human situation. MacIntyre, as mentioned earlier, sees Plato and Sophocles as

---

9. Most modern readers view Neoptolemus sympathetically, a tendency Calder vigorously opposes. But for this particular approach, see, for example, Kieffer (1942); Avery (1965); Nussbaum (1976); Vidal-Naquet (1990); Gill (1993); Blundell (1989, 1993); and Williams (1993, 87–88).

philosophically opposed on the resolution of moral dilemmas and thus on some basic principles of moral philosophy as well. MacIntyre's Sophocles holds that:

> There are indeed crucial conflicts in which different virtues appear as making rival . . . claims upon us. But our situation is tragic in that we have to recognize the authority of both claims. There *is* an objective moral order, but our perceptions of it are such that we cannot bring rival moral truths into complete harmony with each other . . .[10]

But Plato, MacIntyre avers, denies that "rival goods [can be] at war with each other. [So] it is just what Plato takes to be impossible which makes tragic drama possible."[11] On this reading, both view the moral realm as ordered rationally; but Plato, unlike Sophocles, considers the human agent capable of discerning this rational order and thus of resolving apparent conflicts. For Plato, the world of the Forms is neatly structured, governed by the Form of the Good. The philosopher can rationally determine which ideals would be prior to others, which is why only the philosopher is suited to make judgments of any moral or political consequence. MacIntyre's Sophocles can find no training or cast of mind adequate for adjudicating conflicting moral claims, thus the tragedy of the human situation. But in the *Philoctetes* Sophocles in fact is much closer to Plato.

In order to see this, however, we must begin with a more precise idea of a moral dilemma than that deployed in most current treatments of tragedy, though the nature of a moral dilemma, let alone its implications for moral psychology and the reality of moral values, is itself a complex problem. Aaron Ridley, in his "Tragedy and the Tender-Hearted,"[12] describes a moral dilemma as a situation in which a person is forced "to choose between two courses of action each of which involves a moral violation." And, as we have seen, MacIntyre takes a dilemma as a situation in which we must choose between "rival claims" with apparently equal authority. On these notions, then, a moral dilemma is a circumstance forcing us to choose between an ineluctably conflicting set of values, imperatives, or principles.

At first glance, this would seem to preclude the possibility of such situations for Plato and other cognitive moral realists who view the moral realm as rationally structured and at least some human minds as capable of discerning the relations among its constituents. For Plato, the Form of the Good orders the

---

10. MacIntyre (1981), 134.
11. MacIntyre (1981), 133. For an interesting discussion of this and of the problem of moral dilemmas more generally, see Gowans (1987, 3–33).
12. Ridley (1993).

realm of the Forms, which determines the relative priority of one good or imperative over another. To use a Platonic example, all things being equal, we ought not to lie. But when lying protects the integrity of the state, we must choose to protect the state. Thus, the noble lie of the *Republic* is morally unproblematic. The priority of one good over the other eliminates the dilemma. Some dilemmas dissolve less neatly. But, for Plato, the astute and rationally trained agent can make determinations by discerning which value takes priority over another. The flaws in the defective souls of Books 8 and 9 arise from the mistaken priorities of values that each assigns in life, errors made by emotionally clouded judgments. So, the timocratic soul, with its excessively robust *thumos*, will choose honor over integrity, which arguably Sophocles's Odysseus does. So, for Plato, we have criteria for resolving these matters.

However, some philosophers conclude that we have no criterion for deciding these issues, or if there is one, we cannot know it. Both the antirealist, represented by the Protagorean relativist and the skeptic, by MacIntyre's Sophocles, would have recourse to either social or religious conventions. One could indeed construe the Heracles deus ex machina scene in *Philoctetes* as indicating precisely such an attitude. The appeal to convention, however, leaves the dilemmas fundamentally unsolved, for no one value or principle can be definitively subordinated to another, and the distinction between nature and convention therefore collapses.

For some realists, too, the dilemmas remain unsolved in that even if one principle has some greater claim on a person, it does not follow that its rival has *no* claim. Moreover, Ruth Barcan Marcus argues that "moral dilemmas can arise even if one assumes the consistency of moral rules."[13] For her, the Platonist or other "single-principle" thinkers should be just as uneasy as the antirealist or skeptic. She has in mind the sort of case in which one principle demands that the agent perform two actions, only one of which is possible. *Antigone* would present a clear instance of this. Antigone arguably is motivated by her allegiance to the obligations of the *oikos*. But if she buries her brother, she cannot marry, a conflict that fills her with great anguish. Or, the horrific decision forced on Sophie in *Sophie's Choice* would be another good example. Marcus's analysis is important for our concerns, for it does reveal one crucial point of contention between Sophocles and Plato. Though both are, as will emerge, non-skeptical moral realists, Sophocles does not rule out the possibility of tragedy.

For Plato, the human situation is not—or at least need not be—tragic. The Platonic philosopher is both intellectually and emotionally suited to cope with such situations. For Sophocles, the human agent (like Antigone, for example)

---

13. Barcan Marcus (1980).

may have tragically unfulfilled possibilities. But there being unfulfilled possibilities does not mean that the agent is left with "dirty hands," that in solving the dilemma and therefore acting rightly, she is nonetheless acting wrongly at the same time.[14] For Sophocles, it simply means that the agent, being human, can actualize only one set of possibilities, though all things being equal, she would be happier actualizing both. This is yet one more insidious lie that Plato can find in tragedy and yet one more lamentable element of the human situation that Sophocles can find in the human condition. But as for their realism and cognitive analysis of dilemmas, they are on a par, as we shall see.

However one analyzes moral dilemmas, they are part of life. Even Plato would agree, I wager, that confronting, rather than evading, them can transform our moral landscapes and take us to new vantage points. This emerges in E.J. Lemmon's now classic "Moral Dilemmas,"[15] in which he distinguishes three types of moral dilemma. While much work has been done since the appearance of his article, his taxonomy remains helpful and his analysis more nuanced than many more recent ones. His treatment will prove helpful for our understanding of the *Philoctetes*, especially for the contrast between Neoptolemus and Philoctetes.

Lemmon offers a threefold classification of moral dilemmas. The first sort is what philosophers usually mean when they refer to a moral dilemma. It is a situation in which one ought to do something and ought not to do it. This can arise from a conflict between duty and obligation, duty and principle, obligation and principle, or between any two of these. He illustrates this with the famous Platonic case of returning a weapon to a mad friend, which he construes as a conflict between a principle and an obligation.[16] Another instance of the first sort would be when one's duty to perform a given job conflicts with one's moral principles. Such dilemmas can be solved either by considering whether we hold duty prior to obligation, obligation to principle, or the like, or by considering our moral priorities more generally, for instance which duties are prior to others and so forth. More often, though, these clashes require us to figure out our priorities and ultimately our "ends" or "goods." For how we order our principles reflects our hierarchy of values.

The second and third types of dilemma are more complex and show the acuity of Lemmon's moral psychological insight. In the first type, one's imperatives are clear and they conflict. In the second type, one has "some, but not conclusive, evidence" that one ought to do such and such. So a "given ordering of

---

14. The problem of dirty hands is neatly explained by Stocker (1986).
15. Lemmon (1962), reprinted in Gowans (1987). Page references to Lemmon are to (1962).
16. Lemmon (1962, 139–143) sorts out the concepts of duty, obligation, and principle.

one's duties and obligations and the like" will not resolve the dilemma, because "part of the very dilemma is just one's uncertainty as to one's actual moral situation." He illustrates this kind of dilemma with the famous Sartrean case of the student who does not know whether he should join the Free French Forces or remain with his mother. He thinks it his duty to fight, "but can it really be his duty, given his obligation to his mother," Lemmon asks. Interestingly, to solve the dilemma *is* to determine one's obligations. In cases of sufficient gravity or intensity, this resolution can lead to "a changed moral outlook." As Lemmon justly notes, most philosophers have ignored the psychological interest such dilemmas hold in that they can—but need not—lead to a new moral vision. Lemmon insightfully compares this with the way a certain aesthetic encounter might lead to a new artistic insight or appreciation.

The third type of dilemma, the most grave and rare, is a situation in which a person confronts a situation for which he is "completely unprepared . . . by his moral outlook" so that it challenges one to "meet unprecedented moral needs." He appeals to the example of Chamberlain dealing with Hitler, in which he morally failed, because—Lemmon speculates—he deceived himself as to Hitler's nature. In this case, the agent's moral outlook did not include such moral monstrosities, and he perhaps lacked the moral courage to develop a new vision. Such a case, "if correctly resolved . . . forces [one] to develop a new morality." Lemmon likens this type of dilemma to a case in which an artist stumbles on a new artistic problem and thus must develop new canons of aesthetic creativity. This third type requires a personal authenticity, "to be true to oneself and one's character." Interestingly, this third type of dilemma might escape the problem of dirty hands, for in resolving the dilemma by formulating a canon of morality, the agent may well erase the conflict that emerged from the old canon.

Both the second and third cases can be evaded by bad faith, and both demand for their resolution the moral bravery to be authentic or "true to oneself." While both call for "basic moral rethinking," they differ in that in the second case, the problem is "the applicability of his moral outlook to his present situation," while in the third, the problem is "to create a new moral outlook to meet unprecedented moral needs." In the second case, the agent *might* transform that outlook in successfully resolving the situation, but in the third, the agent *must*, and must do so radically.

Lemmon's taxonomy will illuminate the *Philoctetes*, and especially the profound moral contrast between Neoptolemus and Philoctetes. Though many philosophical interpreters of the play take it to depict the moral transformation of Neoptolemus, we shall see that he is not transfigured by working through a moral conflict, nor can he be; but Philoctetes is. This will take us to the ethical heart of the play. As my analysis will show, Neoptolemus faces three critical moral moments in the play, each one of which corresponds to one of Lemmon's types of dilemma, while Philoctetes basically faces one, which corresponds to the third. In each of Neoptolemus's crucial situations, he acts in bad faith and thus ethically stagnates. In Philoctetes's situation, he struggles, acts authentically, and moves to a new ethical level. Ironically, it is, to speak in Lemmon's terms, Philoctetes, not Neoptolemus, who is "true to" himself, despite the constant references to Neoptolemus's nature[17] and his professed concern to act in accordance with it.

THE CHARACTER OF NEOPTOLEMUS

Neoptolemus, at first glance, seems a likely figure to find at the center of Sophocles's play. Not only is he the man destined to share Philoctetes's glory at Troy, but Sophocles was, Dio Chrysostom tells us,[18] the first tragedian to include Neoptolemus in his dramatization of the myth.[19] Perhaps few would go as far as Lewis Campbell, who describes this character as "one of the most beautiful figures in Greek poetry,"[20] but many assess him sympathetically, at worst, an innocent victim of Odysseus. This view has prevailed, despite William Calder's cogent, though widely ignored, interpretation of Neoptolemus as a nefarious deceiver.[21] Though I diagnose Neoptolemus's impairment differently, my conclusions are in the spirit of Calder's.

On one standard reading, however, the play depicts Neoptolemus's journey to a new moral plateau. Two recent treatments of note chart the philosophical parameters of the play along just these lines. Martha Nussbaum, for one,

---

17. The play emphasizes Neoptolemus's *physis*, which has been the focus of much interpretive debate. The notion is clearly related to the attribution of *gennaios* to him. Both issues are fraught with complicated problems: *physis* because his *physis* seems (at least to some scholars) not unmixedly admirable; *gennaios*, because the notion seems to have transformed with the ethical culture, and some have argued cogently that different characters use the term differently in the play. Nussbaum (1976, 32) appealing to a later Aristotelian usage, maintains that *gennaios* means fidelity to one's nature, and in Neoptolemus's case, this nature is commendable. Calder, who points out that Sophocles uses the term rarely in his other plays, but uses it six times in this one, argues that the way the different characters use the term reflects their different moral standards (1971, 171–172). Avery (1965, 289), whom Calder cites, interprets the play in terms of the way Neoptolemus comes to embody the true, rather than Odyssean, sense of *gennaios*. See also Creed (1972).
18. Dio Chrysostom, *Discourse* 52.
19. See Kieffer's comments on this, which he describes as "Sophocles' great stroke of originality" (1942, 45).
20. Campbell (1881/1969). See Introduction to the *Philoctetes* (vol. 2, 358).
21. Calder (1971).

takes Neoptolemus to be struggling with two competing attitudes towards political justice: Odysseus's in terms of the common good and Philoctetes's in terms of the individual.[22] Neoptolemus, she argues, synthesizes the two ideals and so is transformed from a docile youth to a noble moral agent, who has actualized his best potential as a son of Achilles.[23] Mary Whitlock Blundell, in her more extensive analysis,[24] views Neoptolemus as having to choose "from various [ethical] paradigms" of Odysseus, Philoctetes, and "the background figure of Achilles."[25] He successfully comes to express his *physis* by embodying "the best of Achillean honesty and persuasiveness, while avoiding the concomitant vices of recalcitrance and treachery. [Moreover, Achilles's] forthright pursuit of honor is tempered in him by an unselfish concern for pity, justice, and friendship."[26] This interpretative line receives some support from the structuralist analysis of Pierre Vidal-Naquet, who argues that the play portrays Neoptolemus's transformation from an ephebe to a hoplite. While this approach does not underscore Neoptolemus's development as a moral agent, it does see him as completing a rite of passage, as progressing into manhood.

This line of interpretation faces insurmountable difficulties.[27] Moral development is a form of growth, an actualization of one's ethical potential. Neoptolemus, as Sophocles's audience knew, would go on to commit heinous acts of injustice and hubris. Blundell, like many scholars, finds allusions to his enormities in Heracles's admonitions to him to be pious even in taking Troy. Heracles reminds the two warriors that standards of justice are timeless and universal, transcending cultural difference (1440–1444). How can Neoptolemus have attained moral maturity when he would go on to flout so intemperately those ethical standards?

Blundell tries to accommodate this by ascribing to Sophocles an Aristotelian conception of virtue, with many of its finer nuances. Neoptolemus, she suggests, would act with nobility on Lemnos, but would not go on to do so dispositionally.[28] The play, on this reading, is Neoptolemus's tragedy of a beautiful

---

22. Nussbaum (1976).
23. Nussbaum (1976) tempers her praise of (what she alleges to be) Neoptolemus's noble respect for Philoctetes' personhood with an acknowledgment of his ambitiousness.
24. Blundell (1987, 1989, 1993).
25. Blundell (1987), 307.
26. Blundell (1993), 112.
27. Vidal-Naquet (1990).
28. This is disturbingly procrustean. Aristotelian virtue requires not only promise, but practice. If "one swallow does not make a summer" (*EN* I.7 1098a18), then we need to observe Neoptolemus's subsequent actions, desires, and responses to assess his moral nature.

shoot gone to seed. William Calder, however, adduces powerful evidence against the modern, favorable view of Neoptolemus, which he describes as "a glaring anomaly in the orthodox tradition of the hero and Troy."[29] And, for reasons different from mine, Calder contends that Sophocles's Neoptolemus is far from a paragon of virtue. We should reflect too on the frequent references to Neoptolemus's *physis* as a son of Achilles.[30] Achilles, the centrifugal force of the *Iliad*, has a strength of personality and conviction that Neoptolemus never attains. In the *Iliad* (ix. 312ff) Achilles rails against deception. As Stanley Lombardo so effectively translates him, "I hate like hell/The man who says one thing and thinks another."[31] His directness is essential to his character. Sophocles's Neoptolemus espouses the sentiment, but drops it quickly when Odysseus dangles before him other enticements.

Neoptolemus faces three critical moments in the play: (1) the decision whether he should lie in order to obey his military superior, (2) the decision as to whether he should return the bow of Philoctetes, and (3) the decision whether he should agree to take Philoctetes home rather than to Troy. Interestingly, each of these corresponds to one or another type of moral dilemma in Lemmon's scheme, almost as if Sophocles were offering a similar taxonomy. (1) falls under the first type, because Neoptolemus feels conflicted between his duty as a soldier to obey his superior and his principle that he ought not to lie. (2) falls under the third type, for as we shall see, Neoptolemus has never witnessed suffering of the intensity and magnitude displayed by Philoctetes. Thus, he encounters a situation for which his moral outlook has left him unprepared. (3) falls under the second type, for he feels conflicted, but not between two warring imperatives—he is simply not sure what he ought to do in this case. In none of these situations, however, does he authentically wrestle with the dilemma, let alone resolve it. Taking one route or another, as he does, is not sufficient for having dealt with the moral problem. As Lemmon points out, it is by struggling with dilemmas that one arrives at a new morality or clarifies (and by implication renews) a commitment to one's established morality. As he puts it, "it is hard to see what else would be likely to bring about a change of moral outlook other than having to make a difficult moral decision."[32] Though so many commentators see Neoptolemus as coming to age ethically by tackling such a dilemma, he avails himself of none of the opportunities presented to

---

29. Calder (1971), 168.
30. This is a complex issue that requires close scrutiny on its own. Many scholars addressed the Achillean presence in the play, some taking Philoctetes as embodying it rather than Neoptolemus.
31. See Lombardo's masterful translation (1997).
32. Lemmon (1962), 155.

him, as we shall see. The ethical man he is at the beginning is no different from the man whom Heracles urges to be pious and moderate. Let us examine each of his moral opportunities.

(1) At the start of the play, Neoptolemus evinces a certain moral outlook articulated by both him and Odysseus: He has no qualms about capturing the lame Philoctetes, especially by physical force (86–91) or persuasion (103), though he objects to doing so by verbal trickery. Thus, Neoptolemus remarks, "ἔφυν γὰρ οὐδὲν ἐκ τέχνης πράσσειν κακῆς," (88) indicating his concern not so much with the deed but with the mode of performing it. Deception, as even Odysseus acknowledges, is distasteful to him (79–91; 94–95). On the other hand, he respects his political duties, one of which is to obey his military superior (93–95). Thus, he has a clash between a principle and a duty—between his commitment to honesty and his commitment to fulfill his duty as soldier.

On Lemmon's perspicuous analysis, one resolves such dilemmas (of the first sort) by clarifying the priority of one's values or principles. But Neoptolemus does not deliberate and choose the Odyssean path in *that* way. Scholars have generally overlooked two crucial points about this early situation. First, however strongly Neoptolemus objects to verbal treachery, he has no scruples about using physical force. Despite his later compassion for Philoctetes, he does not hesitate to act with gratuitous violence at Troy. He does not develop any enduring sense of justice or compassion. Secondly, Odysseus, psychologically astute as ever, easily persuades Neoptolemus to adopt his strategy of craft. He first appeals to a broader consequentialist ideal (111), but Neoptolemus's honesty is untethered to any broader moral view. He cannot bring into focus the structure of his moral outlook, because he has no stable outlook. Thus, Odysseus persuades Neoptolemus by reminding him of the glory that he will gain if they take Philoctetes and the bow back to Troy, and he explains that because Philoctetes has the bow, he cannot prevail over him with force. Odysseus seduces Neoptolemus with the promise not only of victory, but also reputation (100–120). Odysseus assures him that he will be *called* wise and good (119). At that Neoptolemus directly agrees to do it.

While many rightly identify Odysseus with the sophists, given his instrumentalist respect for rhetorical virtuosity, Neoptolemus is a stronger model of anti-Socratic, sophist morality,[33] with his preference for appearing good over being good. Ironically, his preference for moral appearance over moral reality is itself a form of dishonesty, and it reveals how superficially he grasps the

---

33. His shifts from one moral criterion to another also suggests this, as does the value he places on *sumpheron*.

value he espouses. As for the first type of moral dilemma, Neoptolemus does not use it, then, to clarify the structure of his moral beliefs; rather he jettisons them and adopts, without acknowledging it, an ethic of honor. So, he has not confronted the dilemma put before him. He does not genuinely choose duty— he quickly forgets it when tempted by honor.

(2) Neoptolemus's next moral reversal occurs once he confronts, existentially, Philoctetes' suffering. It is the chorus hearing his moans, who first expresses pity for the wounded man and implores Neoptolemus to abandon his plot (180–190; 209–211). Before he has a chance to respond, Philoctetes enters, undoubtedly looking pathetic and limping, which makes the audience share the sympathies of the chorus for him.[34] Philoctetes, still human, wants first to hear human discourse. Despite this touching expression of his humanity, Neoptolemus proceeds to execute Odysseus's plot. After Neoptolemus pretends to befriend him, Philoctetes becomes exhausted from a weird, otherworldly seizure of pain and gives Neoptolemus his bow, *the* bow, for safekeeping. Here Neoptolemus begins to question what he should do (895). He discloses his real intentions to Philoctetes who embarks on a justifiable tirade against him. Neoptolemus once again asks what he is to do, because a terrible pity has overcome him (ἐμοὶ μὲν οἶκτος δεινὸς ἐμπέπτωκέ τις [969]). But before he can reverse his course, Odysseus appears and naturally clashes with him over the bow. Neoptolemus purports to have no fear of him. Why should he? He now has the bow as well as the confidence that he is as necessary to Odysseus as are Philoctetes and the bow.

Neoptolemus' situation here is resonant of Lemmon's third type of dilemma in that Philoctetes' pain is of an intensity that Neoptolemus has never encountered. His situation, as Lemmon says, creates "unprecedented moral needs," requiring him to "create a new morality" to meet those needs, indeed a new canon of morality. Neoptolemus is understandably perplexed: How can he integrate this experience into a worldview in which violence is acceptable? At the beginning of the play, he would not hesitate to take a cripple by physical force nor is he unwilling to set aside his reservations about lying if he can thereby appear good in the eyes of others. One would expect Neoptolemus now to integrate his pity into his ethical landscape and so to transform it, just as earlier one would have expected this noble (*gennaios*) youth to value being true to himself rather than gaining the esteem of others. But in this case, too, he fails. Though he is swayed by emotion here—for he does, after all, return the bow— his act does not betoken a reassessment of his moral universe, for which his circumstances afforded him the opportunity. Given the gratuitous acts of violence he would commit at Troy, this is just an arbitrary act.

---

34. See Gardiner (1987). Cf. Poe (1974), 37.

(3) Neoptolemus's final moral moment occurs when he decides to take Philoctetes home rather than to Troy, though he has tried to persuade Philoctetes to come to Troy to take both the cure and the enemy. This could be subsumed under Lemmon's second type of dilemma in which one is not sure of one's obligations, and in solving the dilemma one clarifies what they are. But Neoptolemus does not try to sort out whether he should act from political interests, concern for Philoctetes's desires, or an obligation to keep his promise. He has not fashioned a new moral outlook incorporating any of these values, though he has the chance. His moral motivations are just as self-serving and, more significantly, haphazard as they were at the start. He agrees to take Philoctetes home only after securing from him a vow of protection against the Greeks (1404–1408). Philoctetes, after all, has the bow. Neoptolemus seems swayed here by the force of Philoctetes's personality and his bow, and, possibly, his own earlier unreflective commitment to honesty. Notice, however, that he will respect his pledge *only* if he feels assured of Philoctetes's protection. Neoptolemus thus shows no special moral courage or integrity here. Neoptolemus's decision to take Philoctetes home arises from what Bernard Williams terms an "egoistic micro-motivation" to cooperate.[35] His act gratifies Philoctetes, but it arises not from an externally directed concern with Philoctetes himself as would a "non-egoistic" one; nor does it arise from a commitment to a broader social concern, as would a "macro-motivation," either egoistic or non-egoistic. Finally Heracles appears and commands Philoctetes to go to Troy where he will find redemption, healing, and glory.

Each of the situations affords Neoptolemus an opportunity for moral growth, but he avails himself of none of them. Neoptolemus is striking not so much for his pity for the wounded hero, but for the instability of his motivations. At one time vanity and self-interest take command, at another pity, and yet another, fear. Neoptolemus prefigures a personality Plato describes in his *Republic*—the democratic soul, the person whose values are all on a par, with none prior to another, the person whose choices are arbitrary, as if selected by lot (*Rep.* 8 561a-562a). This encapsulates Williams's insight about egoistic micro-motivations, namely, that "it is the mark of this kind of motivation . . . in a pure form, that there will be no motivational momentum from one case . . . to the next."[36] His beliefs and commitments have no cohesive foundation; rather he may be governed by prudence one day, pleasure another, and an outpouring of benevolence the next. This person's weak, impressionable personality and unreliability make him as dangerous as the most flagrant villain, especially in the eyes of a perceptive Athenian in 409. In this light, Neoptolemus's actions

---

35. Williams (1995), 118.
36. Williams (1995), 118.

after Lemnos seem easily compatible with Sophocles's depiction of him. He has an exterior luster that masks the disease festering in his interior. With Philoctetes, we shall find the reverse. Let us now turn to a scrutiny of his character as an anticipation of the Platonic ideal.

THE VIRTUE OF PHILOCTETES

The Platonic ideal aristocratic soul is governed by rationality, which gives the philosopher-king an internal harmony. This precludes the vacillations we find in Neoptolemus—though not rational deliberation—and also the ethical excesses one finds in Odysseus, or for that matter in Achilles. While Philoctetes does not exactly mirror the Platonic aristocrat, he does exemplify many of his key attributes. He may seem an improbable ancestor of this ethical figure. First, the chorus, Neoptolemus, and Odysseus all vilify Philoctetes as inflexible, severe, and recalcitrant (for example, 1045–1048; 1095– 1100; 1318–1323). Then, too, he might seem perversely vindictive in refusing to go to Troy, where he will be cured. Surely, being healed should be more important than indulging his spite. He has, moreover, good reason to trust Neoptolemus once the bow is returned. But Philoctetes is neither stubborn, vindictive, nor perverse.[37] In order to see this, let us consider Philoctetes's dilemma and how he deals with it. Then we shall examine the notion of the Platonically just soul and how Philoctetes exemplifies it.

Philoctetes, like Neoptolemus, asks at a critical juncture, τί δράσω (1350). Neoptolemus is urging him to go to Troy to win glory and health. Philoctetes wants to go home. On the one hand, he trusts Neoptolemus, but, on the other hand, he cannot even conceive of trusting the people who abandoned him, nor that the universe would be so structured as to allow such morally deformed men to triumph.[38] He is facing a situation for which, in Lemmon's terms, he is "completely unprepared . . . by his moral outlook." A natural reaction to such a situation as Lemmon indicates, is self-deception or bad faith. Overlooking the unprecedented moral claims is easier than "develop[ing] a new morality" or "basic moral rethinking." What Lemmon seems to have in mind is developing radically new principles or dramatically restructuring the framework of those one has (which would require new higher-order principles). As Lemmon contends, this requires a personal authenticity and moral courage. This, too, is a Socratic point: in the early dialogues, Socrates emphasizes the difficulty, but

---

37. Many commentators defend Philoctetes's virtue and heroism, but Poe (1974) takes up his cause against charges such as these using Fryean categories. For a different take, see Biggs (1966).
38. See Poe (1974), 45–46.

importance of jettisoning one's beliefs in order to improve or to develop ethically. Philoctetes faces a situation requiring him to do just that. His dealings with Neoptolemus and, even more so, with Odysseus are rather like Chamberlain having to confront Hitler. But Philoctetes does not fail in his task. He views the Greeks as his enemies and Neoptolemus as his friend. He is unprepared for a friend with divided loyalties, because his concept of *philia* does not encompass the political realm, only the personal. He does not grasp the notion of political *philia*, a loyalty necessary for the existence of the polis. This tension in the play between personal and political claims parallels the tension in so many other Greek dramas between the *oikos* and the polis. In the *Republic*, the guardians must tell the noble lie (414d-e) precisely because the less enlightened souls cannot separate personal and political affection; thus, this myth subsumes political under personal *philia*.

Sophocles, unlike Plato, seems not to have a tidy solution to this problem because he considers the friction between the *oikos* (private domain) and the polis (public domain) to be an inevitable condition of social life. But, interestingly, his treatment does show an awareness of two distinctions subsumed under the private and political: (1) personal and political loyalties; for example, the loyalties one has toward a friend and those toward an anonymous fellow citizen, and (2) self-regarding and other-regarding concerns; for example, the interest one has in self-preservation and the interest one has in preserving the life of a friend or relative.

Philoctetes is about to leave for home when Heracles appears and persuades him to go to Troy. He appeals to his self-regarding interests by confirming that this will indeed bring him a cure and glory. But it is Philoctetes's other-regarding, but nonpolitical, personal loyalty that makes him trust Heracles's veracity and reasoning.[39] His bond of personal *philia* engenders one of political *philia*. In a sense, Heracles compels him to acknowledge the necessity of others, of the polis, even an unjust one, for a civilized individual life. The demands of the polis may conflict with one's individual desires, but this conflict can arise within a personal friendship as well, as that is a smaller-scaled polis. Human interaction, political or personal, may thwart the gratification of some self-regarding desires; but ultimately it gratifies broader ones, and the very possibility of genuine personal loyalty (as Philoctetes evinces towards Heracles) shows the possibility of extending them more broadly. In leaving Lemnos, Philoctetes is leaving a moral landscape. His decision betokens a rationality,

---

39. Cf. Blundell (1989), 220–25. Blundell also sees friendship as a crucial motif, but assesses the character and configuration of their emotional bonds differently than I do. She also sees, as indicated earlier, a genuine friendship between Neoptolemus and Philoctetes at the end of the play.

flexibility, and magnanimity that so many deny he has. He has reassessed his moral world and, in doing so, shows great integrity. Were he truly stubborn and spiteful, he would not have listened to Heracles, or at best would have left grudgingly. He would have been more concerned with saving face than acting in line with his revised beliefs, had he a smaller cast of mind. The problem has allowed him to manifest his natural aristocratic bent of character.

How does this relate him to the aristocratic soul of the *Republic*? His sheer survival on Lemnos would not have been possible without the self-sufficiency and rational control of his passions that belongs to the Platonic aristocrat. Moreover, as seen, he shares the aristocrat's nobility of spirit. It will be helpful to recall how Plato develops his ethical ideal in the *Republic*. Socrates must rise to Glaucon's challenge to prove that the person who acts justly is happier than the one who acts unjustly while suffering no adverse consequences. The conventional ideal is to appear good while acting unfairly. If performed on a large enough scale, such actions can lead to the pinnacle of happiness. The conventional or vulgar notion of justice is to avoid violating the moral and legal rights of others and to obey the laws, all of which allegedly bridle the human acquisitive and passionate impulses.

Plato develops a concept of justice as an internal harmony of the soul, with reason governing *thumos* and appetite. Integrity is a higher-order virtue that emerges from the proper functioning of this triad. Temperate action, for example, emerges from the fundamental integrity of the Platonic soul. Thus integrity is the consistency of the well-governed soul to which Plato refers. Platonic justice guarantees conventional justice because the rationally governed person will not desire the goals that would require her to violate the rights of others. The relationship between Platonic and conventional justice and their respective eudaimonistic rewards have been controversial since the publication of David Sachs's groundbreaking essay.[40] But Plato clearly relies on his aristocrat to be impervious to the blandishments that bring down others. The Platonic aristocrat is rather guided by her rational commitment to her view of the good, not by fear or desire for honor. She exemplifies, most saliently, self-sufficiency and integrity.

Philoctetes is not a philosopher of the sort Plato delineates in Books 5–7 in that he does not devote himself to a logical investigation of reality. (He is kept rather busy just trying to survive.) Nonetheless he does have an integral soul with reason at the helm. While this may not appear to be so, the following considerations make this evident: (1) As for his refusal to go to Troy, even Odysseus realizes how outrageous it would seem to ask him, which is why he needs Neoptolemus—someone not part of the group that left him marooned for

---

40. Sachs (1963).

ten years.[41] (2) When Philoctetes is preparing to kill Odysseus (1299ff), his concern is not to avenge an enemy, but to protect his autonomy. To appeal to Plato's political metaphor, even a well-governed, peaceful state needs an army to defend it. Even a philosophical soul needs the passion of *thumos* to act in self-defense. (3) Heracles never indicates that he finds Philoctetes irascible, just misguided. Philoctetes's anger towards the Greeks contrasts markedly with that of Achilles in the *Iliad*. As Blundell and others have indicated, Achilles is a silent presence in this play. Even if one views Philoctetes as responding as ferociously as Achilles, which seems hyperbolic to say the least, Philoctetes is not dispositionally wrathful, and he has far greater cause than Achilles to growl at the Greeks. (4) Philoctetes, even after ten years as an outcast, has not become a thorough misanthrope, as is clear when he first encounters the Greeks (219ff). His pleasure at human contact attests to this. (5) His initial reluctance to go to Troy suggests an unwillingness to act for purely opportunistic motives, and thus a moral independence. He resembles the Platonic philosopher in his self-sufficiency, integrity, and rationality. His conventionally ethical behavior flows from a deeper, Platonically aristocratic nature, which becomes further actualized as he comes to grips with his dilemma. For such a person to be shunned by his compatriots coheres neatly with the Platonic picture. Plato's aristocrat will be an outcast in an imperfect society and will face the ridicule heaped on the escaped prisoner who returns to the cave or on Socrates by the Athenians.

Once we notice how Philoctetes exemplifies a fundamental mythic archetype, we shall find additional support for this interpretation. Though scholars have not explored this,[42] Philoctetes resembles the god Hephaistos, the crippled god, whose lameness is no fault of his own. Robert Garland describes this god as a symbol of the disabled:

> [He is] a solitary misfit among an unageing population of divinely perfect deities. A variety of theories have [*sic*] been proposed to account for the god's lameness. One is that it is a consequence of his status as a "magician" . . . whereby a special defect is redeemed . . . by a special gift or talent . . . Hephaistos' lameness is thus compensated for by his magical power to infuse life into inanimate materials and forge armour of incomparable excellence.[43]

The resemblance to Philoctetes is obvious: he may be lame, but he has the unerring bow. As with any mythic figure, stories vary as to Hephaistos's circum-

---

41. It is extraordinary that critics find fault with Philoctetes's refusal to go to Troy. For a more insightful approach, see Poe (1974, 16).
42. Segal is an exception. See his (1981, ch. 6, 310–311).
43. Garland (1995), 61.

stances. But consistently, he is the son of Hera, cast off Olympus to fall for days until he landed on Lemnos. Philoctetes, in fact, speaks of Lemnos and its fire as Hephaistos-made ('Ηφαιστότευκτον 986-987). The deformed god exacted revenge on his mother by fashioning for her a golden throne on which she became trapped. Only he could free her. The gods sent Dionysus to retrieve him. They knew he would be reluctant to return; who wants to be included only for necessity? Dionysus made him lose his reason through wine and brought him back. François Lissargue notes that this procession was a prominent scene on Attic vases, that indeed we have nearly 130 extant examples.[44] Lissargue finds these significant in that: "This set of images celebrates both the return of a god under the influences of wine and the triumph of Dionysus."[45]

Sophocles's Philoctetes alludes to the myth of Hephaistos. The play is a poetic equivalent of a processional vase. But notice that Philoctetes is not brought to Troy by trickery or force. Unlike Hephaistos, he does not lose his rationality. Rather, Heracles induces him rationally, by appealing to his own situation and trusting in Philoctetes' reasonable trust in his friend's counsel. Hephaistos is a craftsman, which is an activity of a civilized creature. His lameness, or disability, connects him to the realm of humanity, a realm of imperfection. Philoctetes's bow signifies his humanity, his superiority to the beasts, but the bow also connects him to the divine, the realm of Heracles. Unlike Hephaistos, however, who is lured away by being reduced to bestial irrationality, Philoctetes is induced rationally and by his connection to a god.

In choosing to accept Heracles's counsel, he is not mindlessly succumbing to divine authority, as MacIntyre (1981) would have it. Rather he is learning from a now deified friend, whose greater experience he respects. While the Platonic philosopher arguably ranks *philia* lower than Philoctetes does,[46] both recognize the paradoxical loneliness of political life. The Platonic aristocrat transcends this by minimizing his emotional needs, but he nonetheless can be an outcast within the city. Sophocles dramatically portrays the tension between self-regard and regard for others, on the one hand, and the personal and private domains on the other. But these inevitable frictions are not the only source for the tragic vision Sophocles conveys in this play. Philoctetes goes to rejoin men for whom he has no respect and will earn their esteem by helping these moral monstrosities.[47] This changes his moral worldview. When he leaves Lemnos

---

44. Lissargue (1987), 40.
45. Lissargue (1987), 41.
46. Cf. Peters (1989).
47. This point is poignantly developed by Poe (1974, 44–48). Poe believes, as I do, that Sophocles expresses in this play a bleak view of the human condition, especially the necessity and allure of human companionship.

and addresses the island, he asks to be sent without blame (ἀμέμπτως; 1465). He has perhaps lost some of his enthusiasm being among people, but has moved to a new plateau. In asking to go without blame, he is accepting his new moral outlook, which leaves his hands clean. Sophocles does not see any sullying residue in his act. With the help of Heracles, Philoctetes learns that one can navigate through the obstacles that await the person of integrity in a less than ideal community. Perhaps the Sophoclean insight about the guidance that personal *philia* can offer is what Plato would come to embrace in his *Phaedrus*.

Both Sophocles and Plato portray ethical ideals of a rational soul whose primary value is integrity and the self-sufficiency that naturally accompanies it. Both accept the existence of moral facts and the human ability to grasp them. For Sophocles, the human agent can glean the laws of the gods, but she cannot understand why the gods arrange matters as they do. Plato too thinks us ultimately ignorant of why moral reality is as it is. Even if the philosopher completes the arduous task of grasping the Form of the Good, Plato does not indicate that the philosopher can know why it has the character it has. He does not, that is, seem to have modified the skepticism expressed in the *Phaedo* (99c-e) about the human capacity to know final causes, in spite of the greater epistemic optimism implicit in the philosophical method of the *Republic*.

Sophocles, then, artistically foreshadows some crucial Platonic motifs and even a poetic gesture in the ironically reversed portraiture. Philoctetes, like Socrates or like the philosopher of the *Republic*, has a misleadingly ugly appearance that conceals an inner luster; Neoptolemus, in contrast, appears radiant with health and beauty, but is diseased and corrupt within. Sophocles's portrayal rests on a moral realism and a confidence in the human moral epistemic faculties. But this does not, for Sophocles, minimize the tragedy of the human condition. Though Sophocles usually does not spring to mind as a pre-Platonic philosopher who, one might speculate, may have even influenced Plato, our reading of the *Philoctetes* has shown him to be not only a dramatic poet, but also a philosophical thinker of great subtlety.

Bibliography

Allen, R. E. (1997). *Plato's Parmenides,* 2d ed. New Haven, CT: Yale University Press.

Anton, John, and Kustas, G., ed. (1971). *Essays in Ancient Greek Philosophy I.* Albany: State University of New York Press.

Asmis, E. (1986). *Epicurus' Scientific Methodology.* Ithaca, NY: Cornell University Press.

Avery, Henry C. (1965). "Heracles, Philoctetes, Neoptolemus," *Hermes* 93:279–297.

Baccou, Robert (1951). *Histoire de la science grecque de Thalès à Socrate.* Paris.

Baldes, R. W. (1975). "Democritus on Visual Perception: Two Theories or One?" *Phronesis* 20:93–105.

———. (1978a). "Democritus on the Nature and Perception of 'Black' and 'White'," *Phronesis* 23:87–100.

——— (1978b). "Subjectivism and Objectively True Observation Statements in Democritus." *The Ancient World* 1:89–95.

——— (1981). "Democritus on Empirical Knowledge: Reflections on DK 68B125 and on Aristotle *Metaphysics* 4.5." *The Ancient World* 4:17–34.

Barnes, Jonathan (1979). *The Presocratic Philosophers*, two vols. London: Routledge and Kegan Paul; 1982: 2d ed.

Belfiore, Elizabeth (1992). *Tragic Pleasures: Aristotle on Plot and Emotion.* Princeton, NJ: Princeton University Press.

Berkeley, George (1710). *Principles of Human Knowledge.* London: Aaron Rhames.

Biggs, Penelope (1966). "The Disease Theme in Sophocles's *Ajax, Philoctetes,* and *Trachiniae.*" *Classical Philology* 61:223–335.

Blundell, Mary Whitlock (1987). "The Moral Character of Odysseus in *Philoctetes.*" *Greek, Roman, and Byzantine Studies* 28:307–329.

——— (1989). *Helping Friends and Harming Enemies: A Study in Sophocles and Greek Ethics.* Cambridge: Cambridge University Press.

——— (1993). "The *Phusis* of Neoptolemus in Sophocles's *Philoctetes,*" in Ian McAuslan and Peter Walcott, eds., *Greek Tragedy.* Oxford: Oxford University Press. 104–115. Reprint from *Greece and Rome* 35 (1988):137–148.

Bodnár, I. M. (1988). "Anaximander's Rings." *Classical Quarterly* 38:49–51.

Bollack, Jean (1965–1969). *Empédocle,* vol. I–IV (Paris: Editions de Minuit) (1965 = vol. I)

Bolotin, David (1993). "Continuity and Infinite Divisibility in Aristotle's *Physics.*" *Ancient Philosophy* 13:323–340.

Booth, N. B. (1957a). "Were Zeno's Arguments A Reply to Attacks Upon Parmenides?" *Phronesis* 2:1–9.

——— (1957b). "Were Zeno's Arguments Directed Against the Pythagoreans?" *Phronesis* 2:90–103.

Bousset, W. (1901). "Die Himmelsreise der Seele," *Archiv für Religions-
wissenschaft*, 136–169 and 229–273 (repr. Darmstadt).

Brumbaugh, R. S. (1981). *The Philosophy of Greece*. Albany: State University
of New York Press.

Burch, George (1949–1950). "Anaximander, the First Metaphysician," *Review
of Metaphysics* 3:137–160.

Burkert, Walter (1963). "Iranisches bei Anaximander." *Rheinisches Museum
für Philologie* 106:97–113.

——— (1962). *Weisheit und Wissenschaft: Studien zu Pythagoras, Philolaos
und Platon*. Nürnberg: H. Carl.

——— (1972). *Lore and Science in Ancient Pythagoreanism* (Cambridge, MA),
tr. by Edwin Minar of a revised edition of *Weisheit und Wissenschaft*.

——— (1977). "Air-Imprints or Eidola: Democritus' Aetiology of Vision." *Illi-
nois Classical Studies* II, 96–109.

Burnet, John (1930). *Early Greek Philosophy*, 4th ed. London: Black.

Calder, William (1971). "Sophoclean Apologia: *Philoctetes*," *Greek, Roman,
and Byzantine Studies* 12:153–174.

Campbell, Lewis (1881/1969). *Sophocles: The Plays and Fragments* (edited
with Notes and an Introduction, 2 vol.) Hildesheim: George Olms
reprint.

Cassin, Barbara (1992). " 'Barbariser' et 'citoyenner' ou On n'échappe pas à
Antiphon." *Rue Descartes (Collège international de philosophie)*, Janvier
1992, 3, 19–34. Incorporated (with modifications) in B. Cassin (1995),
L'Effet Sophistique. Paris: Gallimard. 161–184.

Castertano, Giovanni (1978). *Parmenide. Il metodo, la scienza, l'esperienza*.
Naples: Loffredo Editore.

Chalmers, A. (1997). "Did Democritus Ascribe Weight to Atoms?" *Aus-
tralasian Journal of Philosophy* 75: 279–287.

Clagett. M. (1989). *Ancient Egyptian Science. A Source Book*, vol. 1, *Knowledge and Order*. Philadelphia: American Philosophical Society.

Classen, C. J. (1986). *Ansätze: Beiträge zum Verständniss der frühgriechischen
Philosophie*. Würzburg: K&N and Amsterdam: Rhodopi.

Conche, M. (1991). *Anaximandre. Fragments et Témoignages*. Paris: Presses
Universitaires de France.

Conley, Thomas M. (1985). "Dating the Dissoi Logoi: A Cautionary Note." *Ancient Philosophy* 5.1:59–65.

Cornford, F. M. (1934). "Innumerable Worlds in Presocratic Philosophy." *Classical Quarterly* 28:1–16 .

——— (1952). *Principium Sapientiae.* Cambridge: Cambridge University Press.

Couloubaritsis, L. (1980). "Considérations sur la notion de *Noũs* chez Démocrite," *Archiv für Geschichte der Philosophie* 62:129–145.

Couprie, Dirk L. (1995). "The Visualization of Anaximander's Astronomy." *Apeiron* 28:159–181.

——— (1996). "Het universum volgens Kant," *Algemeen Nederlands Tijdschrift voor Wijsbegeerte.* 88:18–30.

Creed, J. L. (1972). "Moral Values in the Age of Thucydides." *Classical Quarterly* ns 23:213–231.

Cullen, C. (1996). *Astronomy and Mathematics in Ancient China: The Zhou bi suan jing.* Cambridge: Cambridge University Press.

Curd, Patricia Kenig (1991). "Knowledge and Unity in Heraclitus." *The Monist* 74:531–549.

——— (1993). "Eleatic Monism in Zeno and Melissus." *Phronesis* 38:1–22.

——— (1998). *The Legacy of Parmenides: Eleatic Monism and Later Presocratic Thought.* Princeton, NJ: Princeton University Press.

Dancy, R. M. (1984). "The One, the Many, and the Forms: *Philebus* 15b1-8." *Ancient Philosophy* 4:160–193.

Decleva Caizzi, Fernanda (1989). "Antipho," in Francesco Adorno et al., eds. *Corpus dei papiri filosofici greci e latini.* Florence: Olschki. 176–236.

DeLacy, P. (1958). "*où μᾶλλον* and the Antecedents of Ancient Scepticism." *Phronesis* 3:59–71.

De Santillana, Giorgio (1961). *The Origins of Scientific Thought.* New York: Mentor Books.

——— (1963). *Prologue to Parmenides.* Cincinnati: University of Cincinnati.

Dicks, D. R. (1966). "Solstices, Equinoxes, and the Presocratics." *The Journal of Hellenic Studies* 86:26–40.

——— (1970). *Early Greek Astronomy to Aristotle.* Ithaca, NY: Cornell University Press.

Diels, Hermann (1897). "Ueber Anaximanders Kosmos." *Archiv für Geschichte der Philosophie* 10:228–237. Reprinted in H. Diels (1969) *Kleine Schriften zur Geschichte der Philosophie.* Hildesheim: Georg Olms. 13–22.

Diels, H., and Kranz, W. (1951/1961/1989). *Die Fragmente der Vorsokratiker,* 6th ed. Berlin: Weidmannsche Buchhandlung. = DK.

Dixsaut, Monique, ed. (1999). *Études sur le Philèbe de Platon,* 2 vols. Paris: Vrin.

Dreyer, J.L.E. (1906/1953; 2d ed.). *A History of Astronomy from Thales to Kepler.* Cambridge: Cambridge University Press and New York: Dover.

Duchesne-Guillemin, J. (1966). "D'Anaximandre à Empédocle: Contacts Gréco-Iraniens." *Atti del convegno sul tema: la Persia a il mondo Greco-*

Romano (Roma, 11–14 aprile 1965). Roma: Accademia Nazionale di Lincei. 423–431.

Dumont, J.-P. (1988). *Les Présocratiques*. Paris: Gallimard.

Ebeling, E. (1931). *Tod und Leben nach der Vorstellung der Babylonier. I.Teil, Texte*. Berlin/Leipzig: De Gruyter.

Eggermont, H. L. (1973). "The Proportions of Anaximander's Celestial Globe and the Gold-Silver Ratio of Croesus' Coinage," in M. A. Beek, et al., eds., *Symbolae Biblicae et Mesopotamicae Francisco Mario Theodoro De Liagre Böhl Dedicatae*. Leiden: E. J. Brill. 118–128.

Eisler, R. (1910). *Weltenmantel und Himmelszelt*. München: Beck.

English, R. B. (1915). "Democritus' Theory of Sense Perception." *Transactions of the American Philological Association* 46:217–227.

Engmann, Joyce (1991). "Cosmic Justice in Anaximander." *Phronesis* 36:1–25.

Farrar, C. (1988). *The Origins of Democratic Thinking*. Cambridge: Cambridge University Press.

Forbiger, Albert (1842). *Handbuch der alten Geographie*, Band I. Leipzig: Verlag von Mayer und Wiegand.

Frank, Erich (1923). *Plato und die sogenannten Pythagoreer*. Halle: Neimeyer.

Furley, David J. (1967). *Two Studies in the Greek Atomists*. Princeton, NJ: Princeton University Press.

———— (1974). "Zeno and Indivisible Magnitudes," in Mourelatos (1974).

———— (1981). "Antiphon's Case Against Justice," in G. B. Kerferd, ed., *The Sophists and Their Legacy*. Wiesbaden: *Hermes* Einzelschriften 44:81–91.

———— (1983). "Weight and Motion in Democritus' Theory." *Oxford Studies in Ancient Philosophy* 1:193–209.

———— (1987). *The Greek Cosmologists*, vol. 1. Cambridge: Cambridge University Press.

———— (1989). *Cosmic Problems*. Cambridge: Cambridge University Press.

———— (1993). "Democritus and Epicurus on Sensible Qualities," in J. Brunschwig and M. Nussbaum, eds., *Passions and Perceptions: Studies in Hellenistic Philosophy of Mind*. Cambridge: Cambridge University Press, 72–94.

Gagarin, Michael (1990). "The Ambiguity of *Eris* in the *Works and Days*," in M. Griffith and D. J. Mastronarde, eds., *Cabinet of the Muses: Essays on Classical and Comparative Literature in Honor of Thomas G. Rosenmeyer*. Atlanta, GA: Scholars Press. 173–183.

———— (1994). "Probability and Persuasion: Plato and Early Greek Rhetoric," in Ian Worthington, ed., *Persuasion. Greek Rhetoric in Action*. London: Routledge. 46–68.

———— (1997). *Antiphon, the Speeches* (edition and commentary). Cambridge: Cambridge University Press.

Gagarin, Michael, and Paul Woodruff (1995). *Early Greek Political Thought from Homer to the Sophists.* Cambridge: Cambridge University Press.

Gardiner, Cynthia P. (1987). *The Sophoclean Chorus: A Study of Character and Functionk.* Iowa City: University of Iowa Press.

Garland, Robert (1995). *The Eye of the Beholder: Deformity and Disability in the Greco-Roman World.* Ithaca, NY: Cornell University Press.

Germain, G. (1954). *Homère et la mystique des nombres.* Paris.

Gill, Christopher (1993). "Bow, Oracle, and Epiphany in Sophocles' *Philoctetes,*" in Ian McAuslan and Peter Walcott, eds., *Greek Tragedy.* Oxford: Oxford University Press, 95–103, reprint from (1980) *Greece and Rome* 2nd series 27:137–146.

Gosling, J.C.B. (1975). *Plato: Philebus.* Oxford: Clarendon Press.

Gowans, Christopher W. (1987). "The Debate on Moral Dilemmas," in C. W. Gowans ed., *Moral Dilemmas.* Oxford and New York: Oxford University Press.

Graham, Daniel (1988). "Symmetry in the Empedoclean Cycle." *Classical Quarterly* 38:297–312.

Greenhalgh, P.A.L. (1973). *Early Greek Warfare. Horsemen and Chariots in the Homeric and Archaic Ages.* Cambridge: Cambridge University Press.

Guthrie, W.K.C. (1962). *A History of Greek Philosophy,* vol. 1. Cambridge: Cambridge University Press.

———— (1965). *A History of Greek Philosophy,* vol. 2. Cambridge: Cambridge University Press.

———— (1971). *The Sophists* (Originally part I of vol. III of *A History of Greek Philosophy*). Cambridge: Cambridge University Press.

Haack, Susan (1978). *Philosophy of Logics.* Cambridge: Cambridge University Press.

Hackforth, R. (1954). *Plato's Examination of Pleasure.* Cambridge.

Hahn, R. (1978). "On Plato's *Philebus* 15B1-8." *Phronesis* 23:158–172.

———— (1995). "Technology and Anaximander's Cosmical Imagination: A Case-Study for the Influence of Monumental Architecture on the Origins of Western Philosophy/Science," in J. C. Pitt, ed., *New Directions in the Philosophy of Technology.* Dordrecht/Boston/London: Kluwer, 95–138.

Hall, J. J. (1969). "πρηστῆρος αὐλός." *The Journal of Hellenic Studies* 89:57–59.

Hampton, Cynthia (1988). "Plato's Late Ontology: A Riddle Unresolved." *Ancient Philosophy* 8.1:105–116.

———— (1990). *Pleasure, Knowledge and Being.* Albany: State University of New York Press.

Heath, Sir Thomas (1913). *Aristarchus of Samos.* Oxford: Clarendon.

Heinemann, F. (1945). *Nomos und Physis.* Basel: F. Reinhardt.

Heitsch, Ernst (1969/1976). "Ein Buchtitel des Protagoras." *Hermes* 97:292–96. Reprinted with additional bibliography in C. J. Classen, ed., *Sophistik.* Darmstadt: Wissenschaftliche Buchgesellschaft. 298–305.

Hölscher, U. (1970). "Anaximander and the Beginnings of Greek Philosophy," in D. J. Furley and R. E. Allen, *Studies in Presocratic Philosophy*, vol. 1, *The Beginnings of Philosophy.* New York: Humanities Press. 281–322.

Huffman, Carl (1985). "The Authenticity of Archytas Fr. 1," *Classical Quarterly* 35:344–348.

———— (1993). *Philolaus of Croton.* Cambridge: Cambridge University Press.

———— (1999). "Limite et illimité chez les premiers philosphes grecs," in Dixsaut (1999) vol. II:11–31.

Hume, David (1896). *A Treatise of Human Nature.* Ed. L. A. Selby-Bigge. Oxford: Clarendon Press. First published in 1739–1740.

———— (1902). *Enquiries*, Ed. L. A. Selby-Bigge. Oxford: Clarendon Press. First published in 1777.

Inwood, Brad (1992). *The Poem of Empedocles.* Toronto: University of Toronto Press.

Jameson, M. H. (1956). "Politics and the *Philoctetes.*" *Classical Philology* 51:217–227.

Jones, K. G. (1971). "The Observational Basis for Kant's Cosmogony: A Critical Analysis." *Journal of the History of Astronomy* 2:29–34.

Kahn, Charles H. (1960). *Anaximander and the Origins of Greek Cosmology.* New York: Columbia University Press.

———— (1969). [Review of] Jean Bollack (1965). *Gnomon* 41:442.

———— (1970) "On Early Greek Astronomy." *The Journal of Hellenic Studies* 90:99–116.

———— (1985) "Democritus and the Origins of Moral Psychology." *American Journal of Philology* 106:1–31.

———— (1993) "Pythagorean Philosophy Before Plato," in A.P.D. Mourelatos, ed., *The Pre-Socratics*, 2d ed. Princeton, NJ: Princeton University Press, 161–185.

Kant, I. (1755/1981). *Allgemeine Naturgeschichte und Theorie des Himmels.* Königsberg und Leipzig [anonymous]. Transl. by S. L. Jaki (1981) *Immanuel Kant. Universal Natural History and Theory of the Heavens.* Edinburgh: Scottish Academic Press.

Kerferd, G. B. (1955/1956). "Gorgias on Nature or That Which Is Not." *Phronesis* 1:3–25.

———— (1965). "Recent Work on Presocratic Philosophy." *American Philosophical Quarterly* 2:130–140.

———— (1981). *The Sophistic Movement.* Cambridge: Cambridge University Press.

Kieffer, John S. (1942). "Philoctetes and 'Arete'." *Classical Philology* 37:38–50.

Kingsley, Peter (1994). "Empedocles and his Interpreters: The Four-Element Doxography," *Phronesis* 39:235–254.

———— (1995). *Ancient Philosophy, Mystery and Magic: Empedocles and the Pythagorean Tradition.* Oxford: Oxford University Press.

Kirk, G. S. (1955). "Some Problems in Anaximander." *Classical Quarterly* N. S. 5:28–32.

Kirk, G. S., and Raven, J. E. (1957). *The Presocratic Philosophers.* Cambridge: Cambridge University Press.

Kirk, G. S., Raven, J. E., and Schofield, M. = KRS (1983). *The Presocratic Philosophers*, 2d ed. Cambridge: Cambridge University Press.

Kline, A. D., and Matheson, C. A. (1987). "The Logical Impossibility of Collision." *Philosophy* 62:509–515.

Konstan, David (1979). "Problems in Epicurean Physics." *ISIS* 70.

Krafft, F. (1971). *Geschichte der Naturwissenschaft I.* Freiburg. 92–120. (The same article: F. Krafft, "Anaximandros," in K. Fassmann, ed., *Die Grossen der Weltgeschichte, I.* München. 1971:284–305, and in F. Krafft: "Anaximander und Hesiodos. Die Ursprung rationaler griechischer Naturbetrachtung." *Sudhoffs Archiv* 55 (1971):152–179.

Lambert, W. G. (1975). "The Cosmology of Sumer and Babylon," in C. Blacker and M. Loewe, eds., *Ancient Cosmologies.* London: Allen and Unwin. 42–65.

Lemmon, E. J. (1962). "Moral Dilemmas." *The Philophical Review* 70:139–158.

Lerner, E. J. (1991). *The Big Bang Never Happened.* London: Times Books.

Lesher, J. H. (1978). "Xenophanes' Scepticism." *Phronesis* 23:1–21.

———— (1983). "Heraclitus' Epistemological Vocabulary." *Hermes* 111: 155–170

———— (1992). *Xenophanes of Colophon: Fragments.* Toronto: University of Toronto Press.

Levi, A. J. (1940). "On Twofold Statements." *American Journal of Philology* 61:292–306.

Lissargue, François (1987). *The Aesthetics of the Greek Banquet: Images of Wine and Ritual*, trans. Andrew Szegedy-Maszak. Princeton, NJ: Princeton University Press.

Lloyd, G.E.R. (1966). *Polarity and Analogy: Two Types of Argumentation in Early Greek Thought.* Cambridge: Cambridge University Press.

———— (1990). "Plato and Archytas in the Seventh Letter." *Phronesis* 35.2: 159–174.

Loenen, J.H.M.M. (1959). *Parmenides, Melissus, Gorgias.* Assen: Royal Van-Gorcum.

Lombardo, Stanley (1997). *Homer, Iliad.* Indianapolis, IN: Hackett Publishing.

Long, A. A. (1974). "Empedocles' Cosmic Cycle in the Sixties," in A.P.D. Mourelatos, *The Presocratics* (1974).

Long, A. A, and Sedley, D. N. (1987). *The Hellenistic Philosophers*. Cambridge: Cambridge University Press.

Luria, S. (1932/1933). "Die Infinitesimaltheorie der antiken Atomisten," *Quellen und Studien zur Geschichte der Mathematik, Astronomie und Physik*, Abt. B: Studien, vol. 2 fasc. 2:106–185.

——— (1970). *Democritea* [Demokrit: Teksty, perevod, issledovanija]. Leningrad: NAUK.

MacIntyre, A. (1981). *After Virtue*. Notre Dame, IN: University of Notre Dame Press.

Makin, Stephen (1989). "The Indivisibility of the Atom." *Archiv für Geschichte der Philosophie* 71:125–149.

——— (1993). *Indifference Arguments*. Oxford: Blackwell Publishers.

Mansfeld, J. (1985). "Historical and Philosophical Aspects of Gorgias' 'On What is Not'," in L. Montoneri and F. Romano, eds., *Gorgia e la Sofistica: Atti del convegno internazionale, Lentini-Catania, 12–15 dicembre 1983*, Siculorium Gymnasium, N.S. a38, nos. 1–2. Catania: Università di Catania, 243–271.

Marcus, Ruth Barcan (1980). in *The Journal of Philosophy* 77:121–36; reprinted in Gowans (1987), 188–204.

Matson, Wallace I. (1980). "Parmenides Unbound." *Philosophical Inquiry* (Athens) 2.1:345–360.

——— (1987). *A New History of Philosophy*, vol. 1: *Ancient and Medieval*. New York: Harcourt Brace Jovanovich.

——— (1988). "The Zeno of Plato and Tannery Vindicated." *La Parola del Passato* (Naples) 43:312–336.

Mau, J. (1954). *Zum Problem des Infinitesimalen bei den antiken Atomisten*. Berlin: Akademie-Verlag.

McAuslan, Ian, and Peter Walcott, eds. (1993). *Greek Tragedy*. Oxford: Oxford University Press.

McDiarmid, J. B. (1959). "Theophrastus, *De Sensibus* 66: Democritus' Explanation of Salinity." *American Journal of Philology* 80:56–66.

McKim, R. (1984). "Democritus Against Skepticism: All Sense Impressions Are True," in L. G. Benakis, ed., *Proceedings of the First International Congress on Democritus*. Xanthi: International Democritean Foundation. 281–290.

McKirahan, Richard D. (1993). *Philosophy Before Socrates*. Indianapolis, IN: Hackett Publishing.

——— (1996). "Epicurean Doxography in Cicero, *De Natura Deorum*, Book I," in G. Giannantoni and M. Gigante, eds., *Epicureismo Greco e Romano, Atti del Congresso Internazionale, Napoli, 19–26 Maggio 1993*. Naples: Bibliopolis. 865–878.

Morrison, J. S. (1963/1976). "The Truth of Antiphon." *Phronesis* 8:35–49. Reprinted with additional bibliography in C. J. Classen, ed., *Sophistik*. Darmstadt: Wissenschafliche Buchgesellschaft. 519–536.

Moulton, C. (1974). "Antiphon the Sophist and Democritus." *Museum Helveticum* 31:129–139.

Mourelatos, A.P.D., ed. (1974). *The Presocratics*. New York: Anchor Books. 2d ed. (1993) Princeton, NJ: Princeton University Press.

Muller, Carl W. (1965). *Gleiches zu Gleichem: Ein Prinzip fruhgriechischen Denkens*. Weisbaden: Otto Harrassowitz.

Naddaf, Gerard (1998). "On the Origin of Anaximander's Cosmological Model." *Journal of the History of Ideas* 51.1:1–28.

Narcy, Michel (1989). "Antiphon d'Athènes," in Richard Goulet, ed., *Dictionnaire des philosophes antiques*. Paris: Editions du CNRS. 225–244.

Navia, Luis E. (1993). *The Presocratic Philosophers: An Annotated Bibliography*. New York: Garland.

Needham, Joseph (1959). *Science and Civilisation in China*, vol. 3. Cambridge: Cambridge University Press.

Neugebauer, O. (1952). *The Exact Sciences in Antiquity*. Princeton, NJ: Princeton University Press.

Neuhäuser, I. (1883). *Anaximander Milesius sive vetustissima quaedam rerum universitatis conceptio restituta*. Bonn: Max Cohen et filium.

Nill, Michael (1985). *Morality and Self-Interest in Protagoras, Antiphon and Democritus*. Leiden: Brill.

Nussbaum, Martha (1976). "Consequences and Character in Sophocles' *Philoctetes*." *Philosophy and Literature* 1:25–53.

———— (1979). "Eleatic Conventionalism and Philolaus on the Conditions of Thought." *Harvard Studies in Classical Philology* 83:63–108.

O'Brien, Denis (1967). "Anaximander's Measurements." *The Classical Quarterly* 61:424–425.

———— (1969). *Empedocles' Cosmic Cycle, A Reconstruction from the Fragments and Secondary Sources*. Cambridge: Cambridge University Press.

———— (1981). *Theories of Weight in the Ancient World*, vol. I: *Democritus on Weight and Size: An Exercise in the Reconstruction of Early Greek Philosophy*. Paris: Les Belles Lettres.

———— (1995). "Empedocles Revisited." *Ancient Philosophy* 15: 403.

O'Keefe, Tim (1996). "The Ontological Status of Sensible Qualities for Democritus and Epicurus," presented at the Central American Philosphical Association meetings (1997). Revised: *Ancient Philosophy* 17:119–134.

O'Meara, D. J. (1989). *Pythagoras Revived. Mathematics and Philosophy in Late Antiquity*. Oxford: Clarendon.

Ostwald, Martin (1990). "*Nomos* and *Phusis* in Antiphon's Περὶ 'Αληθείας," in M. Griffith and D. J. Mastronarde, eds., *Cabinet of the Muses: Essays on Classical and Comparative Literature in Honor of Thomas G. Rosenmeyer.* Atlanta, GA: Scholars Press. 293–306.

O'Sullivan, Neil (1992). *Alcidamas, Aristophanes and the Beginnings of Greek Stylistic Theory. Hermes* Einzelschriften 60. Wiesbaden: Steiner.

Owen, G.E.L. (1958). "Zeno and the Mathematicians." *Proceedings of the Aristotelian Society* 58:199–222.

Parpola, S. (1993). "The Assyrian Tree of Life: Tracing the Origins of Jewish Monotheism and Greek Philosophy." *Journal of Near Eastern Studies* 52:161–208.

Parry, Adam (1957/1981). Logos *and* Ergon *in Thucydides.* Ph.D. Diss., Harvard; Arno Press reprint.

Perelman, Chaim (1963). "The Specific Nature of Juridical Proof," in *The Idea of Justice and the Problem of Argument.* New York: Humanities Press, 98–108.

Peters, James Roberts (1989). "Reason and Passion in Plato's *Republic.*" *Ancient Philosophy* 9:173–187.

Poe, Joe Park (1974). *Heroism and Divine Justice in Sophocles' Philoctetes.* Leiden: E. J. Brill.

Procopé, J. F. (1989). "Democritus on Politics and the Care of the Soul." *Classical Quarterly* 39:307–331.

Randall Jr., J. H. (1970). *Plato, Dramatist of the Life of Reason.* New York: Columbia University Press.

Raphael, D. D. (1983). "Can Literature be Moral Philosophy." *New Literary History* 15:1–12.

Reinhardt, K. (1959). *Parmenides und die Geschichte der griechischen Philosophie,* 2d ed. Frankfurt: Vittorio Klostermann.

Rescher, Nicholas (1958). "Cosmic Evolution in Anaximander?" *Studium Generale* 11:718–731. Reprinted in: Rescher (1969). "Cosmic Evolution in Anaximander," *Essays in Philosophical Analysis.* Pittsburgh: University of Pittsburgh Press.

Ridley, Aaron (1993). "Tragedy and the Tender-Hearted." *Philosophy and Literature* 27:234–245.

Robinson, John M. (1968). *An Introduction to Early Greek Philosophy.* Boston: Houghton Mifflin.

——— (1971). "Anaximander and the Problem of the Earth's Immobility," in Anton & Kustas (1971). *Essays in Ancient Greek Philosophy,* vol. 1.

Robinson, Thomas M. (1979). *Contrasting Arguments.* An Edition of the *Dissoi Logoi.* New York: Ayer.

——— (1987). *Heraclitus of Ephesus, Fragments: Text and Translation.* Toronto: University of Toronto Press.

Rochberg-Halton, F. (1983). "Stellar Distances in Early Babylonian Astronomy: A New Perspective on the Hilprecht Text (HS 229)." *Journal of Near Eastern Studies* 42:209–217.

de Romilly, J. (1988). *Les Grands Sophistes dans l'Athènes de Périclès.* Paris: Fallois.

——— (1992), Tr. J. Lloyd, *The Great Sophists in Periclean Athens.* Oxford: Clarendon Press.

Röper, Gerhart (1852). *Philologus* 7.

Rose, Peter W. (1992). *Sons of the Gods, Children of the Earth.* Ithaca, NY and London: Cornell University Press.

Ross, David (1951). *Plato's Theory of Ideas.* Oxford: Clarendon Press.

Sachs, David (1963). "A Fallacy in Plato's *Republic.*" *Philosophical Review* 72:141–158.

Saltzer, W. (1990). "Vom Chaos zu Ordnung. Die Kosmologie der Vorsokratiker," in U. Schulz, ed., *Scheibe, Kugel, Schwarzes Loch. Die wissenschaftliche Eroberung des Kosmos.* München. 61–70.

Sambursky, Samuel (1956/1987). *The Physical World of the Greeks.* New York: Macmillan.

Sayre, K. (1983) *Plato's Late Ontology: A Riddle Resolved.* Princeton, NJ: Princeton University Press.

——— (1987) "The *Philebus* and the Good." *Proceedings of the Boston Area Colloquium in Ancient Philosophy* 2:45–71.

Schibli, H. S. (1996). "On 'the One' in Philolaus, Fragment 7." *Classical Quarterly* 46.1:114–130.

Schmitz, H. (1988). *Anaximander und die Anfänge der griechischen Philosophie.* Bonn: Bouvier Verlag.

Searle, John R. (1995). *The Construction of Social Reality.* New York: Free Press.

Sedley, David (1992). "Sextus Empiricus and the Atomist Criterion of Truth." *Elenchos* 13 (fasc. 1–2):21–56.

——— (1995). "The Dramatis Personae of Plato's *Phaedo,*" in T. J. Smiley, ed., *Philosophical Dialogues: Plato, Hume, Wittgenstein. Proceedings of the British Academy* 85. Oxford: Oxford University Press. 3–26.

Segal, Charles (1981). *Tragedy and Civilization.* Cambridge, MA: Harvard University Press.

Shamsi, F. A. (1994). "A Note on Aristotle *Physics* 239b5–7: What Exactly Was Zeno's Argument of the Arrow?" *Ancient Philosophy* 14:51–72.

Sharples, R. W. (1996). *Stoics, Epicureans, and Sceptics.* London and New York: Routledge.

Sherry, David M. (1988). "Zeno's Metrical Paradox Revisited." *Philosophy of Science* 55:58–73.

Shwayder, D. S. (1955). "Achilles Unbound." *Journal of Philosophy* 52:449–458.

Smith, Joseph W. (1985). "Zeno's Paradoxes." *Explorations in Knowledge* 2.1:1–12.

Snyder, George S. (1984). *Maps of the Heavens.* New York: Abbeville Press.

Solmsen, Friedrich (1965). "Love and Strife in Empedocles' Cosmogony." *Phronesis* 10:109–148.

———— (1974). "The Tradition About Zeno of Elea Re-Examined," in Moure-latos (1974) 368–393. Originally in *Phronesis* 16 (1971).

Sorabji, Richard (1983). *Time, Creation, and the Continuum.* Ithaca, NY: Cornell University Press.

Spinelli, E. (1996/1997). "On Using the Past in Sextus Empiricus: The Case of Democritus," presented to the Society for Ancient Greek Philosophy, December 1996; revised version (1997): *Hyperboreus* 3:151–173.

Sprague, Rosamond Kent, ed. (1972). *The Older Sophists.* Columbia: University of South Carolina Press.

———— (1990). "Aristotle on Mutilation; *Metaphysics* 5.27." *Syllecta Classica* 2.

Stanford, W. B., ed. (1958). *Aristophanes, The Frogs.* London: MacMillan.

Stephanus, H. (1570). *Diogenes Laertius Opera* 1. Paris: Etienne.

Stewart, Z. (1958). "Democritus and the Cynics." *Harvard Studies in Classical Philology* 63:179–191.

Stocker, Michael (1986). "Dirty Hands and Conflicts of Values and of Desires in Aristotle's Ethics." *Pacific Philosophical Quarterly* 67:36–61.

Stokes, M. C. (1971). *One and Many in Presocratic Philosophy.* Washington, DC: Center for Hellenic Studies.

Striker, G. (1970). *Peras und Apeiron: Das Problem der Formen in Platons Philebos.* Göttingen: Vandenhoeck and Ruprecht.

Stritzinger, H.-W. (1952). *Untersuchungen zu Anaximander* (Inaugural-Dissertation in typescript) (Mainz).

Tannery, Paul (1887, 2d ed. 1930). *Pour l'Histoire de la Science Hellène: de Thalès à Empédocle.* Paris: Alcan.

Taylor, A. E. (1928). *A Commentary on Plato's Timaeus.* Oxford: Clarendon.

———— (1956). *Philebus and Epinomis.* London: Nelson.

Taylor, C.C.W. (1967). "Pleasure, Knowledge and Sensation in Democritus." *Phronesis* 12:6–27.

Teichmüller, Walter (1874/1966). *Studien zur Geschichte der Begriffe.* Berlin: Weidmannsche Buchhandlung. Repr. Hildesheim: Georg Olms.

Thivel, Antoine (1981). *Cnide et Cos? Essai sur les doctrines médicales dans la collection hippocratique.* Paris: Les Belles Lettres.

Thompson, W. H. (1882). "Introductory Remarks on the *Philebus*." *Journal of Philology* 11:1–22.

Thurston, H. (1994). *Early Astronomy.* New York: Springer Verlag.

Treue, W., ed. (1986). *Achse, Rad und Wagen. Fünftausend Jahre Kultur- und Technikgeschichte.* Göttingen: Vandenhoeck and Ruprecht.

Untersteiner, Mario (1961–62). *Sofisti: testimonianze e frammenti,* 4 vols. Florence: La Nuova Italia.

Verdenius, W. J. (1985). *A Commentary on Hesiod* Works and Days, *vv. 1–382.* Leiden: Brill.

Vidal-Naquet, Pierre (1990). "Sophocles' *Philoctetes* and the Ephebeia," in Jean-Pierre Vernant and Pierre Vidal-Naquet, eds., *Myth and Tragedy in Ancient Greece,* trans. Janet Lloyd. New York: Zone Books. 161–179.

Vlastos, Gregory (1945; 1946/1995). "Ethics and Physics in Democritus." *Philosophical Review* 54:578–592 and 55. Reprinted in G. Vlastos (1995) 328–350.

——— (1966a). "A Note on Zeno's Arrow." *Phronesis* 11:3–18.

——— (1966b). "Zeno's Race Course." *Journal of the History of Philosophy,* 4.2:95–108.

——— (1967). "Zeno," in P. Edwards, ed., *The Encyclopedia of Philosophy,* vol. 8. New York: Macmillan. 369–379.

——— (1975). "Plato's Testimony Concerning Zeno of Elea." *Journal of Hellenic Studies* 55:136–162.

——— (1993; 1995). *Studies in Greek Philosophy,* vol. 1: *The Presocratics,* ed. D. Graham. Princeton, NJ: Princeton University Press.

van der Waerden, B. L. (1974). *Science Awakening II: The Birth of Astronomy.* New York: Oxford University Press.

Wardy, R.B.B. (1988). "Eleatic Pluralism." *Archiv für Geschichte der Philosophie* 70:125–146.

Weiss, H. (1938). "Democritus' Theory of Cognition." *Classical Quarterly* 32: 47–56.

West, Martin L. (1969). "The Sayings of Democritus." *Classical Review* 19:142.

——— (1971). *Early Greek Philosophy and the Orient.* Oxford: Clarendon.

Williams, Bernard (1993). *Shame and Necessity.* Berkeley and Los Angeles: University of California Press.

——— (1995). "Formal Structures and Social Reality," in Bernard Williams, *Making Sense of Humanity and Other Philosophical Papers.* Cambridge: Cambridge University Press. 111–122.

Williams, C.J.F. (1982). *Aristotle's De Generatione et Corruptione.* Oxford: Clarendon Press.

Wilson, Edmund (1947). *The Wound and the Bow.* New York: Oxford University Press.

Wright, M. Rosemary (1981/1995a). *Empedocles: The Extant Fragments.* New Haven, CT: Yale University Press; reprinted Indianapolis, IN: Hackett Publishing.

——— (1995b). *Cosmology in Antiquity.* London and New York: Routledge.

Zeller, E. (1892;, 1919; 1963). *Die Philosophie der Griechen,* 6th ed., ed. W. Nestle. Leipzig. Repr. Hildesheim: Olms. Teil 1 Abt. 1: "Vorsokratische Philosophie."

Zuntz, Günther (1939). "Earliest Attic Prose-Style (*On Antiphon's Second Tetralogy*)." *Classica et Mediaevalia* 2:121–144.

Contributors

István M. Bodnár is Associate Professor of History of Philosophy at Eötvös University, Budapest. He presented "Atomic Independence and Indivisibility" at the meeting of the Society for Ancient Greek Philosophy with the Central Division of the American Philosophical Association in 1997. It was published in *Oxford Studies in Ancient Philosophy* XVI (1998) 35–61, and is reprinted here with permission of the Editor and Oxford University Press.

Dirk L. Couprie is a former Associate Professor of Philosophy at the University of Leiden (Netherlands). After a career in university- and higher education management he is now an independent researcher. "Anaximander's Discovery of Space" was presented at the meeting of the Society for Ancient Greek Philosophy in Binghamton, NY, 1996, and is published here for the first time.

Patricia Curd is Professor of Philosophy at Purdue University. Early versions of "Why Democritus Was Not a Skeptic" were presented at the VIIth International Symposium of Philosophy and Interdisciplinary Research in Olympia, Greece, in August 1996, and at the meeting of the Society for Ancient Greek Philosophy in Binghamton, NY, in 1996. The essay is published here for the first time.

Michael Gagarin is Professor of Classics at the University of Texas in Austin. He presented "The Truth of Antiphon's *Truth*" at the meeting of the Society for Ancient Greek Philosophy with the American Philological Association in 1991. It is published here for the first time.

Carol Steinberg Gould is Associate Professor of Philosophy at Florida Atlantic University. She presented an earlier version of "Moral Dilemmas and Integrity in Sophocles' *Philoctetes*" at the meeting of the Society for Ancient Greek Philosophy in Binghamton, NY, in 1995. The essay is published here for the first time.

Carl Huffman is Professor of Classics at DePauw University. He presented an earlier version of "The Philolaic Method: The Pythagoreanism Behind the *Philebus*" at the meeting of the Society for Ancient Greek Philosophy in Binghamton, NY, in 1994. This essay is published here for the first time.

Wallace I. Matson is Professor of Philosophy, Emeritus, at the University of California, Berkeley. At the 1983 meeting of the Society for Ancient Greek Philosophy with the Eastern Division of the American Philosophical Association he presented "Eleatic Motions," subsequently published in *La Parola del*

Passato 43 (1988) 312–336, under the title, "The Zeno of Plato and Tannery Vindicated." "Zeno Moves!" is a revised version of that essay, and is published here with permission of the Direttore of *La Parola del Passato*.

Richard McKirahan is E.C. Norton Professor of Classics and Philosophy at Pomona College. He presented "Anaximander's Infinite Worlds" at the meeting of the Society for Ancient Greek Philosophy in Binghamton, NY, in 1994. The essay is published here for the first time.

Gerard Naddaf is Associate Professor of Philosophy at York University. He presented "Anaximander's Measurements Revisited" at the meeting of the Society for Ancient Greek Philosophy in Binghamton, NY, in 1995. It is a much shorter and revised version of "On the Origin of Anaximander's Cosmological Model," published in the *Journal of the History of Ideas* 59 (1998) 1–28; it is printed here with the permission of the Editors.

Anthony Preus is Professor and Chair of Philosophy at Binghamton University, State University of New York. He is Secretary of the Society for Ancient Greek Philosophy and is the Editor of this volume.

Thomas M. Robinson is Professor of Philosophy at the University of Toronto. He presented "The *Dissoi Logoi* and Early Greek Skepticism" at a conference entitled "Scepticism in the History of Philosophy: A Pan-American Dialogue," at the Centre for Ideas and Society, University of California at Riverside, February 16, 1991, and at the meeting of the Society for Ancient Greek Philosophy in Binghamton, NY, in 1994. It was subsequently published in *Skepticism in the History of Philosophy*, ed. Richard H. Popkin (Dordrecht: Kluwer), 1996, 27–36, and is reprinted here in slightly revised form with the permission of the publisher.

Joel Wilcox is Associate Professor of Philosophy at Providence College. He presented an earlier version of "Homeopathy and 'Whole-Natured Forms' in Empedocles' Cosmic Cycle" at the meeting of the Society for Ancient Greek Philosophy in Binghamton, NY, in 1995. The essay is published here for the first time.

Index of Proper Names

This index includes names of both ancient and modern contributors to the understanding of early Greek philosophy; it also includes a few names of fictional or mythical persons.

Index of Concepts

This index includes many of the Greek words used in this volume. The definitions in parentheses are only suggestive; in many cases more complete discussions of the meanings of the terms occur in the text.

Index of Classical Passages Cited

References to Presocratic fragments and testimonia are inherently complicated. The fundamental collection for the study of the Presocratics is "Diels-Kranz." Where authors of chapters give references to that collection, they are included below under "DK"; such references follow the name of the Presocratic in this index.

Many authors prefer to refer to the original sources from which fragments or testimonia are taken; those references are included under those authors (e.g., "Aetius," "Aristotle." If authors give both references, you will find the same text cited in both places.

When there are several citations to the same chapter of Aristotle (for example), those are gathered together.

DATE DUE

ILL-3 weeks			

Demco, Inc 38-293